Palgrave Series in Indian Ocean World Studies

Series Editor
Gwyn Campbell
McGill University
Montreal, Canada

This is the first scholarly series devoted to the study of the Indian Ocean world from early times to the present day. Encouraging interdisciplinarity, it incorporates and contributes to key debates in a number of areas including history, environmental studies, anthropology, sociology, political science, geography, economics, law, and labor and gender studies. Because it breaks from the restrictions imposed by country/regional studies and Eurocentric periodization, the series provides new frameworks through which to interpret past events, and new insights for present-day policymakers in key areas from labor relations and migration to diplomacy and trade.

More information about this series at
http://www.springer.com/series/14661

Hideaki Suzuki

Slave Trade Profiteers in the Western Indian Ocean

Suppression and Resistance in the Nineteenth Century

palgrave
macmillan

Hideaki Suzuki
Nagasaki University
Nagasaki, Japan

Palgrave Series in Indian Ocean World Studies
ISBN 978-3-319-59802-4 ISBN 978-3-319-59803-1 (eBook)
DOI 10.1007/978-3-319-59803-1

Library of Congress Control Number: 2017944187

Cover illustration: Philip Howard Colomb, *Slave-catching in the Indian Ocean*

Printed on acid-free paper

This Palgrave Macmillan imprint is published by Springer Nature
The registered company is Springer International Publishing AG
The registered company address is: Gewerbestrasse 11, 6330 Cham, Switzerland

Acknowledgements

I first became interested in the Indian Ocean world and its history while I was still a freshman. I saw it as a world of adventure, which I admired although I never stepped into it at that time. For me, adventure had always been confined to Manga comics or video games, so to explore the history of the Indian Ocean world was rather like being able to fulfil a wanderlust which had been present in my mind for a long time; it also came to be closely connected to my physical travels around that same world. Eventually, I fixed my scholarly focus on East African history, largely because it seemed to me that various elements around this maritime world compose history of this coastal society. Following existing literature on the subject, particularly works by Hikoichi Yajima, I focused on the history of migration to East Africa as well as East Africa's place in Arab geography of the medieval period. Several of my professors and colleagues advised me to shift my focus to the slave trade, although the subject seemed to me a rather difficult one for various reasons. First, at the time I was immersed in the medieval history of the Indian Ocean world and I was sure that I would not be able to find enough documents to make any impression on the topic as far as this time period was concerned. If I were to move the period of my focus towards to a much later period, I knew I would find plenty of extant contemporary sources and could much more easily apply my field experience to the task I had set myself; nevertheless, as the subject of the slave trade seemed to be so complicated and, potentially, a minefield, I preferred to stay in the medieval world.

The turning point came in 2004. It was then I met with Professor Masashi Haneda to discuss my Ph.D. project: a proposal to closely examine the Shirazi tradition in the nineteenth century. Since I was unsure whether what I really wanted to do would be acceptable, I had chosen this alternative, as philological study holds an importance place in the tradition of Oriental history in Japan. Professor Haneda simply scanned my proposal and then asked me: 'Do you really want to do this?' So I told him the truth—I wanted to explore my longed-for world of adventure. But, still, the slave trade had no part in this. Almost simultaneously, Professor Yuzo Shitomi, also at the University of Tokyo, suggested I work on the slave trade. He kindly introduced me to some foundation literature on this subject. But I still hesitated. In 2005, I had the opportunity to go to Gujarat as a part of a project on architectural history led by Professors Naoko Fukami and Shu Yamane, who kindly allowed me to stay for a while in Mumbai, where I visited Mahārāshtra State Archives. Exploring the documents there, I gradually realized that investigating the slave trade might allow me to explore my world of adventure—and even challenge conventional understanding of the historical Indian Ocean itself.

In short, many professors and colleagues helped me to arrive at the topic of this book. Needless to say, after I had embarked on my Ph.D. project yet more help has come my way from yet more professors and colleagues. Some individuals—Hiroki Ishikawa, Naofumi Abe, Osamu Otsuka, Ichiro Ozawa, Shizuo Katakura, Yuki Terada, Noriko Kanahara, Yuka Tomomatsu and Kazuaki Sawai—joined the seminars of Professors Haneda and Shitomi, and we spent a great deal of time discussing a wide variety of topics—not merely academic subjects. Yasuhiro Yokkaichi and Yasuyuki Kuriyama both started their work on the Indian Ocean world history before me, and they have most kindly given me much guidance from the beginning. A number of different projects have extended my perspective, particularly 'Minatomachi Kaken' and 'Eurasia Kaken', both organized by Professor Haneda and Grants-in-Aid for Scientific Research, which provided me with critically important opportunities to meet many wonderful scholars as well as to hone my own ideas. I am also extremely appreciative of the help of the leaders of those projects, most notably Professors Yasunori Arano, Yoshihito Shimada, Kazunobu Ikeya, Taku Iida, Shoichiro Takezawa, Kayoko Fujita, Masashi Hirosue,

Takeshi Onimaru, Hiroshi Nawata and Yoko Nagahara. Not forgetting, of course, my fellow students.

Since my first presentation outside Japan in 2007, I have come across others who share similar interests and their works give me real encouragement. For example, Kenneth Cozens is one of my earliest academic friends outside Japan and, to mention them especially, Elisabeth McMahon, Klara Boyer-Rossol, Matthew Hopper, Pedro Machado and Thomas Vernet are at similar stages to me in their academic careers: their conversation is never less than stimulating. Numerous conferences and workshops, especially those organized by the Major Collaborative Research Initiative project led by the Indian Ocean World Centre (IOWC) at McGill University, have given me the chance to encounter wonderful scholars like Michael N. Pearson, James F. Warren and George Michael La Rue, not forgetting Alessandro Stanziani, Lakshmi Subramanian and Stephan J. Rockel. My two-year post-doctoral fellowship at IOWC provided me with unique experiences both inside and also outside the centre's walls; I am most thankful to Peter Hynd, Anna Winterbottom, Rashed Chowdhury, Omri Bassewitch Frenkel, Erin Bell, Veysel Simsek, Tyler Yank, Michael Ferguson, Facil Tesfaye and Lori Callaghan.

Professor Martin A. Klein's broad knowledge covering the entire globe and his sharp arguments always amazed me and have developed my project even further. Professor Edward A. Alpers's energetic works exploring many veiled issues inspired me even before I met him, and I have since found his conversation always fascinates me in terms of his broad perspective and profound knowledge of Africa as well as the Indian Ocean world. As to this book, he also kindly provides helpful suggestions, comments and introduces several references. Professor Gwyn Campbell not only very kindly put me up during my post-doctoral work at IOWC, but his dynamically argued views on the Indian Ocean world have pushed this book project into new realms, while the conferences and workshops he organized offered great opportunities to meet many interesting scholars. I most gladly thank Professor Yuzo Shitomi, who taught me the exactness required in the academic world. But I am most deeply grateful to Professor Masashi Haneda. Professor Haneda has always encouraged me, and talking to him is both enjoyable and stimulating. His sharp criticism always develops and improves my ideas, while his worldwide perspective and the sincerity of his approach to history always make me look very closely at myself and at my project.

I offer my gratitude to those too whom I met during my research elsewhere. Some were looking after the various archives I consulted, others I met simply in the street while travelling in the Indian Ocean world. Some offered me a cup of tea, while others accepted my offer of a bottle of beer or two. Such encounters have been extremely satisfying and have gradually helped my understanding of the profound nature of the history of the Indian Ocean world—and beyond. This book might not reflect my field experience fully enough, but without that fieldwork I am sure I could not have completed it.

Finally, I wish to dedicate this volume to my four grandparents, whom I knew I could always rely on absolutely in any circumstances.

Contents

List of Tables

List of Maps

CHAPTER 1

Introduction: Slave Traders and the Western Indian Ocean

The First Question: Who Profited from the Slave Trade?

This book addresses two main interrelated questions. The first deals with the slave trade, the second with the Indian Ocean world. More precisely, the first question is: 'Who profited from the slave trade in the nineteenth-century western Indian Ocean?' The question might seem absurd because many readers will instantly answer, 'those who traded slaves' or 'slave traders'. These should include transporters, buyers, sellers and users. If we go on to ask for further detail on them, we find there are none, so we reach a dead end. Despite the increase in literature on slavery and the slave trade in the western Indian Ocean, surprisingly few studies focus on slave traders themselves. Thus, to answer the above question, we need to answer another question: 'Who were slave traders?'

While three of the major components of the slave trade in the nineteenth century were slave traders, those who wished to suppress the trade and the slaves themselves, only the latter two have rich historiographies. The campaign of suppression has naturally been a traditional topic for naval historians; for example, Charles R. Low's detailed study traces the progress of the campaign with reference to the Indian Navy, while Gerald S. Graham's work does the same for the Royal Navy and John B. Kelly examines the activities of the Royal Navy in the Persian Gulf.[1] Furthermore, Christopher Lloyd gives the chronology of the campaign in the Indian Ocean.[2] With exception of Lloyd, the question of

H. Suzuki, *Slave Trade Profiteers in the Western Indian Ocean*, Palgrave Series in Indian Ocean World Studies,
DOI 10.1007/978-3-319-59803-1_1

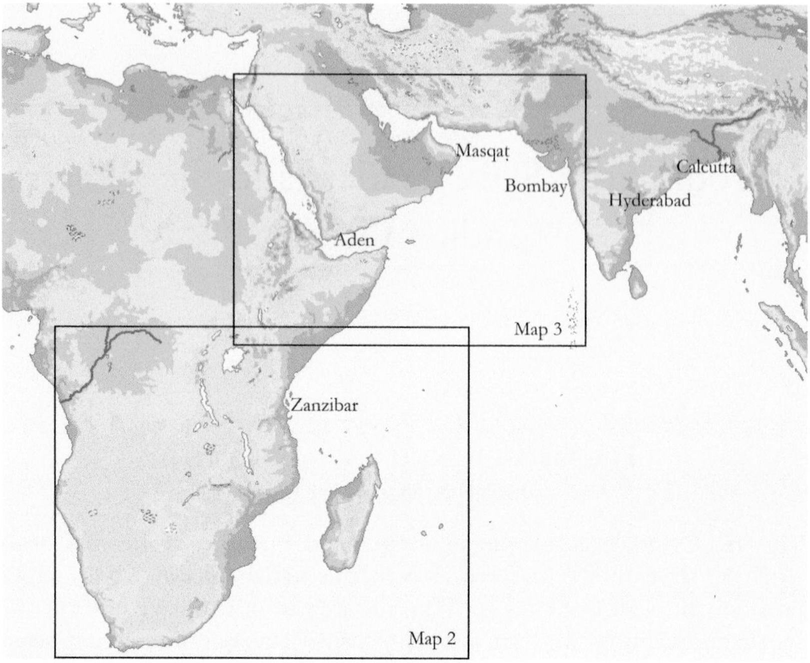

Map 1.1 Western Indian Ocean

the suppression of the slave trade is not these authors' main concern, but rather the entirety of the activities of the navies. Within that framework the campaign to suppress the slave trade is certainly important enough to be included. The studies mentioned vividly describe the progress of the campaign of suppression and locate it in the context of the history of each navy. As for the slaves, over the last twenty years or so much more scholarly attention has been paid to the variety of slavery in the entirety of the Indian Ocean world.[3] One of the core disciplines in support of such increased attention is diaspora studies, and, since the 2000s, Edward A. Alpers, Shihan de Jayasuriya, Matthew S. Hopper and many others have brought to light this undiscovered feature of the slave trade; today the field is growing rapidly.[4] In the literature, regardless of whether dealing with the suppressors or the slaves, slave traders are mentioned frequently; despite that, they are always given only a secondary role, so that the details of their activities are largely ignored. One contribution

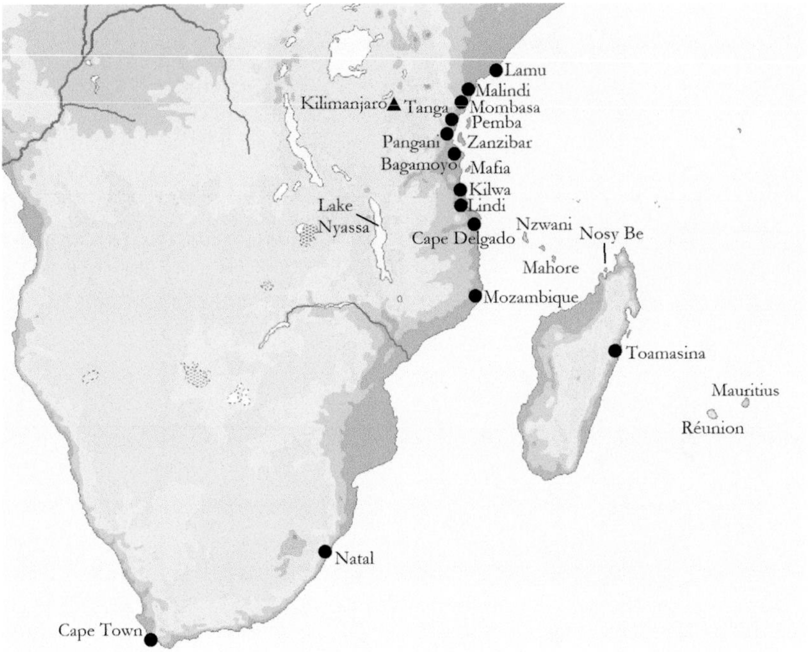

Map 1.2 East Africa and Madagascar

of this book will be to fill that gap in the existing literature. Moreover, in my opinion, this volume has greater importance outside that function. I believe that the three components of the slave trade referred to must have been interrelated and must have impacted on each other. This book therefore looks at slave traders in conjunction with the two other components of the slave trade, and particularly at how they inter-reacted with the suppressors. We shall thereby be able to consider those two other components from a different perspective. Indeed, in including all three, we shall be able to see whether slave traders should merely be portrayed as profiteers, and as we explore the interaction between slave traders and the suppression campaign, we shall come to a certain conclusion.

The time span covered here is principally the fifty or so years between the 1820s and 1870s—the classical era of the subject in the existing literature. The reason for the attention given to the 1820s is twofold, the first being the General Maritime Treaty of 1820, led by the

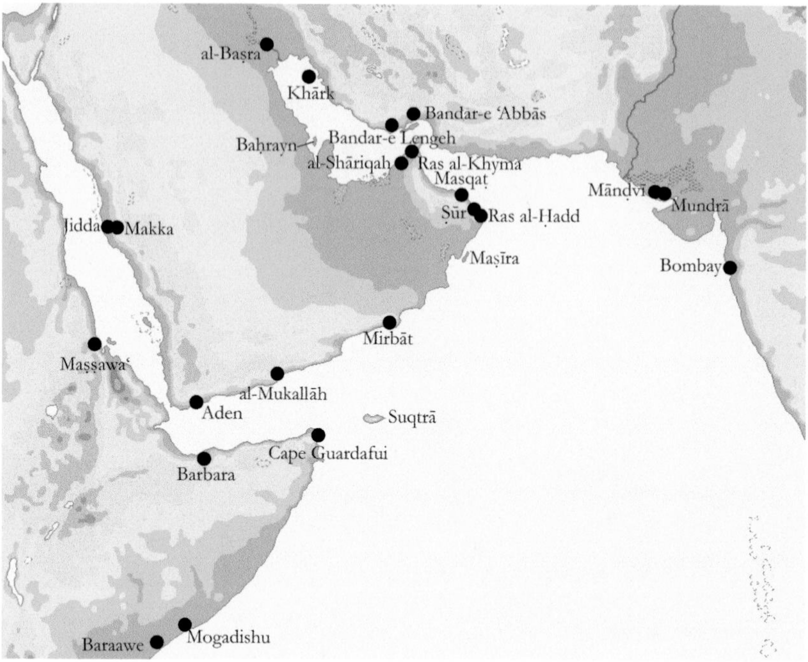

Map 1.3 North-Eastern Africa, the Arabian Peninsula and Indian Subcontinent

Bombay Government, which was concluded by the Arabian shaykhs in the Persian Gulf, and the second the so-called Moresby Treaty of 1822, which was signed on behalf of Britain by Fairfax Moresby, Senior Officer on Mauritius, and by Sayyid Sa'īd bin Sulṭān of the Bū Sa'īd. Both treaties are recognized as making first steps towards the suppression of the slave trade in the western Indian Ocean. The key significant event of the 1870s was the 1873 banning of the slave trade in Zanzibar—the most important entrepôt for the slave trade in the western Indian Ocean. In short, the five decades between the 1820s and the 1870s made up the period when the slave trade was, first of all, greatly shaken up and then had its fate largely sealed with the 1873 ban. When one considers the long history of the slave trade in the Indian Ocean world, that it took as little as 50 years for it to be so affected is indeed remarkable. How did that happen? Of course, slave trading continued in the western Indian Ocean region after 1873, but it was of a very different sort from what had gone on before, not least because it became entirely illegal and clandestine. The Sultan of Zanzibar declared the trade illegal in 1873 and surrendered his rights to control to the Royal Navy.[5] That is in stark contrast with what happened about a couple of decades previously when actual seizures of slaving dhows along the East African coast finally began. Then, the Sultan's secretary Aḥmad b. Na'amān,[6] protested to the British Consul, allegedly saying 'Arabs have carried on the trade since the days of Noah, and they must have slaves.'[7] Related to those events, East Africa gradually lost its supreme position as a slave-exporting region to the rest of the western Indian Ocean; as a consequence, export from Baluchistan to the Persian Gulf has significantly increased since the early twentieth century.[8] Moreover, traffickers' reduced the risk of capture by British patrols if they elected to move their cargoes of slaves by shorter routes.[9] So, the 1873 ban on the slave trade must be marked as an important turning point in the history of slave trading in the region. However, without the actual conflict between slave traders and their suppressors over the preceding five decades, the legal steps towards the ban would not have been taken—and this book mainly examines that struggle. In other words, we must closely investigate the process by which the two sides became entangled. It is a complicated and multifaceted story and, to unravel it, instead of trying to trace a strict chronology from chapter to chapter, we shall consider it from various angles.

The Second Question: Did the Indian Ocean World Collapse?

The other main question addressed in this book is about the Indian Ocean world. There is a varied literature on slavery in the Indian Ocean world, and over the last 10 years or so particularly a great deal has been published on this topic. Many writers have emphasized that knowledge of that particular maritime sphere offers a great opportunity to reconsider the conventional view of slavery, which has largely been influenced by case studies from the Atlantic world.[10] While such literature does, of course, portray the Indian Ocean world as an 'alternative version' of slavery studies—which I fully understand—the challenge I have taken up here is to approach the slave trade in the Indian Ocean world rather differently. This book will attempt to examine what happened in the western Indian Ocean while principally focusing on the transformation in the circumstances of the slave traders. But first, I must explain the logic of my approach, and to do so I must take us back to the question I posed at the beginning of this chapter: 'Who were the slave traders?'

In the existing literature we can find terms such as 'slave traders', 'slavers', 'slave ships', but nowhere do we find any further explanation or definition. More particularly, the terms 'Suri Arab' and 'Northern Arab' are frequently found in the contemporary documents as slave traders and modern scholars use those terms in the same manner, but neither those original documents nor today's scholars can enlighten us as to who those people really were. Nevertheless, the terminology used and the descriptions found in the modern scholarly literature create the impression that the slave business was carried out by traders who dealt only in slaves. Within the framework of a study of the suppression campaign and of the slaves themselves, further information on slave traders is perhaps not strictly necessary, but a lack of concern with that aspect of the subject certainly greatly limits the historical value of the slave trade in the context of Indian Ocean history. The conventional wisdom concerning the slave trade, according to the Atlantic model, always includes such things as large ships specifically adapted for conveying large numbers of bodies and auctions where slaves were forced to endure the indignity of being paraded under the critical gaze of the masses in the slave market. However, such markets were by no means the only spaces for slave transaction in the western Indian Ocean. Moreover, as one naval officer wrote, 'there is no such thing as a slaver [slave ship]'[11] in slave trafficking between Zanzibar and the Persian Gulf; this statement can be applicable to most of other parts of the western Indian Ocean also, where the ships engaged in slave transport were generally smaller than those in the Atlantic. Moreover, the movement of slaves was not carried out separately from other traffic; indeed, as is discussed further in Chap. 2, it can reasonably be claimed that slave traffic in this area was in fact inseparable from other traffic. When we see the reality of slave trafficking in the region, there is no evidence for the frequently repeated claim that slave traffic was a specialized trade. Rather, designating certain groups of people as slave traders leads to serious misunderstanding. Slave auctions were held, but as Chap. 5 shows, small-scale, individual and private slave dealing outside the realm of the 'professionals' was an important feature of the trade we simply cannot afford to ignore. The slave trade was part of the complex whole of Indian Ocean trading in general and most certainly was not isolated from other trading activities. That being so, it follows that attempts at its suppression had effects that were barely distinguishable from those on general trade.

The other advantage for understanding the nineteenth-century western Indian Ocean region's focus on the slave trade is that there is an abundance of sources to explore, while, surprisingly, we lack sufficient sources to examine even the actual volume of general trade in the ports that were under the control of local polities. Ports like Stone Town in Zanzibar might appear to be exceptions, but even for Stone Town those records, although at least available, are only fragmentary. Needless to say, we face further difficulties in trying to explore the detailed activities both of local traders and transporters. Local documents currently available to scholars are indeed scarce, and although there are rich archives of the communications between Salem merchants and local merchants—such as those from Kachchh—it is still difficult to draw a complete picture of the activities of the local merchants from them. By contrast, many more sources are available on the slave trade, left not only by the British but by the consulates and naval officers of other countries, not forgetting the records of European and American merchants. Such records provide information on other trades associated with slaving, and given that, as we have mentioned, the slave trade was inseparable from other trades, the same sources enable us to explore what happened in the western Indian Ocean.

That phrase 'what happened in the western Indian Ocean' is the core of the second question addressed in this book. Despite a recent awakening of academic interest in the history of the Indian Ocean world, which we shall trace in the following section 'Corruption Theory of the Indian Ocean World', we still need to work out how our framework includes the wider nineteenth-century world; here is where we must refer to the so-called 'corruption theory'. In short, the 'corruption theory' suggests that the cohesion of the Indian Ocean world began to collapse around the middle of the eighteenth century as a result of the expansion of the world economy and European colonial expansion. According to the theory, the period after the middle of the eighteenth century is not worthy of consideration within the framework of the Indian Ocean world as a unit of history, simply because this world had collapsed by that time, but I disagree, and I shall discuss the question fully in the following sections. Thus, the significance of the nineteenth century in this book is of particular importance when refuting corruption theory. In addition, bearing in mind that we cannot deny that the maritime world of the western Indian Ocean was, of course, connected with the rest of the world in the nineteenth century regardless of whether or not we agree with 'corruption theory', an examination of the fate of this maritime world during this period can contribute to our understanding of a much broader sphere of history.

Corruption Theory

The idea of looking at the Indian Ocean as a unit of history has been developed since the 1960s when the region found its way out of colonization and various independent nation states emerged in the wake of the international attention it received as a result of its geopolitical importance under the Cold War regime. The first work to advocate that view was by August Toussaint, a Mauritius-born historian whose book, *Histoire de l'Océan Indien*, was first published in French in 1961 and then translated into English in 1966.[12] He was inspired by works on both the Atlantic and the Pacific, which place ocean at the centre of the focus. For Toussaint, to consider his own national history as a Mauritian was no less than to consider the history of the Indian Ocean. Following his early work, a number of symposiums and conferences have been organized by the International Historical Association of the Indian Ocean, and by United Nations Educational, Scientific and Cultural Organization (UNESCO).[13] In due course, therefore, the Indian Ocean, which Toussaint called 'océan méconnu',[14] came to be recognized as a historical unit in its own right.

A common feature highlighted by earlier studies of the Indian Ocean history is what I call 'corruption theory', a term which I devised myself from my reading of Toussaint's work as well as those by subsequent scholars.[15] For example, Kirti N. Chaudhuri argued that the origin of colonialism and western economic imperialism could be found in the 1650s, when people in the Southeast Asian archipelago lost their economic autonomy to the Dutch East India Company, and then in the second half of the eighteenth-century, when British military and naval power, supported by technological innovation in Europe, came to 'redraw the civilizational map of the Indian Ocean'.[16] The Japanese scholar Hikoichi Yajima began to develop his concept of Indian Ocean maritime world (*Indo-yō kaiiki sekai*) at the end of the 1960s, and he too suggested that the maritime sovereignty and economic system established by both the British and the Dutch between the later seventeenth century and the eighteenth century began to undermine the traditional system there.[17] Meanwhile, André Wink divided the history of the Indian Ocean between the seventh and the eighteenth centuries into five stages in his work on the expansion of Islam. Wink paid especially close attention to the Indian subcontinent; according to him, the disintegration of Islamic empires into a number of regional successor polities in the eighteenth century was the last phase of a process and triggered British control over the subcontinent that was the centre of that maritime world. Eventually, said Wink, it caused the ruination of the integrated trading network of the Indian Ocean.[18] Ashin Das Gupta, a distinguished Indian scholar of the Indian Ocean, seemed to agree with all those historians mentioned.[19] A more detailed explanation is offered by Kenneth McPherson, who believed that Europeans in the late seventeenth century, as well as pursuing profits in the Indian Ocean's established internal trade, shifted their target items from purely luxury goods like spices to mass consumption items such as tea and cotton cloth. As a result, the maritime world of the Indian Ocean was rapidly introduced to a capitalist economy that was already operating on a global scale. Furthermore, that development eventually triggered European control over the region's economy and politics; previously European interaction had led merely to the unique development of the region.[20]

Michael N. Pearson, in his book *the Indian Ocean*, published in 2003, covered a good number of pages trying to grasp what he called the 'deep structure' of this maritime world, by which he meant such things as the seasonal monsoon winds, ocean currents, climate and general geography. A remarkable feature in Pearson's work is that it extends its scope right up to the twentieth century, and to that extent, therefore, must be distinguished from earlier works which agree with the corruption theory. Unlike the existing literature, which regarded both the spread of Islam in the seventh century and European expansion in the sixteenth century onwards as epoch-making events, Pearson divided his history into two periods at roughly about the year 1800,[21] thereby still imparting significance to the nineteenth century. Pearson said that the industrial revolution and the development of capitalism caused structural and qualitative change in the Indian Ocean, starting from about 1800, so that gradually his so-called 'deep structure' began to lose its significance from about this point.[22]

Prasannan Parthasarathi and Giorgio Riello also doubt the disconnection and stress continuity in the eighteenth century. However, for them, the framework and links forming the Indian Ocean world in the nineteenth century was dramatically different from those in the previous century.[23] Another recent work related to this subject, Edward A. Alpers' *The Indian Ocean in World History* overviews the history of this ocean until the twentieth century, while it describes 'the long nineteenth century', a long process transforming 'the Indian Ocean from an "Islamic Sea" into what came to be known popularly as a "British lake"' starting from the middle of the eighteenth century.[24]

It is not only scholars of Indian Ocean world history who have seen the significance of the nineteenth century to this area, for those who work on the so-called world system have noted it too. Immanuel Wallerstein's view is that the 'European world economy', which appeared between about the 1450s and the 1550s, developed and reached the same level as other world systems, including that of the Indian Ocean, in the sixteenth century. After overcoming a slump in the seventeenth century, the world system integrated other systems into itself during the age of industrial capitalism which commenced in the late eighteenth century.[25] Fernand Braudel acknowledged the existence of a single world economy in the Indian Ocean region—which he called 'the Far East (Extrême-Orient)'—but eventually in the nineteenth century it became integrated into another world economy, which the Europeans extended into the sphere of the Indian Ocean from the end of the fifteenth century.[26] Andre Gunder Frank tried to reconceptualize the early modern economy on a global scale. Frank both criticized the Eurocentric historical narratives and social theories found in the works of Wallerstein and Braudel, and emphasized the centrality of Asia. However, for him, the nineteenth century was when Asia's long-sustained superiority, which had endured in the global economy since the fifteenth century, was displaced, as the new European-led hegemonic order was established.[27]

Looking, therefore, at the big picture, I think it can be agreed that the nineteenth century was indeed a significantly important period for the Indian Ocean world because it brought full colonial political and economic rule, an enormous change, of course. Indeed, even today it is not at all difficult to find the legacy of this rule all over the Indian Ocean region.

Nevertheless, even if the Indian Ocean did become integrated into the world economy, or was forced into the position of accepting colonial rule, neither of those circumstances would necessarily have meant the dissolution of that world as an established unit of history. In fact, many historians who identify such a dissolution have not fully analysed the process and transition of the Indian Ocean world towards it. Sugata Bose critically points out the problem: '[they are] hampered [by] the development of a historical method that would unsettle the discredited, yet entrenched, notions of a West versus rest and other accompanying dichotomies'.[28] In fact, even general travellers in the Indian Ocean region can find evidence of the inconsistency of the corruption theory. For instance, dhows sailing with seasonal monsoon winds have been repeatedly referred to in the existing literature as a sort of symbol of the ancient and historic world of the Indian Ocean. So, what became of these dhows in the 'post-corruption' period? They clearly have not disappeared, at any rate. The 'traditional' trading dhows have repeatedly been described by all sorts of writers, not just scholars, and many have opined that the well-known local wooden ships are in the final phase of their existence.[29] Of course, the importance of the dhow has declined. As Erik Gilbert's detailed study on the Zanzibar dhow trade makes clear, the role of the vessels has changed. Gilbert examined the transition in the role of the trading dhow in Zanzibar's economy from the second half of the nineteenth century to the early twentieth century, when Zanzibar's economy was being edged towards marginality by the Atlantic economy even while it experienced the expansion of British political influence.[30] Gilbert argues that the anti-slave trade campaign turned the dhow into a pariah, because in the eyes of the authorities dhows had always been an integral part of the slave trade, in both colonial and post-colonial times. The resulting negative image therefore relegated them to a marginal position in the new economy such people wished to see established—in fact in some cases dhows were actually excluded from it. In any case, the dhows were never allowed to recover the central position they had previously enjoyed in the region's shipping.[31]

Today, many dhows can be found functioning exclusively as touristic attractions, no longer a major logistical component of maritime trade. Even so, we still cannot presume the dissolution of the historical network in this ocean. Indeed, although gigantic tankers and air freight have superseded dhows, they are really no more than replacement methods of transport. What the dhows represent, that is, extensive region-wide exchange of goods, people and information, is still carried on, albeit with new modes of transport. Instead of dissolution, therefore, we actually find continuity. Needless to say, continuity has always coexisted with transition and transformation, just Gilbert found. In that regard, I fully agree with the following statement by Ned Bertz, another who has challenged the conventional periodization of the Indian Ocean world history: 'instead of being "destroyed" by colonial power, indigenous residents of the Indian Ocean adapted to the new political structures and continued to travel, trade and interact across the sea in altered relationships mediated, but not dominated, by Europeans'.[32] Adding to this, several keywords for spatial setting, as suggested by Markus P.M. Vink, are worth keeping in mind for future study on Indian Ocean world history: porousness, permeability, connectedness, flexibility, openness of spatial and temporal boundaries and borders.[33]

While we should, of course, agree with the 'macroscopic' debates that have occurred and admit that a significant change in this maritime world took place in the nineteenth century, that change by no means implied dissolution. The main problem, in fact, is lack of 'microscopic' examination of what was really going on. So far, what is certain is that the significant change did not happen as a result of purely endogenous development. Rather, it was the result of a sort of fusion between an existing commerce-based maritime world and an existing western European political and economic order. From that viewpoint, the significance of the slave trade in the western Indian Ocean becomes much clearer, for the trade constituted one of the first direct encounters between the existing commerce of the Indian Ocean and the newly arriving European political order, and, of course, slave traders were at the forefront of those encounters. As we have already seen in the section 'The Second Question', those same individuals were traders in other goods too. We need to focus on the slave traders to understand that macroscopically significant transition in the nineteenth century from its true microscopic perspective.

Structure and Method

This book contains eight chapters apart from this introduction, and a general conclusion. Chapter 2 is an overview of the slave trade in the nineteenth-century western Indian Ocean, and as well as giving an estimate of the overall volume of the trade, trade destinations and other details, explores aspects of 'slavers' that until now have largely been ignored. Chapters 3 and 4 follow on from each other, as both discuss the confrontation between transporters and (British) suppressors. In Chap. 3, while focusing on the period prior to 1860, I have traced the progress of legal restrictions on slave trafficking in the western Indian Ocean and will reveal various methods of resistance against official efforts at suppression. Chapter 4 brings to light a hitherto undiscovered feature of the Royal Navy's campaign of suppression—that it did damage to the indigenous trading network. Thereafter, Chap. 4 is concerned with trying to discover the background to the measures taken by the Royal Navy and clarifying how the damage to the local trading network was done. In fact, it was caused not only by the inseparable nature of the slave trade and general trade, but also by the Royal Navy's experience of suppression in the Atlantic; the connection between their experience there and how they went about the same task in the western Indian Ocean is highlighted.

While scholars frequently place emphasis on the historical extent of the slave trade in the western Indian Ocean,[34] the actual condition of it remains largely unknown, regardless of the particular period. William

G. Clarence-Smith's comment from 1989 that 'nothing has created so much controversy in the history of the slave trade as the disputes over the total number of slaves exported'[35] remains applicable to the current state of knowledge of slave trade, although progress has been made in studies of slaves themselves. Estimation of numbers is, of course, a basic job in comparative study, but all authors ought to ask themselves if their own particular comparison of the numbers is worthwhile if they have not considered the actual local conditions of slave trading, which might well have differed in different regions and which probably differed in different periods. In other words, equal if not more weight should be given to a qualitative over a quantitative approach, because the significance of the statistics is revealed only against an understanding of the local circumstances of the slave trade and its context. To that end, Chap. 5 deals with the actual conditions of the slave trade and is based on the accounts of slaves. The chapter illuminates the trade with a degree of detail entirely absent from studies that have tried to comprehend the volume of it, and shows how slave dealings in this region were widespread not only in a geographical but also a class sense.

A rapid increase in the export of slaves from East Africa from the last quarter of the eighteenth century corresponds to an increase of slave demand in the Caribbean and the rise of the Mascarene Islands' plantation economy. Adding to that, the successful transplanting of cloves and the rise of a plantation economy in Zanzibar from the 1820s—and, for that matter, in several other spots along the East African coast—gave rise to greater demand for slaves. Almost all the scholars who have made estimates of the volume of the East African slave trade find that its peak period occurred in the nineteenth century. In addition to the East African coast's dual role as both exporter of slaves and itself a creator of demand for them, careful observation of contemporary records reveals that the region began to play yet another role around the middle of the century—its coastal society emerged as a new slave ground. Chapter 6 goes on to explore not only how that happened but why, by looking not only the coastal areas but the hinterland too.

Chapter 7 is, in a sense, a supplement to Chap. 6. In order to understand a phenomenon that the coastal society emerged as a new slave ground, one factor that must never be overlooked is the differences in the policies of local sultans. Namely, Mājid b. Sa'īd (1834–1870, r. 1856–1870) adopted a far stricter policy than had his father, Sa'īd b. Sulṭān (1790–1856, r. 1807–1856). Chapter 7 explores the background to the complex political scramble that characterized the post-Sa'īd period.

There we shall observe that this political scramble was not merely a localized affair but involved the Consuls in Zanzibar and in fact became an international trial of strength, so to speak. Such, then, is the context for our further examination of how coastal East Africa turned into a slave ground.

Indian merchants played a major role in commerce on the nineteenth-century East African coast, and with 'dual protection' they had a significant advantage in their efforts at extending their influence. 'Dual protection' meant that they could choose either to be British subjects or to be subjects of the local sultan, depending on how they saw their situation. Chapter 8 then tackles the question of the Indian population's sense of belonging in Bū Saʿīdi East Africa, and examines the extent to which they could benefit from their somewhat ambiguous position as well as the difficulties that flowed from it. The chapter explores too the fact that the dynamics of how slavery and the slave trade were viewed affected the position of the Indians until finally their 'dual protection' was removed. Furthermore, it explores the effects of the dynamic transoceanic diplomatic connections of the British Empire.

In the final chapter before the general conclusion, Chap. 9, the focus is fixed once again on the transporters. The chapter deals with the question of what is called *françisation*. The transporters found that there was an advantage to be had from hoisting the French flag and carrying French registration documents, which practically amounted to a 'special ticket' for free passage from British patrols, regardless of whether the transporters were carrying slaves or not. Chapter 9 concludes by examining, on the one hand, the agency of the maritime transporters in general regardless if conveying slaves or not, which was realized only when they made full use of both their vast network and the suppression measures, and, on the other, looks at British efforts to tackle a situation that had its origins in a tangled international relationship. The final section of the chapter takes us 6000 km away from the western Indian Ocean to Den Haag, where the question was finally settled.

Notes

1. Charles R. Low, *History of the Indian Navy 1613–1863*, 2 vols, Delhi: Manas Publications, 1985; Gerald S. Graham, *Great Britain in the Indian Ocean 1810–1850*, Oxford: Clarendon Press, 1967; John B. Kelly, *Britain and the Persian Gulf 1795–1880*, Oxford: Clarendon Press, 1968.
2. Christopher Lloyd, *The Navy and the Slave Trade: The Suppression of the African Slave Trade in the Nineteenth Century*, London: Longmans, Green, 1949.

3. For recent studies on slavery, see Gwyn Campbell (ed.), *The Structure of Slavery in Indian Ocean Africa and Asia*, London and Portland: Frank Cass, 2004; Jan-Georg Deutsch, *Emancipation without Abolition in German East Africa c.1884–1914*, Oxford: James Curry, 2006; Henri Médard and Shane Doyle (eds.), *Slavery in the Great Lakes Region of East Africa*, Oxford: James Curry, 2007; Elisabeth McMahon, *Slavery and Emancipation in Islamic East Africa: From Honor to Respectability*, Cambridge: Cambridge University Press, 2013. Also, for recent contributions from archaeology, see Paul J. Lane and Kevin C. Macdonald (eds.), *Slavery in Africa: Archaeology and Memory*, Oxford: Oxford University Press, 2012; Samuel A. Nyanchoga et al. (eds.), *Slave Heritage and Identity at the Kenyan Coast*, Nairobi: CUEA Press, 2014.
4. Edward A. Alpers, 'Recollecting Africa: Diasporic Memory in the Indian Ocean World', *African Studies Review* 43, 1 (2000); Shihan de S. Jayasuriya and Richard Pankhurst (eds.), *The African Diaspora in the Indian Ocean*, Trenton: Africa World Press, 2003; Shihan de S. Jayasuriya, 'Identifying Africans in Asia: What's in a Name?' *African and Asian Studies* 5, 3–4 (2006); Kenneth X. Robbins and John McLeod (eds.), *African Elites in India: Habshi Amarat*, Ahmedabad: Mappin Publishing, 2006.
5. House of Commons Parliamentary Papers (hereafter HCPP): Correspondence respecting Sir Bartle Frere's Mission to the east coast of Africa, 1872–1873, 1873 (C.820), LXI, 924–925.
6. In the document, this figure was spelt in different forms such as 'Ahmed bin Nahman', 'Ahmed bin Ammon', or 'Ahamed bin Aman'. Nicholls follows the spelling of 'Nahman' (Christine S. Nicholls, *The Swahili Coast: Politics, Diplomacy and Trade on the East African Littoral, 1798–1856*, London: George Allen and Unwin, 179). However, the correct spelling would be Aḥmad b. Na'amān (1784–1869). We can identify this figure with the captain of the *Saltana*, which sailed to New York in 1840–1841. He was frequently mentioned as secretary to Sa'īd (cf. Norman R. Bennett and George E. Brooks, Jr (eds.), *New England Merchants in Africa: A History through Documents, 1802 to 1865*, Boston: Boston University Press, 1965, 223 [Water to Waters, Zanzibar, 17 December 1839]; ibid., 477 [Ward to Abbot, Zanzibar, 13 March 1851]; Zanzibar National Archives (hereafter ZZBA) AA12/2/11-12 [Rigby to the Bombay Government, Zanzibar, 5 September 1861]. See also, Bennett and Brooks, *New England Merchants*, 223, n. 16).
7. ZZBA AA12/2/12 [Rigby to the Bombay Government, Zanzibar, 5 September 1861].
8. Behnaz A. Mirzai, 'Slavery, the Abolition of the Slave Trade, and the Emancipation of Slaves in Iran (1828–1928)' (Ph.D. dissertation, York University, 2004), 56–59; Matthew S. Hopper, 'The African Presence in Arabia: Slavery, the World Economy, and the African Diaspora in

Eastern Arabia, 1840–1940' (Ph.D. dissertation, University of California, Los Angeles, 2006), 93–95; Matthew S. Hopper, *Slaves of One Master: Globalization and Slavery in Arabia in the Age of Empire*, New Haven and London: Yale University Press, 2015, 203–206.

9. Indeed, purchasers' preference for African descendants is clearly found in the Baluchi slave trade just as in the East African slave trade. Hideaki Suzuki, 'Baluchi Experiences under Slavery and the Slave Trade of the Gulf of Oman and the Persian Gulf, 1921–1950', *Journal of the Middle East and Africa* 4, 2 (2013).
10. Gwyn Campbell, 'Introduction: Slavery and Other Forms of Unfree Labour in the Indian Ocean World', in Campbell (ed.), *The Structure of Slavery*; Campbell, 'Slave Trade and the Indian Ocean World', in John Hawley (ed.), *India in Africa, Africa in India: Indian Ocean Cosmopolitanisms*, Bloomington: Indiana University Press, 2008; Edward A. Alpers, 'The African Diaspora in the Indian Ocean: A Comparative Perspective', in Jayasuriya and Pankhurst (eds.), *The African Diaspora*; Alessandro Stanziani, *Sailors, Slaves, and Immigrants: Bondage in the Indian Ocean World, 1750–1914*, New York: Palgrave, 2014.
11. Oriental and India Office Collection, British Library (hereafter OIOC) IOR R/15/1/171/22 [Report on the Slave Trade in the Persian Gulf extending from 1 January 1852 to 30 June 1858 compiled by H. Disbrowe].
12. Auguste Toussaint, *Histoire de l'Océan Indien*, Paris: Presse Universitaires, 1961; Toussaint, *History of the Indian Ocean*, tr. June Guicharnaud, London: Routledge and Kegan Paul, 1966.
13. Neville H. Chittick and Robert I. Rotberg (eds.), *East Africa and the Orient: Cultural Synthesis in Pre-Colonial Times*, New York: Africana Publishing, 1975; UNESCO (ed.), *Historical Relations across the Indian Ocean: Report and Papers of the Meeting of Experts organized by UNESCO at Port Louis, Mauritius, from 15 to 19 July, 1974*, Paris: UNESCO, 1980.
14. The title of the first chapter in Toussaint, *Histoire de l'Océan Indien*.
15. Toussaint, *Histoire de l'Océan Indien*, 152, 167–168, 192.
16. Kirti N. Chaudhuri, *Asia before Europe: Economy and Civilisation of the Indian Ocean from the Rise of Islam to 1750*, Cambridge: Cambridge University Press, 1990, 387. To grasp his perspective on the history of the Indian Ocean, see Chaudhuri, *Trade and Civilisation in the Indian Ocean: An Economic History from the Rise of Islam to 1750*, Cambridge: Cambridge University Press, 1985.
17. Hikoichi Yajima, *Umi ga tsukuru bunmei: Indo-yō kaiiki sekai no rekishi*, Oosaka: Asahi shinbunsha, 1993, 53.
18. André Wink, *Al-Hind, the Making of the Indo-Islamic World, Volume 1: Early Medieval India and the Expansion of Islam 7th-11th Centuries*, Leiden: Brill, 1996, 3.

19. Ashin Das Gupta, 'Introduction II: The Story', in Das Gupta and Michael N. Pearson (eds.), *India and the Indian Ocean*, Calcutta: Oxford University Press, 1987, 39.
20. Kenneth McPherson, *The Indian Ocean: A History of People and the Sea*, Oxford: Oxford University Press, 1993, 198–252. See also, Milo Kearney, *The Indian Ocean in World History*, New York and London: Routledge, 2004, 6–7, 103–135.
21. Michael N. Pearson, *The Indian Ocean*, London and New York: Routledge, 2003, 11, 190.
22. Pearson, *The Indian Ocean*, 11–12.
23. Parthasarathi, Prasannan and Giorgio Riello, 'The Indian Ocean in the Long Eighteenth Century', *Eighteenth-Century Studies* 48, 1 (2014), 1–19.
24. Edward A. Alpers, *The Indian Ocean in World History*, Oxford: Oxford University Press, 2014.
25. For example, for a case study of the economic integration of India, see Immanuel Wallerstein, *The Modern World-System*, 3 vols, New York: Academic Press, 1974–1989, Vol. 3, 129–184.
26. Fernand Braudel, *Civilisation matérielle, économie et capitalisme: XVe-XVIIIe siècle*, 3 vols, Paris: Armand Colin, 1979, Vol. 3, 607–669.
27. Andre Gunder Frank, *ReOrient: Global Economy in the Asian Age*, Berkeley, Los Angeles and London: University of California Press, 2000, 258–320. In addition, several works examine the Indian Ocean in world system framework. Janet L. Abu-Lughod sought the origin of Modern World-System and examined the thirteenth century world system which consisted of European, Mediterranean and the Indian Ocean economies (Janet L. Abu-Lughod, *Before European Hegemony: The World System A.D. 1250–1350*, Oxford: Oxford University Press, 1989). More recently, Philippe Beaujard examines gradual process of the Indian Ocean placing itself in the central space of an Afro-Eurasian world system. His de-tailed analysis and description end with the sixteenth century when capitalism world system developed in Europe began to influence over Afro-Eurasian world system (Philippe Beaujard, *Les mondes de l'océan indien*, 2 vols., Paris: Armand Colin, 2012. See also, Philippe Beaujard, 'The Indian Ocean in Eurasian and African World-Systems before the Sixteenth Century', *Journal of World History* 16, 4 (2005), 411–465; Philippe Beaujard, 'The Worlds of the Indian Ocean', in Michael Pearson (ed.),*Trade, Circulation, and Flow in the Indian Ocean World*, New York: Palgrave, 2015, 15–26). Although scope of Beaujard's work extendsup to the sixteenth century, he also remarks the nineteenth century as turing point when European economies outcompeted Asian economies relying on arguments of the California school (Beaujard, 'The Worlds of the Indian Ocean', 24. See also Roy Bin Wong, *China Transformed: Historical Change and the Limits of European Experience*, Ithaca: Cornel University Press, 1997;

Kenneth Pomeranz, *The Great Divergence: China, Europe and the Making of the Modern World Economy*, Princeton: Princeton University Press, 2000).

28. Sugata Bose, 'Space and Time on the Indian Ocean Rim: Theory and History', in Leila Tarazi Fawaz and Christopher A. Bayly (eds.), *Modernity and Culture: From the Mediterranean to the Indian Ocean*, New York: Columbia University Press, 2002, 376. See also, Ned Bertz, 'Indian Ocean World Travellers: Moving Models in Multi-Sited Research', in Helen Basu (ed.), *Journey and Dwellings: Indian Ocean Themes in South Asia*, Hyderabad: Orient Longman, 2008, 27–28.
29. As for academic contributions, see Adriaan H.J. Prins, *Sailing from Lamu: A Study of Maritime Culture in Islamic East Africa*, Assen: Van Gorcum, 1965; D.N. McMaster, 'The Ocean-Going Dhow Trade to East Africa', *East African Geographical Review* 4 (1966); Alan Villiers, *Sons of Sinbad; An Account of Sailing with the Arabs in their Dhows, in the Red Sea, around the Coasts of Arabia, and to Zanzibar and Tanganyika; Pearling in the Persian Gulf; and the Life of the Shipmasters, the Mariners, and Merchants of Kuwait*, New York: Scribner, 1969; Hikoichi Yajima, *The Arab Dhow Trade in the Indian Ocean: Preliminary Report*, Tokyo: Institute for the Study of Languages and Cultures of Asia and Africa, 1976; Esmond B. Martin and Chryssee P. Martin, *Cargoes of the East: The Ports, Trade and Culture of the Arabian Seas and Western Indian Ocean*, London: Elm Tree Books, 1978; Ko'ichi Kamioka and Hikoichi Yajima, *Indo-yō nishikaiiki ni okeru chiikikan kouryuu no kōzō to kinō: Dau chōsa hōkoku 2*, Tokyo: Institute for the Study of Languages and Cultures of Asia and Africa, 1979; Erik Gilbert, 'The Zanzibar Dhow Trade: An Informal Economy on the East African Coast, 1860–1964' (PhD dissertation, Boston University, 1997); Erik Gilbert, *Dhows and the Colonial Economy of Zanzibar, 1860–1970*, Oxford: James Curry, 2004.
30. Gilbert, *Dhows and the Colonial Economy*, 59–83.
31. Gilbert summarized this development as follows: 'as political control of Zanzibar went over to the British, the naval anti-slavery campaign was transformed into a bureaucratic anti-dhow campaign' (Gilbert, *Dhows and the Colonial Economy*, 83).
32. Bertz, 'Indian Ocean World Travellers', 28.
33. Markus P.M. Vink, 'Indian Ocean Studies and the "New Thalassology"', *Journal of Global History* 2 (2007), 52.
34. Raymond W. Beachey, *The Slave Trade of Eastern Africa*, London: Rex Collings, 1976, 3; Campbell, 'Introduction', ix; Mark Horton and John Middleton, *The Swahili: The Social Landscape of a Mercantile Society*, Oxford: Blackwell Publishers, 2000, 73.
35. William G. Clarence-Smith, 'The Economics of the Indian Ocean and Red Sea Slave Trades in the 19th Century', in Clarence-Smith (ed.), *The Economics of the Indian Ocean Slave Trade in the Nineteenth Century*, London: Routledge, 1989, 1.

CHAPTER 2

The Slave Trade in the Nineteenth-Century Western Indian Ocean: An Overview

Introduction

Historically, slaves have been found in almost all strands of society in the western Indian Ocean region—from farmer's field to royal court and harem—and their main role differed from place to place. For example, the general term for 'slave' in Kiswahili is *mtumwa*, which is the passive voice of the verb *(ku)tuma*, meaning 'to use, dispatch', with the prefix *m* indicating the person. Thus, *mtumwa* literally means 'one who is used or dispatched', which indicates to speakers of Kiswahili that a slave was originally a domestic servant rather than an agricultural labourer.

Recent studies on Indian Ocean slavery have emphasized that the slave trade there existed long before its Atlantic counterpart. Indeed, the earliest known legal documents concerning the sale of a slave are on an Ur-Nammu tablet from *c.*2100–2050 BCE,[1] although the nineteenth century is recognized as the peak period of the trade. Various estimates of slave exports from the East African coast to the Gulf of Oman and the Persian Gulf, the main artery of slave trade in western Indian Ocean, agree that there was a sharp increase between the end of the eighteenth century and the first half of the following century, although certain discrepancies can be found which we will discuss later. A fundamental reason for the increase was the rise of the plantation economy, to which the Mascarene Islands, north-western Madagascar and the East African coast transitioned connecting to the global market. Once the plantation economy was on track, the profits from it were invested in both land and

H. Suzuki, *Slave Trade Profiteers in the Western Indian Ocean*, Palgrave Series in Indian Ocean World Studies,
DOI 10.1007/978-3-319-59803-1_2

manpower to facilitate greater wealth from increased production capability. In Mauritius, expansion of sugar production began about 1815, and the 1825 Trade Bill of Mauritius encouraged it, eventually allowing Mauritius sugar to compete with West Indian sugar in Britain.[2] Thus, figures for both acreage of sugar production and new purchases of slaves by estate holders show sharp increases in the 1820s.[3]

Three Major Entrepôts and Modes of Enslavement

There were three major entrepôts for nineteenth-century slave transport across the western Indian Ocean. Even though we must bear in mind the significance of non-African slaves circulating in the western Indian Ocean region throughout the long history of the slave trade there, as far as the nineteenth century is concerned the major entrepôts were concentrated along the African coast.[4] One was the coastal area around the Horn of Africa, with places such as Maṣṣawaʿ (Massawa), another was the East African coast, notably Kilwa and Zanzibar, and the third was on both sides of the Mozambique Channel, including Mozambique Island.

As we shall see from the details given in Chap. 5, individual cases show that slaves' paths towards slavery were varied and intricate. Nonetheless, it might be helpful to give a general impression here. Many of the slaves brought to ports in the Horn of Africa facing the Gulf of Aden and the Red Sea were transferred to the opposite coast, often purchased by Muslim pilgrims as popular souvenirs. On the other hand, a good number of slaves who had been brought to Barbara and also places south of Cape Haafun and Cape Guardafui were taken over to the Gulf of Oman and the Persian Gulf.[5] Furthermore, substantial numbers of slaves from the Horn of Africa went to Egypt.[6]

Different ethnicities satisfied different market demands. There are a number of surviving instruction manuals on the purchase of slaves in medieval Arabic literature which confirm this, as do nineteenth-century documents. Slaves from the Horn of Africa were generally preferred, especially in the Arabian Peninsula. Often appearing as 'Hab(u)shi' in the contemporary documents, they tended to fetch much higher prices than slaves from the East African coast, who were often called 'Si(d)di'.[7] Slaves from the Horn of Africa tended to be treated better too.

Slave transport along the East African coast changed greatly throughout the nineteenth century. In the first half, many slaves who reached the East African coast were sent to the Gulf of Oman and the Persian Gulf, and to a lesser extent to north-west India via Zanzibar and Kilwa. Along the Arabian side of both gulfs, particularly between Baḥrayn Island and Ras al-Ḥadd, there was great demand not only for household slaves, concubines or slaves for military service (common roles in slavery), but also for slaves to work in maritime industries including fishing and shipping, and as sailors.[8] In addition, slaves were needed to construct and maintain the irrigation system which supplemented a chronic shortage of rainfall, and as a labour force for the region's date cultivation, which connected the area with world markets. Pearl fishing also required a large labour force.[9] According to a report in the early twentieth century, about a third of pearl divers were of African origin.[10] As such, in this region there was high demand for a labour force from external sources,[11] largely because there was insufficient local labour, apart from nomads who visited the coast seasonally and provided temporary labour. In addition to the demand within the region, demand for slaves existed in the hinterlands too, including Istanbul and the Iranian plateau. There, it was widely observed that rulers, rich administrators and merchants in urban areas customarily possessed slaves, such as those of the Royal Harem of the Ottoman sultans.[12] In addition, according to the 1867 Census, slaves and servants made up 13% of total population in Tehrān.[13] It was frequently reported that pilgrims to Makka (Mecca) and Kalbalā' purchased slaves.[14] Albeit only in relatively small numbers, slaves were continuously re-exported to the Indian subcontinent.[15]

One important change that took place in nineteenth-century East African port towns was related to slave distribution. Large-scale cultivation of coconuts and cloves was introduced there as late as the 1830s, and triggered new demand for labour. As a result, there was an accumulation of slaves from the interior in the port towns along the East African coast, with some being re-exported overseas, but many remaining on the coast. Paul E. Lovejoy estimates the total number of slaves brought from East Africa during the nineteenth century at 1,651,000, with 769,000 (46.6%) actually employed along the coast.[16] Another estimate by Abdul Sheriff shows that 19,800 per year were brought from the mainland to Zanzibar and 12,000 of them were not re-exported but remained on the island in the 1860s.[17] Also, the port record between May and December of 1866, provided by the Stone Town Customs to the British Consulate in Zanzibar, states that 20,711 slaves were brought through customs during that time and 11,882 of them (57.4%) remained on the island.[18]

The other region important for the export of slaves in the nineteenth century was the Mozambique Channel—both sides of it. Gwyn Campbell estimates that throughout the nineteenth century Portuguese East Africa exported 1900 slaves annually while Madagascar exported over 400 slaves annually to the south–west Indian Ocean region.[19] Until recently scholars believed that most slaves from Portuguese East Africa were exported via the Atlantic trade to places like the Caribbean islands,[20] and paid little attention to exports within the western Indian Ocean.[21] However, as Campbell shows, a much larger number of slaves than previously thought were used to meet the demand in the Mascarene Islands as well as on Madagascar.[22] Pedro Machado, meanwhile, estimates that roughly 1000 slaves a year were shipped to places in Portuguese India such as Goa, Diu and Daman.[23]

Sugar production rose enormously in Mauritius during the first half of the nineteenth century, and as Vijaya Teelock has made clear that increase required a large number of slaves. In 1825, Mauritius produced 217,397 tons of sugar, but just ten years later, its output increased threefold.[24] Production relied largely on slave labour: slaves from Portuguese East Africa had been the largest group among this population until the 1820s, when the Creoles overtook them.[25] Robert T. Farquhar, the Governor of Mauritius, tried to expand agricultural production even more and, following the abolition of slavery, attempted to introduce Chinese workers from Southeast Asia as well as convicts from the Indian subcontinent. However, neither plan worked well, and eventually he was forced to rely on labour from Africa.[26] Both the number of imported slaves and the average price of them more than doubled between 1825 and 1829, but as a system of indentured labour had been reintroduced in the 1830s the labour force on Mauritius gradually shifted from slaves to indentured labourers.[27] French-controlled Réunion Island (Bourbon Island) also began to rely on indentured labour after slavery was abolished there in 1848. Although we tend to assume that this was the turning point from an African to an Asian labour force, a significant number of labourers still came from the East African coast, Portuguese East Africa and Madagascar.[28]

Madagascar exported slaves mainly to the Mascarene Islands as well as to the East African coast. According to Pier M. Larson, Madagascar exported over half a million slaves between 1500 and 1930 and he claims that Malagasy speakers formed possibly the single largest native speech community among slaves scattered around the western Indian Ocean.[29] The nineteenth century is noted as the period when the trade increased dramatically, despite a type of 'closed-door policy' during the reigns of Radama I (1793–1828, r. 1810–1827) and his successor Ranavalona I (1788–1861, r. 1828–1861).[30] In 1845, an insufficiency in the supply of labour for the sharply expanding sugar industry in the Mascarene Islands prompted a joint British and French force to attempt an attack on Toamasina, a Malagasy port connected to the islands.[31] The attempt failed, and in fact strengthened the Imerina 'closed-door policy'. Campbell gives it as a cause for Mascarene plantation owners to seek new sources for their labour force.[32] Although it exported slaves, Madagascar also imported slaves, for it experienced its own demand for them,[33] especially on its north-western coast. There, the influence of the Sakalava is still great today, and there are people called 'Makoa'. That name recalls the Makua who inhabit Mozambique and its environs; indeed, many of the Makoa claim that their ancestors were brought from Lake Nyasa via Mozambique Island or Kilwa.[34]

Recently, scholars have begun to explore the links between the slave trades in the western Indian Ocean and in the Atlantic. Richard B. Allen has estimated a sharp increase in slave exports on board French ships on the Indian Ocean, from about 52,169 to 56,485 between 1670 and 1769, to 160,572–186,816 in 1770–1810, and thereafter 123,379–144,959 in 1811–1830.[35] The Atlantic plantation economy contributed to the increased demand for slaves in the western Indian Ocean between the late eighteenth century and the early nineteenth, with Rio de Janeiro absorbing a large number of slaves from Mozambique. According to Herbert S. Klein, ever-rising demand for slaves in Brazil coincided with severe droughts (between 1790 and 1830) and the *mfecane* movement in south-eastern Africa.[36] Moreover, after 1811 the Portuguese government gave Brazilian slavers access to trade freely from all its East African ports, which opened the floodgates for the demand for slaves there. Klein estimated that as many as 386,000 East Africans were forced to migrate to America from 1811 onwards, and Mozambique became the nineteenth century's third largest supplier of slaves to America.[37]

People were enslaved almost everywhere and in a variety of ways. Obvious ways included being captured in war, being kidnapped or as a result of debt bondage, and these happened often. However, we should not ignore certain natural disasters people faced such as drought or plagues of insects, or other factors, which sometimes made voluntary enslavement a relatively attractive option in order to survive. In such circumstances some people chose to surrender themselves or their families to enslavement,[38] so although it is possible to categorize the mode of enslavement, the reality was often more complex. A notable and well-known example is given by Edward A. Alpers, who discovered the story of a girl called Swema in the missionary archives in Paris. Swema, a Yao girl, grew up in a relatively wealthy family. Her father died in a hunting accident and some time after that her family's arable land was severely damaged by a plague of locusts. Swema's family's neighbours lent them millet seed but the crop failed. In the end, to clear Swema's family's debt the neighbours sold her to a slave caravan heading for the coast.[39]

Trade Volume and Gender Ratio

While we know the main entrepôts and can confirm that demand for slaves existed throughout the western Indian Ocean world and even beyond, and link the former with the latter, it remains rather more difficult to be sure of either the route, the volume of the trade or the gender ratio in an accurate manner. We will explore routes further in Chap. 5. The volume of the trade, meanwhile, is one of the major points of disagreement in studies of the slave trade in the western Indian Ocean[40]; the major estimates from the East African coast to the Gulf of Oman and the Persian Gulf are given in Table 2.1.

There are several reasons for the differing estimates. First of all, because, unlike for the Atlantic slave trade, we have no records made by the traders themselves, we are forced to rely largely on British records of their programme of suppression. However, the reliability of those records is highly questionable in many cases. They contain many exaggerations and not a few of them are based completely on rumours. A number of naval and consular records show the actual number of slaves rescued, but reading through them carefully it is clear that large numbers of slaves remained in captivity. Therefore, the records chosen by scholars for attention, and how much they were relied upon, mean there is great variation in results. The problems are rather similar to those on that arise when attempting to discover accurate trading routes. Referring to the number of slaves exported from Zanzibar and Kilwa, for example, we cannot discover their destinations. Shipping routes were changeable and in most cases ships called at several ports before reaching their final destinations. We must therefore consider the possibility that slaves were disembarked en route as well as at a ship's destination. As Chap. 5 shows, slaves themselves were often involved in the chain of reselling, thus making it even more difficult to determine what their final destinations were. That slaves were disembarked at their ship's final port of call by no means meant that they would not be transferred again elsewhere.

As for gender ratio, conventionally scholars agree that, in contrast to the trans-Atlantic slave trade, more females than males were taken as

Table 2.1 Estimates of average numbers of slaves exported from east coast of Africa to the Gulf of Oman and the Persian Gulf

Martin and Ryan 1977		*Austen 1981*		*Sheriff 1987*		*Austen 1989*		*Ricks 1989*	
		1700–1815	2250						
1770	2500							1722–1782	500–600
-1829		1815–1875	6625	1st half of 19c.— early 1870s	Gradual decrease from 3000 to 1000			1782–1842	800–1000
1830s	3500					1830–1866	2700–3100		
1840s	4000							1842–1872	2000–3000
1850–1873	6500								
								1872–1902	50–100

Source Ralph A. Austen, 'From the Atlantic to the Indian Ocean: European Abolition, the African Slave Trade, and Asian Economic Structures', in David Eltis and James Walvin (eds.), *The Abolition of the Atlantic Slave Trade: Origins and Effects in Europe, Africa and the Americas*, Madison: University of Wisconsin Press, 1981; Ralph A. Austen, 'The 19th Century Islamic Slave Trade from East Africa (Swahili and Red Sea Coasts)', in Clarence-Smith (ed.), *The Economics of the Indian Ocean Slave Trade*, 29; Esmond B. Martin and T.C.I. Ryan, 'A Quantitative Assessment of the Arab Slave Trade of East Africa, 1770–1896', *Kenya Historical Review* 5 (1977); Ricks, 'Slaves and Slave Traders in the Persian Gulf', 67; Sheriff, *Slaves, Spices and Ivory*, 40

slaves in the Indian Ocean trade.[41] However, a number of contemporary records from East Africa challenge this view.[42] For example, the list of slaves emancipated in 1860–1861 from the Indian population in Bū Sa'īdi East Africa by Christopher P. Rigby, the second British Consul in Zanzibar (1858–1861), shows that 53.12% were male.[43] That might be explained as an exception by the fact that, by the 1860s, Zanzibar had already transformed itself into a plantation-based economy, unlike many other regions in the western Indian Ocean world, and plantations generally required more males than females, as shown by Caribbean and American examples. However, considering slave demand in the East African coast was so significant in the nineteenth-century western Indian Ocean-wide context, case studies there must be considered significant when addressing the question of the gender ratio in the entire region in that period. In addition, the Persian Gulf also required a large number of males, especially for its pearl fishing industry. As far as I have been able to discover, no Persian Gulf pearling ships ever allowed females on board, pearl diving being exclusively an occupation for males. Although we have insufficient data on the slave population in the nineteenth-century Persian Gulf, data we do possess for the first half of the twentieth century confirms that there were more male slaves than female.[44] Ultimately, the question of the gender ratio requires more data; however, it is fair to say at this stage that we should not overestimate the number of female slaves in the western Indian Ocean world, especially in the nineteenth century. Considering these obstacles to any accurate knowledge of both the trade volume and its gender ratio, I am forced to admit the inherent limitations of so much estimating in this overview; however, it must be acknowledged that it would be next to impossible to reach the same sort of numerical accuracy as Atlantic studies have been able to achieve. A productive approach at this stage is a qualitative analysis which will clarify the actual condition of the slave trade with as much detail as possible. Chapter 5 addresses that challenge.

Slave Transport, Trade and Usage

Now, as the last topic in this chapter, we can explore the actual conditions of slave transport, trade and usage in the western Indian Ocean world. These following quotations are of prime importance in tackling the question. James Felix Jones, who served as Political Agent at Bandar-e Būshehr between 1855 and 1858, wrote that:

> In fact the term 'slaver' is scarcely one applicable to these vessels in its full sense, for assumedly in proportion to the general cargo, pertaining, perhaps to a variety of owners, the slaves brought in their form but a small part. They are in short quite a distinct class of vessels from those expressly fitted slavers dealing so largely in the inhuman traffic on the west coast of Africa.[45]

The second quotation is from a 'report on the slave trade in the Persian Gulf extending from January 1, 1852 to June 30, 1858' compiled by Herbert F. Disbrowe, *Assistant* Political Resident for the *Persian Gulf*:

> The term 'slaver', it is not unworthy of remark, is scarcely applicable to vessels that engage in slave trade between Zanzibar and the Persian Gulf. No such thing as a slavers, that is, a ship specially rigged for, or solely occupied in, the transport of human flesh, is to be found in these tracts. The slaves that may be on board constitute but a minimum part of the cargo in the vessel.[46]

Certainly, carrying slaves promised large profits in the western Indian Ocean; nevertheless, slave transporters did not deal only in slaves.[47] Traders did not sail long distances directly, such as between the East African coast and the Gulf of Oman or the Persian Gulf. Non-stop sailing between those regions by trading dhow has occurred only relatively recently. Hikoichi Yajima and Ko'ichi Kamioka, who surveyed the dhow trade in the region in the 1970s, claim that such non-stop voyages by dhow are a phenomenon of 'the last few years'[48] and it is probable that they became possible only as dhows began to be motorized during the same decade. Thus, before motorization, dhows had to rely entirely on seasonal monsoon winds. It was then common for owners to maximize their use of what was a fairly reliable system of durable winds, and, to do so, they sailed from port to port and carried on trading along the way until they reached their final destination. In fact, James Christie, who was in Zanzibar in the early 1870s to investigate cholera epidemics along the East African coast, stated:

> In the absence of steam communication, the trade and other connections between Zanzibar and the regions to the north and south depend entirely upon the prevalence of the north-east and south-west winds, no native craft being able to beat in either direction against the monsoons ... Many of these native vessels having trade communications with other places

> besides Zanzibar, arrive with the first of the monsoon, and, after discharging, take in fresh cargo and proceed to the ports south of Zanzibar, such as Madagascar or Mozambique. At the southern ports they take in return cargo, and leave with the first of the south-west monsoon for Zanzibar, where they discharge and load for their respective ports.[49]

A similar observation was made by Alan Villiers in the middle of the following century.[50] Putting together those quotations then, it should come as no surprise to us that B.W. Montrion listed coffee, grains and roof timbers, along with slaves, as general cargo on board a ship from Zanzibar to the Persian Gulf in his letter to A. Clarke, Consul at Aden, dispatched from Bandar-e Būshehr on May 3, 1854.[51]

Considering other contemporary sources, as well as my own interviews with local elders in Ṣūr, Oman, which I carried out in September 2005 and August 2009, we can list as general cargoes in the trade from the Gulf of Oman and the Persian Gulf to the East African coast notably salt, salted fish and cloth. Salted fish, locally called *māliḥ* (literally 'salted'), remains a staple in Ṣūr and whole of coastal Oman today.[52] Generally, the surplus catch of shark and kingfish is salted and dried, and along the East African coast, it is called *n'gonda* and is a popular foodstuff for the coastal people. Nowadays, locally produced *n'gonda* is common; however, the older folk in Stone Town remembered imported *n'gonda*, which came from the Gulf of Oman and was common in the days before independence. Today, imported *n'gonda* from Oman or Somalia is highly valued in Zanzibar, especially by those who remember those days. Quite a number of nineteenth-century writers observed that salted fish was imported along the East African coast and some mentioned it as one of the items exported from Oman. Edmund Roberts, who visited Masqaṭ in the early 1830s, listed it, as well as salt, as export items to East Africa.[53] According to Charles Guillain, a French naval officer who directed a commercial survey along the East African coast in the 1840s, dhows from the Omani coast moved southward to the Banaadir coast (eastern Somali coast) and the East African coast while fishing; wherever they stopped they sold fish which had been salted on board and was an important trade item in such ports as Mombasa and Mogadishu.[54] He also stated salt was an important trading item from the Persian Gulf to east coast of Africa, and that the Somalis especially used it for preparing hides.[55] A detailed account by Samuel B. Miles reveals that salt and salted fish from al-Ḥikmān Peninsula or the bay of Ghubba Ḥashīsh were carried to the East African coast.[56]

Salted fish was cheap source of rich animal protein. For example, according to research on commodity prices on the market in Zanzibar, an ounce of salted shark meat cost 1 Paice per 1 oz piece, which was almost the same price as one of the coconuts that were abundant on the island.[57] Therefore, salted shark meat was one of the staples of the diet there, especially for the slaves.[58] Another interesting observation was made in Zanzibar by William H. Ingrams, who was the Colonial Administrator there between 1919 and 1927. He recorded that while the local inhabitants knew how to produce salt,[59] they actually relied entirely on imported salt except in cases of emergency, such as when trade was suspended for some reason.[60] Similar reports of the dependency of Zanzibar on exported salt are found in accounts from the middle of the nineteenth century.[61]

As indicated in Chap. 1, technically any dhow could be a 'slaver'. In fact, the term 'dhow' in English represents, as Gilbert explains, various types of local vessels.[62] As far as the documents related to the slave trade are concerned, types of dhows frequently mentioned are buggalow (also spelled by European and American travellers baghla, bghala, bugala, bugalow, bugara, bugarah, buggarah), bateel (batel, batillah), bedan and kotia. Clearly, arriving at any sort of typology for dhows has a certain difficulty, as Dionisius A. Agius discusses,[63] not least because usage of terms differs from place to place. For example, in Suez, Richard F. Burton recorded that there were two types of local vessel ('sambuk' and 'baghlah') and people distinguished between them according to size rather than design. Thus, while modern scholars usually differentiate between 'sambuk' (or *sanbūq* in Arabic) and 'baghlah' (or *baghla*), since the former is categorized as a fishing boat and the other is an ocean-going cargo vessel, in Suez when Burton was there a 'sambuk' was merely smaller version of 'baghlah'.[64] Therefore, the following summary for each type of dhows can be no more than a general one.

The buggalow can be identified with the Arabic *baghla*, which was the largest type of Arab dhow,[65] often rigged with two or three masts and ocean-going. Agius emphasizes its size in his detailed study of dhows on the Arabian side of the Gulf of Oman and the Persian Gulf, listing some ancient *baghla*s as over 500 tons.[66] Likewise, modern scholars tend to give relatively large tonnages for the type.[67] However, as far as the nineteenth century is concerned, standard *baghlas* seem to have been much smaller. Using statistics from 1893 for the local trading boats Gilbert suggests that ocean-going vessels were usually between 50 and 150 tons.[68] Guillain also supposed that most of the vessels of his time were around 50 or 60 tons.[69]

The kotia or *kūtiyya* resembled the buggalow in size and shape, but in the Persian Gulf, because of the similarity between two, the name *baghla* often replaced the name *kūtiyya*.[70] There is a suggestion that the Arabic term *kūtiyya* is etymologically derived from Indian languages,[71] and certain scholars claim that an Indian influence can be discerned in the vessels themselves.[72]

The name bateel is *battīl* in Arabic, and in the Persian Gulf the bateel was known as a pirate ship as well as a man-of-war.[73] A double-ended boat, this dhow was renowned for its speed, while a shallow draught enabled cargo-carrying examples to escape from British patrolling ships, which were usually too large to enter shallow water.[74] George L. Sullivan, a naval officer who saw repeated action in the suppression campaign, stated it was the largest type of ship engaged in the slave trade. As Aḥmad al-Bishr al-Rūmī and Gilbert claim, that type of dhow is no longer found today, so it is difficult to confirm Sullivan's observation. While Miles stated the average size is between 100 and 200 tons,[75] al-Rūmī claims that the general size of sailing bateel is between 15 and 20 tons.[76]

Finally, the bedan (*badan*) was generally used for fishing, but could withstand long-distance sailing. It carried two sails for use when carrying cargo, but fishing was done under oars.[77] Generally, it was smaller than other types. According to the description of a bedan included in the album published after Guillain's French expedition along the East African coast, the range of tonnage for a bedan was from 15 to 20 tons, similar to the average tonnage estimated by Miles.[78] Apart from those types, a dhow called a *mtepe*—of so-called 'sewn' construction, actually a method of using timber, and with a square sail—was reported as being used for slave transport along the East African coast.[79]

As well as considering the various sizes of these different types of dhow, it must be remembered that slaves were only one of the types of cargo which might have been found on board ships in the region. Furthermore, the overall scale of slave transport by dhow should not be overestimated: Table 2.2 shows that the average number of slaves on board each dhow was 36 and the majority carried fewer than 20 at a time.

Table 2.2 Numbers of slaves on board dhows, 1837–1880, featuring 326 dhows

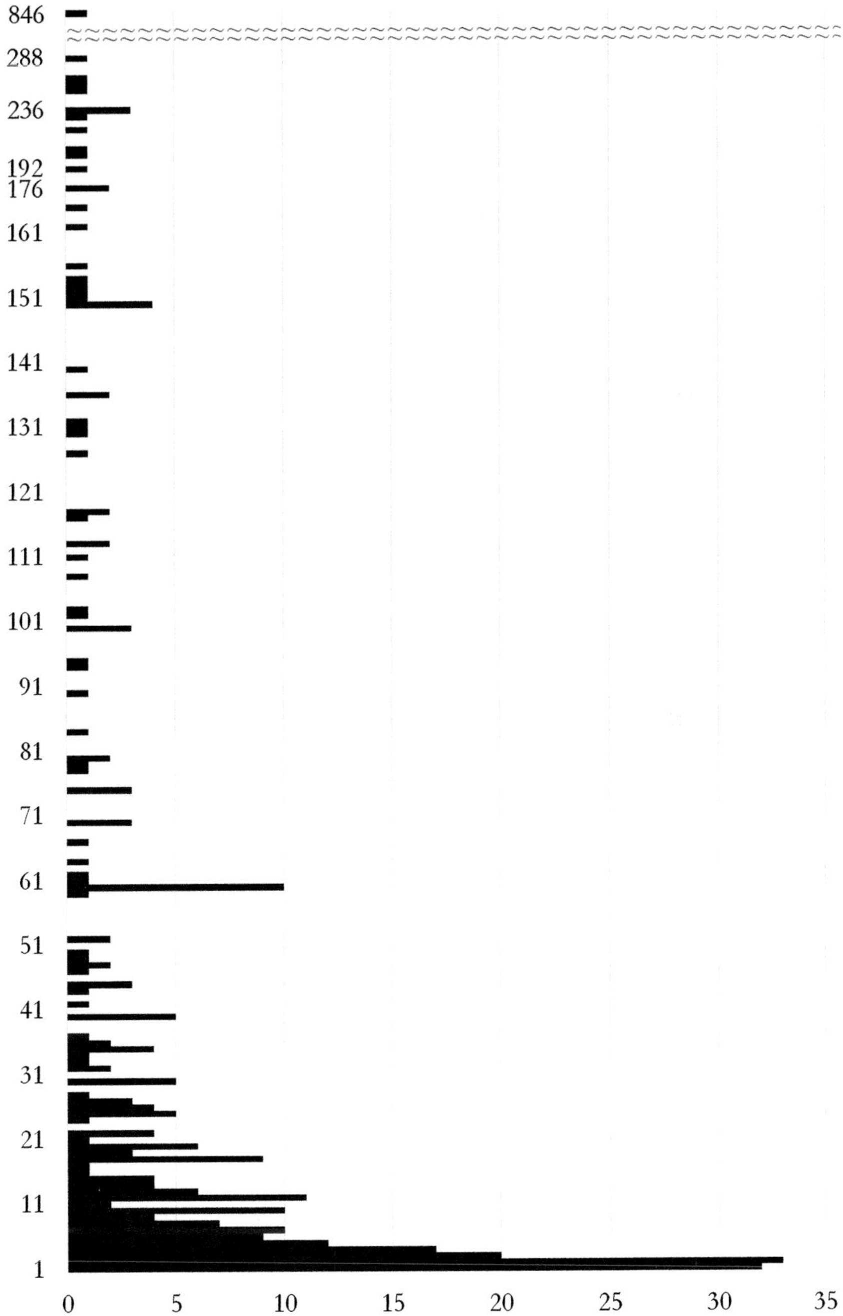

(*Continued*)

Table 2.2 (*Continued*)

Source BPP, Slave Trade, Vol. 24, Class D, 28, 33, 69, 380; ibid., Vol. 25 Class A, 363–364, 380–381, 383–384, 386, 388, 423–424; ibid., Vol. 39, Class B 198, 203–205; ibid., Vol. 40, Class B, 367, 371–375; ibid., Vol. 41, Class B, 292–294, 304; ibid., Vol. 46, Class A, 85–88; ibid., Vol. 48, Class A, 12–13, 29–31, 164; ibid., Vol. 49, Class A, 42–43, 188, Class B, 73, Class C, 64–65, 68, 180, Class D, 120, 125; ibid., Vol. 50, Class A, 15, 17–18, 91, 99–100, 102, 104–105; ibid., Vol. 51, Class A, 10, 68, 71; ibid., Vol. 52, Class A, 86; ibid., Vol. 91, 138, 187–189, 198–199, 203, 488; MAHA PD/1837/78/854/393-400; MAHA PD/1855/1457/93, 115; MAHA PD/1856/93/28/203; MAHA PD/1864/54/704/279; MAHA PD/1864/54/942/14; MAHA PD/1865/52/780/13; MAHA PD/1877/149/689/66; NAUK ADM123/179/n.d.; NAUK FO84/1090/86-98, 105; NAUK FO84/1224/205; NAUK FO84/1245/189; NAUK FO84/1325/166; NAUK FO84/1344/139; NAUK FO800/234/66, 93; NAUK FO881/1703/3, 6; NAUK FO881/3342/5-7; OIOC IOR/L/P&S/9/42/349-351; OIOC IOR/L/P&S/18/B84/65, 72, 81; OIOC IOR/R/15/1/123/13, 14, 17, 22, 25, 26, 27, 29–30; OIOC IOR/R/15/1/127/3, 22, 25, 27; OIOC IOR/R/15/1/134/1, 5; OIOC IOR/R/15/1/143/306-314; OIOC IOR R/15/1/157/226; OIOC IOR R/15/1/168/119; OIOC IOR R/15/1/177/11; OIOC IOR R/20/A1A/255/9; OIOC IOR R/20/A1A/255/26; OIOC IOR/R/20/A1A/285/77; OIOC IOR R/20/A1A/318/90-91, 143; ZZBA AA12/2/9-10; ZZBA AA12/29/32; Jerome A. Saldanha, 'Précis on Slave Trade in the Gulf of Oman and the Persian Gulf, 1873–1905 (With a Retrospect into Previous History from 1852)', in Jerome A. Saldanha (ed.), *The Persian Gulf Précis*, 8 vols, Gerrards Cross: Archive Editions, 1986 (1st. in 18 vols., Calcutta and Simla, 1903–1908), Vol. 3, 90

As to the price of slaves, the principle rule was that the longer it took to transport them, the higher the price. Comparing the prices at Zanzibar and at Bandar-e Būshehr in 1842, for instance, at Zanzibar, a slave cost 14–25 Maria Theresia Thaler (MT$),[80] while at Būshehr the price was 35–40 MT$.[81] The rise in the price of slaves in line with the distance they had to be moved was, in fact, quite frequently remarked on.[82] One of the reasons for it was simply cost. A greater distance obviously required much more time and that implied more food for the slaves, for one thing. In fact, as Hopper shows,[83] owners and captains of dhows did indeed receive higher transport fees for long journeys. Another reason for higher prices was the intermediate margin. As Chap. 5 shows, slaves were a commodity and could be seen as an investment to gain profit from resale. Finally, there was risk of capture by naval patrols or consulate staff, including native agents.

From the traders' point of view, the main threat to the value of slaves as an investment was that they might become too old to be sold, or might simply die. In fact, in the western Indian Ocean, it was rare for slaves over 30 to be sold[84]; the majority of slaves for investment were likely to be children, something discussed further in Chap. 5. Although there is no solid quantitative dataset that would enable us to say anything definitive on the question at present, there are plenty of contemporary observations showing that purchasers preferred children.[85] An important background point to this was that host societies tended to assimilate slaves,[86] and that, apart from in a few spots along the East African coast and the Persian Gulf, slaves were not used in industries requiring a large-scale labour force. As a matter of fact, even in those places such industries had appeared only relatively recently considering how long slavery had flourished there. Rather than merely a labour force, slaves, in a sense, represented their master's standing. They would be required to accompany their masters and to accede to their every demand. Assimilation, specifically, means acquiring the language, customs and manners of a host society, so if a slave acquired such knowledge and developed skills to a level high enough to meet his master's requirements, he or she could expect to be treated much better than others who perhaps could not.[87] In order to facilitate the assimilation process, purchasers thus preferred children to adults as slaves, because, of course, children are much more adaptable.

Notes

1. Adolf Leo Oppenheim, *Ancient Mesopotamia: Portrait of a Dead Civilization*, rev. Erica Reiner, Chicago and London: University of Chicago Press, 282; Jack Goody, 'Slavery in Time and Space', in James L. Watson (ed.), *Asian and African Systems of Slavery*, Berkeley and Los Angeles: University of California Press, 1980, 18.
2. For the impact of the 1825 Trade Bill, see Vijaya Teelock, *Bitter Sugar: Sugar and Slavery in 19th Century Mauritius*, Moka: Mahatma Gandhi Institute, 1998, 42–46.
3. Ibid., 72, 83–84.
4. The data on non-African slaves in the nineteenth-century western Indian Ocean is still insufficient. However, the limited available sources do reveal their distribution (as Chap. 3 examines), while the National Archives of the United Kingdom (hereafter NAUK) FO84/1325/89 [Kirk to Principal Secretary of State for Foreign Affairs, Zanzibar, 15 February 1870] report the existence of Turkish and Georgian slaves in Zanzibar. See also Mirzai, 'Slavery, the Abolition of the Slave Trade, and the Emancipation of Slaves', 18–63.
5. OIOC IOR/R/20/A1A/318/85 [Memorandum for the guidance of Mr. Rutherford, I.N., Commanding HMS *Fanny*, 9 March 1861].
6. Al-Qāhira (Cairo) held not only slaves imported by sea. For example, according to Terence Walz, who investigated Sub-Saharan habitants in this city based on the 1848 census, the number of Ethiopians brought via the Red Sea was lower than those brought along the Nile, including

from southern Kurdfān or Dārfūr (Terence Walz, 'Sketched Lives from the Census: Trans-Saharan Africans in Cairo in 1848', paper presented at Tales of Slavery Conference, University of Toronto, 20–23 May 2009, n.p.).

7. 'Hab(u)shi' derives from *habashī* in Arabic and *habshī* in Persian (Henry Yule and Arthur C. Burnell, *Hobson-Jobson: A Glossary of Colloquial Anglo-Indian Words and Phrases, and of Kindred Terms, Etymological, Historical, Geographical and Discursive*, 1886; London: James Murrey, 1903 (1st. 1886), 428, s.v. Hubshee), while 'Si(d)di' derives from *sīdī* in Hindi, which means 'master', 'ruler', 'owner' and 'descendent of prophet', or *sayyid* in Arabic. According to Yule and Burnell, 'Si(d)di' was used for Africans at the ports and in the ships in West India (ibid., 806, s.v. Seedy). Burton explains that 'Si(d)di' indicates 'Negro Muslim' (Richard F. Burton, *The Book of the Thousand Nights and a Night*, ed. Leonard C. Smithers, 12 vols, London: H.S. Nichols, 1894, Vol. 4, 231). As for these terms, see Shihan de S. Jayasuriya and Richard Pankhurst, 'On the African Diaspora in the Indian Ocean Region', in Jayasuriya and Pankhurst (eds.), *The African Diaspora*, 8. See also James R. Wellsted, *Travels in Arabia*, 2 vols, London: J. Murray, 1838, 388–389.
8. For example, see James S. Buckingham, 'Voyage from Bushire to Muscat, in the Persian Gulf, and from Thence to Bombay', *Oriental Herald* 22–67 (1829), 93; William Heude, *A Voyage up the Persian Gulf and a Journey Overland from India to England in 1817*, London: Longman, 1819, 22; Robert Mignan, *Winter Journey through Russia, the Caucasian Alps, and Georgia; thence across Mount Zagros, by the Pass of Xenophon and the Ten Thousand Greeks, into Koordistaun*, 2 vols, London: Richard Bentley, 1839, Vol. 2, 240; Samuel B. Miles, *The Countries and Tribes in the Persian Gulf*, London: Bentley, 1919, 401; OIOC IOR/L/P&S/18/B84/72 [Report by Mr. Rothery respecting Dhows lately captured by Her Majesty's ships 'Peterel' and 'Nymphe'].
9. As for slave usage in the Persian Gulf, see also Thomas M. Ricks, 'Slaves and Slave Traders in the Persian Gulf, 18th and 19th Centuries: An Assessment', in Clarence-Smith (ed.), *The Economics of the Indian Ocean Slave Trade*, 65. Furthermore, Matthew S. Hopper clarified the contribution of pearl fishery and date cultivation to connect the Persian Gulf region to the world economy as well as to the (slave) labour demand of these industries, which continued until the early twentieth century. See Hopper, *Slaves of One Master*. In addition, recent work done by Benjamin Reilly shows the large-scale employment of African slaves in agricultural areas of the Arabian Peninsula. See Benjamin Reilly, *Slavery, Agriculture, and Malaria in the Arabian Peninsula*, Athens: Ohio University Press, 2015.

10. Abdul Sheriff, *Slaves, Spices and Ivory in Zanzibar: Integration of an East African Commercial Empire into the World Economy, 1770–1873*, Oxford: James Curry, 1987, 37.
11. However, unlike conventional assumptions associated with the 'revolt of Zanj', that the lower basin of both the Tigris and the Euphrates historically contained a large population of agricultural slaves, Albertine Jwaideh and James W. Cox claim that as far as the nineteenth and early twentieth centuries are concerned, few African slaves were employed in agriculture in either place. (Albertine Jwaideh and James W. Cox, 'The Black Slaves of Turkish Arabia during the 19th Century', in Clarence-Smith (ed.), *The Economics of the Indian Ocean Slave Trade*, 50–51.)
12. For example, according to his study on slavery and its abolition in the nineteenth-century Ottoman Middle East, Ehud R. Toledano claimed that a majority of slaves from east coast of Africa were female, and in general they were less valued than female slaves from other regions such as Georgia, the Caucasus and Ethiopia (Ehud R. Toledano, *Slavery and Abolition in the Ottoman Middle East*, Seattle: University of Washington Press, 1998, 13). In addition, referring to a report made by Kemball in 1856, in the case of slaves who were brought from Kuwayt to Ottoman Arabia, those from the east coast of Africa were sold with a 50% mark-up of their original price, while Ethiopian slaves were sold at three times their original price (OIOC IOR/R/15/1/130/292-293 [Kemball to Malet, Bushire, 12 November 1856]).
13. Thomas Ricks, 'Slaves and Slave Trading in Shi'i Iran, AD 1500–1900', in Maghan Keita (ed.), *Conceptualizing/Re-Conceptualizing Africa: The Construction of African Historical Identity*, Leiden: Brill, 2002, 84.
14. For example, *British Parliamentary Papers*, Slave Trade, 95 vols, Shannon: Irish University Press, 1968–, Vol. 24, Class D, 26 [Kemball to Robertson, Karrak, 8 July 1842] (hereafter known as *BPP*); OIOC IOR/R/15/1/143/353-354 [Kemball to Anderson, Bushire, 12 April 1854]; ibid., 355 [Abdool Nubbee to Kemball, s.l., received 9 April 1854].
15. *BPP*, Vol. 24, Class D, 71–72 [Memorandum explanatory of the cases cited by the Earl of Aberdeen, in his note to Ali Bin Nasir, dated 6 August 1842]; Dady R. Banaji, *Slavery in British India*, Bombay: Taraporevala Sons, 1933, 74–76; Kelly, *Britain and the Persian Gulf*, 416–417. As Philip H. Colomb, who engaged in naval suppression as a captain, reported, on the Indian subcontinent with its large population, generally speaking demand for labour from outside was not high (Philip H. Colomb, *Slave-Catching in the Indian Ocean: A Record of Naval Experiences*, New York: Negro Universities Press, 1873, 100). See also Graham, *Great Britain in the Indian Ocean*, 152–153; Sheriff, *Slaves, Spices and Ivory*, 40.

16. Paul E. Lovejoy, *Transformations in Slavery: A History of Slavery in Africa: Third Edition*, Cambridge: Cambridge University Press, 2012, 151.
17. Sheriff, *Slaves, Spices and Ivory*, 226–231.
18. NAUK FO84/1279/43-46 [Tables settling for the legitimate slave trade at the port of Zanzibar].
19. Calculated by the author, based on Gwyn Campbell, *An Economic History of Imperial Madagascar, 1750–1895: The Rise and Fall of an Island Empire*, Cambridge: Cambridge University Press, 2005, 238, Table 9.3.
20. The latest study by Pedro Machado shows a dramatic increase in Mozambique slave exports to Brazil from the early 1810s due to increasing demand for sugar production (Pedro Machado, *Ocean of Trade: South Asian Merchants, Africa and the Indian Ocean, c.1750–1850*, Cambridge: Cambridge University Press, 2014, 218).
21. Campbell, *An Economic History of Imperial Madagascar*, 213–214.
22. Ibid., 213–242.
23. Pedro Machado, 'A Forgotten Corner of the Indian Ocean: Gujarati Merchants, Portuguese India and the Mozambique Slave-Trade, *c.* 1730–1830', in Campbell (ed.), *The Structure of Slavery*, 19–26. It should be noted that Machado's estimate excludes slaves exported to other regions of India, such as Kachchh.
24. Teelock, *Bitter Sugar*, 82–83.
25. Ibid., 63.
26. Ibid., 64–73.
27. Ibid., 73; Hugh Tinker, *A New System of Slavery: The Export of Indian Labour Overseas 1830–1920*, 1974; London: Hansib, 1993 (1st. 1974, London: Oxford University Press), 53–56. Prior to abolition of slavery in 1835, the Indian population of Mauritius was quite small. For example, in 1826/7 Indians amounted to only 6.4% of the total population; however, in 1871 they numbered 216,258 while the Creole population was 99,784 (Tinker, *A New System of Slavery*, 56. See also, Richard B. Allen, 'The Mascarene Slave-Trade and Labour Migration in the Indian Ocean during the Eighteenth and Nineteenth Centuries', in Campbell (ed.), *The Structure of Slavery*, 36).
28. Hai Quang Ho, *Histoire économique de l'île de la Réunion (1849–1881): Engagisme, croissance et crise*, Paris: L'Harmattan, 2004, 69–88; Edith Wong-Hee-Kam, *La diaspora chinoise aux Mascareignes: le cas de la Réunion*, Paris: L'Harmattan, 1996; Sudel Fuma, *L'esclavagisme à La Réunion 1794–1848*, Paris: L'Harmattan, 1992, 184–185; Lovejoy, *Transformations in Slavery*, 220. For example, in Bourbon, between 1848 and 1859, 7500 indentured labourers were brought from Madagascar and the surrounding islands yearly (Campbell, *An Economic History of Imperial Madagascar*, 215–216). For similarities between the living and labour conditions of indentured labourers and slaves, see Tinker, *A New System of Slavery*. In addition, until 1858, the

contracts of African indentured labourers did not include an end date (Ho, *Histoire économique de l'île de la Réunion*, 89).

29. Pier M. Larson, 'Enslaved Malagasy and "Le Travail de la Parole" in the Pre-Revolutionary Mascarenes', Journal of African History 48 (2007), 457–479.
30. Campbell, *An Economic History of Imperial Madagascar*, 215. Campbell, *An Economic History of Imperial Madagascar*, 213–215.
31. Export of sugar from Mauritius continued to expand steadily until the middle of the 1860s. See Table 2.1 in Richard B. Allen, *Slaves, Freedmen, and Indentured Laborers in Colonial Mauritius*, Cambridge: Cambridge University Press, 1999, 23.
32. Campbell, *An Economic History of Imperial Madagascar*, 215.
33. Ibid., 229.
34. For recent studies of them, see Klara Boyer-Rossol, 'Le stigmatisation des *Makoa* ou *Masombika*: les séquelles de l'esclavage à Madagascar (XIXe–XXe siècles)', in Laurant Médéa (ed.), *Kaf: Etude pluridisciplinaire*, Sainte-Clotilde: Zarlor éditions, 2009, 31–37; Klara Boyer-Rossol, 'L'histoire orale de Makoa: un pont entre les deux rives du canal de Mozambique', paper presented at Tales of Slavery Conference, University of Toronto, 20–23 May 2009.
35. Richard B. Allen, 'Satisfying the "Want for Laboring People": European Slave Trading in the Indian Ocean, 1500–1850', *Journal of World History* 21, 1 (2010), 67. He revised his estimate later, but still sharp increase is found (Richard B. Allen, *European Slave Trading in the Indian Ocean, 1500–1850*, Athens: Ohio University Press, 2014, 23).
36. Herbert S. Klein, *The Atlantic Slave Trade*, Cambridge: Cambridge University Press, 2010 (1st. 1999), 71.
37. Ibid., 72. See aslo, Edward A. Alpers, '"Moçambiques" in Brazil: Another Dimension of the African Diaspora in the Atlantic World', in José C. Curto and Renée Soulodre-La France (eds.), *Africa and the Americas: Interconnections during the Slave Trade*, Trenton and Asmara: Africa World Press, 2005, 44.
38. Edward A. Alpers, 'The Story of Swema: Female Vulnerability in Nineteenth-Century East Africa', in Claire C. Robertson and Martin A. Klein (eds.), *Women and Slavery in Africa*, Madison: University of Wisconsin Press, 1983, 190, n. 5; Campbell, *An Economic History of Imperial Madagascar*, 220; Frederick Cooper, *Plantation Slavery on the East Coast of Africa*, Portsmouth: Heinemann, 1997 (1st. 1977, New Haven: Yale University Press), 126–129; Samuel Mateer, *Native Life in Travancore*, London: W.H. Allen, 1883, 300.
39. Alpers, 'The Story of Swema'.
40. Clarence-Smith, *The Economics of the Indian Ocean Slave Trade*, 1.

41. Hopper, 'The African Presence in Arabia', 10.
42. Cooper, *Plantation Slavery*, 221–222; Sheriff, 'Localisation and Social Composition of the East African Slave Trade, 1858-1873', in Clarence-Smith (ed.), *The Economics of the Indian Ocean Slave Trade*, 139–141.
43. For details of this list, see Hideaki Suzuki, 'Enslaved Population and Indian Owners along the East African Coast: Exploring the Rigby Manumission List, 1860–1861', *History in Africa* 39 (2012).
44. Hideaki Suzuki, 'Baluchi Experiences under Slavery and the Slave Trade of the Gulf of Oman and the Persian Gulf, 1921–1950', *Journal of the Middle East and Africa* 4, 2 (2013).
45. OIOC IOR/R/15/1/157/208 [Jones to Anderson, Bushire, 28 August 1856].
46. OIOC IOR R/15/1/171/22-23.
47. Joseph Miller, 'A Theme in Variations: A Historical Schema of Slaving in the Atlantic and Indian Ocean Regions', in Campbell (ed.), *The Structure of Slavery*, 176.
48. Kamioka and Yajima, *Indo-yō nishi-kaiiki*, 45.
49. James Christie, *Cholera Epidemics in East Africa; An Account of the Several Diffusions of the Disease in that Country from 1821 till 1872*, London: Macmillan, 1876, 8–9. See also, ibid., 102, 111; Cooper, *Plantation Slavery*, 32; Victor Fontanier, *Voyage dans l'Inde et dans le Golfe Persique par l'Égypte et la Mer Rouge*, 2 vols, Paris: Paulin, 1844, Vol. 1, 264; Arnold B. Kemball, 'Paper Relative to the Measures Adopted by the British Government, between the Years 1820 and 1844, for Effecting the Suppression of the Slave Trade in the Persian Gulf', in R. Hughes Thomas (ed.), *Arabian Gulf Intelligence*, Bombay: Bombay Education Society's Press, 1856, 651; Wellsted, *Travels in Arabia*, Vol. 1, 23–24.
50. Alan Villiers, 'Some Aspects of the Arab Dhow Trade', *Middle East Journal* 2, 4 (1948), 399–416.
51. OIOC IOR/R/15/1/143/319. See similar cases in NAUK FO84/1279/83-84 [Majid to Seward, s.l., 9 Shawwāl 1283].
52. John Malcolm, *Sketches of Persia*, 2 vols, London: J. Murray, 1849, Vol. 1, 9; Joseph B.F. Osgood, *Notes of Travel or Recollections of Majunga, Zanzibar, Muscat, Aden, Mocha, and Other Eastern Ports*, Salem: George Creamer, 1854, 76; Edmund Roberts, *Embassy to the Eastern Courts of Cochin-China, Siam, and Muscat; in the U.S. Sloop-of-War Peacock, David Geisinger, Commander, during the Years 1832-3-4*, Wilmington: Scholarly Resources, 1972 (1st. 1937, New York: Harper), 353; David Wilson, 'Memorandum Respecting the Pearl Fisheries in the Persian Gulf', *Journal of Royal Geographical Society of London* 3 (1833), 283.
53. Roberts, *Embassy to the Eastern Courts*, 351, 361. See also, Bennett and Brooks, *New England Merchants*, 157 [Roberts to McLane, Washington,

14 May 1834]; Richard F. Burton, *Zanzibar; City, Island, and Coast*, 2 vols, London: Tinsley Brothers, 1872, Vol. 2, 415; Lewis Pelly, 'Remarks on the Tribes, Trade and Resources around the Shore Line of the Persian Gulf', *Transaction of Bombay Geographical Society* 17 (1863), 66–67; Osgood, *Notes of Travel*, 76, 82; OIOC IOR/R/15/1/143/258 [Kemball to Anderson, Bushir, 1 July 1854].

54. Charles Guillain, *Documents sur l'histoire et le commerce de l'Afrique Orientale*, 2 parts, Paris: Arthus Bertrand, 1856–1858, Part 2, Vol. 2, 335.
55. Guillain, *Documents*, Part 2, Vol. 1, 537; Burton, *Zanzibar*, Vol. 2, 415; Nicholls, *The Swahili Coast*, 78.
56. Miles, *The Countries and Tribes*, 489, 542.
57. Burton, *Zanzibar*, Vol. 2, 422. According to ibid., 418, 8 Paica was equal to 1 Anna and 16 Anna was equivalent to 1 MT$. The coconut price was calculated here based on the price of coconuts in the same report (ibid., 422), 1000 coconuts for 7.5 MT$.
58. ZZBA AA12/29/44 [Hamerton to Secretary to Bombay Government, Zanzibar, 2 January 1842].
59. For local method in the middle of the nineteenth century to obtain salt, see Richard F. Burton, *The Lake Regions of Central Africa: A Picture of Exploration*, 2 vols, California: The Narrative Press, 2001 (1st. 1860, London: Longman, Green, Longman, and Roberts), Vol. 2, 342.
60. William H. Ingrams, *Zanzibar: Its History and its People*, London: Taylor & Francis, 1967, 285.
61. Mahārāshtra State Archives (hereafter MAHA) PD/1859/188/1123/82 [Rigby to Anderson, Zanzibar, 10 May 1859 (Report on the Dominions of His Highness the Sultan of Zanzibar and Sowahil, agreeably to Mr. Hart's Circular No. 3391 of 1859 dated 16 November 1855); Burton, *The Lake Regions of Central Africa*, Vol. 2, 342.
62. Gilbert, *Dhows and the Colonial Economy*, 37.
63. Dionisius A. Agius, *In the Wake of the Dhow: The Arabian Gulf and Oman*, Ithaca: Reading, 2002, 183–189.
64. Richard F. Burton, *Personal Narrative of a Pilgrimage to Mecca and Medina*, 3 vols, Leipzig: Bernhard Tauchnitz, 1874, Vol. 1, 171.
65. Agius, *In the Wake of the Dhow*, 49; Miles, *The Countries and Tribes*, 412.
66. Agius, *In the Wake of the Dhow*, 51.
67. Aḥmad al-Bishr al-Rūmī's work on Kuwayti dhows claims that this type of dhow never exceeded 400 tons (Aḥmad al-Bishr al-Rūmī, *Muʿjam al-muṣṭalaḥāt al-baḥrīya fī al-Kuwayt*, Kuwayt: Markaz al-Buḥūth wa al-Dirāsāt al-Kuwaytīya, 2005, 15), while Yaʿqūb Yūsuf al-Ḥijjī identifies the range of tonnage of this type between 120 and 400 tons (Yaʿqūb Yūsuf al-Ḥijjī, *Ṣināʿa al-sufun al-sharāʿīya fī al-Kuwayt*, Kuwayt: Markaz al-Buḥūth wa al-Dirāsāt al-Kuwaytīya, 2001, 40).

68. Gilbert, *Dhows and the Colonial Economy*, 37.
69. Guillain, *Documents*, Part 2, Vol. 2, 357.
70. Agius, *In the Wake of the Dhow*, 55.
71. Yajima, *The Arab Dhow Trade*, 29, n. 14.
72. Agius, *In the Wake of the Dhow*, 56–57.
73. Ibid., 63; al-Ḥijjī, *Ṣināʿa al-sufun al-sharāʿīya*, 30.
74. Agius, *In the Wake of the Dhow*, 63.
75. Miles, *The Countries and Tribes*, 412.
76. Al-Rūmī, *Muʿjam al-muṣṭalaḥāt al-baḥrīya*, 15.
77. Agius, *In the Wake of the Dhow*, 102.
78. Guillain, *Documents*, album, pl. 51–52; Miles, *The Countries and Tribes*, 413.
79. William C. Devereux, *A Cruise in the 'Gorgon'; or, eighteen months on H. M. S. 'Gorgon', engaged in the suppression of the slave trade on the east coast of Africa. Including a trip up the Zambesi with Dr. Livingstone*, London: Dawsons, 1869, 122.
80. Bennett and Brooks, *New England Merchants*, 253 [Memorandum of Richard P. Waters dated 18 October 1842].
81. *BPP*, Vol. 24, Class D, 30 [Edwards to Kemball, Bushire, 9 July 1842].
82. *BPP*, Vol. 25, Class A, 363 [The Acting Resident in the Persian Gulf to Secretary to Bombay Government, Karrac, 6 October 1840]; *BPP*, Vol. 24, Class D, 26 [Kemball to Robertson, Karrak, 8 July 1842]; *BPP*, Vol. 51, Class B, 131 [Pelly to Anderson, Bandar Lenge, 5 December 1863].
83. Hopper, 'The African Presence in Arabia', 42; Hopper, *Slaves of One Master*, 49.
84. *BPP*, Vol. 24, Class D, 32 [Wilson to Government, n.p., 28 January 1831].
85. See also, Alpers, 'The Story of Swema'; Fred Morton, 'Small Change: Children in the Nineteenth-Century East Africa Slave Trade', in Gwyn Campbell, Suzanne Miers and Joseph C. Miller (eds.), *Children in Slavery though the Ages*, Athens: Ohio University Press, 2009.
86. Campbell, 'Introduction', xviii–xix.
87. Hideaki Suzuki, 'Distorted Variation: Reconsideration of Slavery in the Nineteenth Century Swahili Society from Masters' Perspective', in Alice Bellagamba and Martin Klein (eds.), *African Slaves, African Masters: Politics, Memories and Social Life*, Trenton: Africa World Press, 2017.

CHAPTER 3

Resistance of Transporters and Insufficiency of the Indian Navy's Suppression Prior to 1860

Introduction

The campaign against the slave trade proceeded by means of two different but closely interrelated processes: practical and legal. By practical I mean the naval campaign of patrols, seizures and confiscation, which were often violent means. The legal campaign preceded the practical campaign and included various orders, proclamations and treaties issued and concluded against the slave trade. In principle, the practical measures were taken within the framework and limits fixed by the legal preparations, which had been under way since the beginning of the nineteenth century. However, practical steps against the trade were not taken in earnest before the 1840s.

In the western Indian Ocean region, the nineteenth century marked the peak of the slave trade, largely because of labour demand as a result of economic growth—the rise of a plantation-based economy along the East African coast is a notable example—while the increased prosperity the economic growth brought with it enabled people to buy slaves to bolster their social status. Clove mania in Zanzibar started sometime in the 1830s, while demand for slaves in the Persian Gulf remained high. Thomas M. Ricks concisely explains the reasons behind the demand for slaves in Iran by pointing out that in the second half of the eighteenth century the Zandīyeh dynasty subjugated southern Iran and regions beyond, including al-Baṣra and Baḥrayn Island. Under the reign of Karīm Khān Zand (*c.*1705–1779), commerce was encouraged, and many

H. Suzuki, *Slave Trade Profiteers in the Western Indian Ocean*, Palgrave Series in Indian Ocean World Studies,
DOI 10.1007/978-3-319-59803-1_3

merchants who had left Iran earlier in the eighteenth century because of political instability then returned; at the same time a start was made on the construction of suitable infrastructure. Thus, demand for labour increased for both agriculture and artisanal production but a shortage of available labour force in Iran was a severe hindrance to the recovery process. Slaves from East Africa were the answer.[1]

In this chapter, we shall begin by tracing the development of the legal measures intended to suppress slave trade. After that, the focus will turn to the period of slavery's practical suppression until 1860. This year was the turning point for suppression because that was when the Royal Navy joined the suppression campaign, replacing the Indian Navy. While Chap. 4 looks more closely at the activities of the Royal Navy, this chapter examines the period during which the Indian Navy played the major role in the suppression campaign. Put simply, the Indian Navy's activities were insufficient and far from successful for two main reasons: one being the nature of the Indian Navy itself, the other being resistance by the people transporting the slaves.

Legal Process of Suppression in the Western Indian Ocean

A number of proclamations and orders related to the slave trade were issued in India, and one of the earliest in Bombay Presidency was the order of 1805,[2] which prohibited the import of slaves to any of the ports in the British East India Company's Bombay district. The order had been made 2 years before the British Parliament passed the Slave Trade Act (47 Geo. III, Sess. 1 *Cap.* 36); 6 years after the Slave Trade Act, another Act of Parliament of 1811 (51 Geo. III, *Cap.* 23) made engagement in the slave trade a felony. In the same year, similarly, the government of Bengal passed Regulation X which prohibited the movement of slaves for sale into the East India Company's territory of India, and it created a solid legal ground against the slave trade there.[3] Eventually, in 1843, slavery was abolished in the entirety of the Indian territories under the control of the East India Company.[4]

The first step in British efforts at legal suppression of the slave trade in the Indian Ocean region outside India was the General Maritime Treaty, concluded in 1820 with the shaykhs on the Arabian side of the Persian Gulf. As a matter of fact the treaty was far from voluntary, for immediately after defeating the Qawāsim, on the pretext of suppressing piracy, the British 'encouraged' the shaykhs to sign and thereby took up a position as their protectors in the Persian Gulf.[5] Indeed, the treaty is widely recognized as an important milestone on the Persian Gulf's absorption into Britain's 'informal' empire.[6] It is a milestone along another road too, for it pushed forward Britain's attempt to suppress the slave trade in the western Indian Ocean, as Article 9 of the treaty relates to the slave trade. It says '[t]he carrying off of slaves, men, women, or children from the coasts of Africa or elsewhere, and the transporting them in vessels, is plunder and piracy, and the friendly Arabs shall do nothing of this nature'.[7] Following it, the British concluded the so-called Moresby Treaty in 1822.[8] That treaty was signed by Sa'īd b. Sulṭān, the Imam of the Bū Sa'īd, who had not signed the General Maritime Treaty. At first glance, the treaty seems to have been intended to stop the transport of slaves to Christian countries, but in fact it also obliged all dhows to carry a certificate showing the port of departure as well as that of destination (Article 6). Britain requested the establishment of a zone within which the Bū Sa'īd was obliged to take responsibility for any ships without certificate found carrying slaves to the direction of Christian countries, while Britain reserved to herself the right to seize those outside of that zone (Article 6).[9] An addendum, 5 days after the treaty was first signed, defined the area over which Britain had charge,[10] and extension came when the treaty was renewed in 1839 (Article 1).[11] Raymond W. Beachey evaluated the treaty thus:

> [T]he Moresby Treaty fell far short of complete abolition, but it was a surprising achievement in the light of slow progress made later in the nineteenth century to end the East African slave trade.[12]

Another important element of the treaty was that it was one of the earliest to force local polities in the western Indian Ocean to recognize maritime boundaries.[13] Even so, there was no way it could have led to the abolition of slavery in this area, largely because of the insufficiency of the naval forces available as well as other treaties with local polities were not yet concluded or only affected insufficiently.

Eighteen years after the Moresby Treaty, by agreements entered into with all the shaykhs on the Arabian coast—with the exception of those of Kuwayt and Baḥrayn—British cruisers were authorized to detain and search any vessels belonging to those shaykhs or to their subjects if they suspected them of having any individuals on board who might have been kidnapped. In 1845, after a new treaty known as the Hamerton Treaty was concluded, which banned slave traffic between Asia and Africa,[14] such traffic was limited to the East African territory of the Bū Saʿīd. To ensure that prohibition was put into effect, the Cape of Good Hope squadron of the Royal Navy took charge of the area south of the 4th southern parallel while a squadron of the Indian Navy patrolled north of it.[15] Eventually, by 1848, Britain had concluded a series of treaties with most of the polities along the Gulf of Oman and the Persian Gulf, banning the slave trade between Africa and Asia.[16] However, in practice suppression efforts did not progress accordingly. Although nominally both the Royal Navy and the Indian Navy took part in the campaign, in reality, until the beginning of the 1860s, the Indian Navy took a leading role because the Royal Navy needed to devote itself to the suppression of the Atlantic slave trade.[17] The Indian Navy's direction of the campaign was inadequate for reasons we shall now discuss.

The Indian Navy and the Anti-Slave Trade Campaign Prior to 1860

The Indian Navy established naval bases on Bandar-e ʻAbbās and Khārk Island as well as in Aden.[18] However, they failed to seize even a single vessel between 1820 and 1842.[19] After the Hamerton Treaty was signed their performance improved but only very slowly, and even by the 1850s they had liberated only a small number of slaves. As Table 3.1 shows, 71 slaves were rescued in 1856, which was the most successful year for the Indian Navy in the period covered by the data on that table; in 1855 no slaves were rescued and the average number rescued per year during the entire period was just 25.

Table 3.1 Slaves liberated between 1852 and the end of June 1858

Year	*The number of liberated slaves*
1852	3
1853	50
1854	25
1855	0
1856	71
1857	25
1858	2

Source OIOC IOR/R/15/1/171/29–33

In fact, many scholars agree that the British anti-slave trade efforts up to the mid-1860s were inefficient.[20] Lindsay Doulton argues that Indian Government feared that active suppression would result in an outbreak of hostilities which would ultimately disrupt trade in general.[21] Related to that, another large obstacle to efficient suppression was simple lack of resources.[22] The 'Indian Navy List for 1858'[23] shows the navy had 252 officers and 31 vessels, and that number represents the entire force available for the whole area of their responsibility, which at that time covered the vast region from the South China to the East African coasts. Moreover, as a comprehensive study by Charles R. Low makes clear, they were required to engage in emergency operations such as the Anglo-Burmese Wars (1824–1826, 1852–1853) and the Opium Wars (1839–1842, 1856–1860).[24] As well as that, in 1856 for example, the Qajar invaded Herāt, which Britain regarded as an important bulwark against possible Russian inroads southward towards India. The Indian Navy was consequently ordered to assemble a force in the Persian Gulf in preparation for an emergency.[25] Moreover, because of continuous tribal conflict in the Persian Gulf and rampant 'piracy' as they called it, the Indian Navy was unable to maintain a stable peace in an area which had significant importance for Britain as part of her commercial and communications routes. Its strength was still insufficient to control the region in the 1850s, fully three decades after the General Maritime Treaty had been concluded.[26] There was a chronic lack of patrol vessels and those allotted to the task were usually obsolete. It frequently happened that Indian Navy craft were too slow to catch slave ships, even if they received reports of them.[27] If the navy's outdated vessels did give chase, local vessels could escape by virtue of the superior seamanship of their crews and their use of camouflage, along with other measures discussed later in this chapter. Repeated requests for reinforcements from officers serving in the suppression campaign eventually led to gradual improvement from the early 1850s, but, as we saw earlier, this did not reach the level required.[28]

To understand why progress was so slow, it is not enough to point simply to lack of motivation in Bombay and poor equipment levels of the navy. It is also essential to consider the process employed by the Indian Navy when they seized a 'slaver'. In 1861, for example, once a naval ship's captain had captured a 'slaver' he had to bring the suspect vessel itself for trial to Bombay where the Prize Court of the Vice-Admiralty was located.[29] If the case was approved, the successful captain might

Table 3.2 Number of slaves on board ships confiscated by the Indian Navy Patrol, 1837–1859, featuring 80 dhows

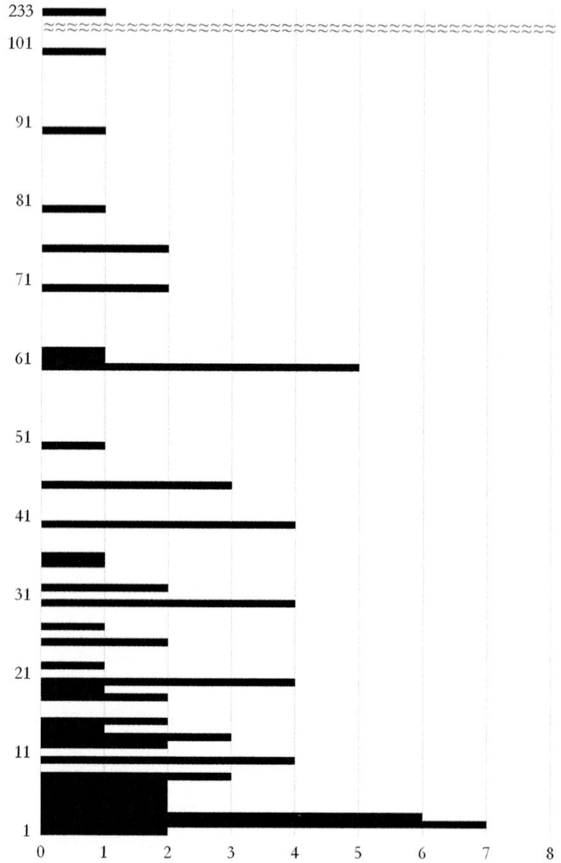

Source BPP, Slave Trade, Vol. 24, Class D, 33, 69, ibid., Vol. 25, Class A, 363–364, 380–381, 383–384, 386, 388, 423–424; ibid., Vol. 39, Class B, 198, 203–205; ibid., Vol. 40, Class B, 375, 367, 371–374, 375; ibid., Vol. 41, Class B, 292–294, 304; ibid., Vol. 46, Class A, 85–88; MAHA PD/78/854/1837/393–400; MAHA PD/1855/70/1457/93, 115; MAHA PD/1856/93/28/203; NAUK F084/1090/86–98, 105; OIOC IOR/R/15/1/123/13, 14, 17, 22, 25, 26, 27, 29–30; OIOC IOR/R/15/1/127/3, 22, 25, 27; OIOC IOR/R/15/1/134/1, 5; OIOC IOR R/15/1/143/306–314; OIOC IOR R/15/1/157/226; OIOC IOR R/15/1/168/119; OIOC IOR R/15/1/177/11; OIOC IOR R/20/A1A/255/9; ZZBA AA12/29/32; Saldanha, 'Précis on Slave Trade', 90.

receive a bounty of £5 for each slave on board, but he was detained at Bombay and also required to pay all expenses while the court deliberated.[30] Those deliberations sometimes took 2 years to be concluded.[31]

That troublesome process and the lengthiness of the deliberations were 'a great cause of discouragement to the officers of the Indian Navy engaged in suppressing the slave trade'.[32] Furthermore, the regulations of the Indian Navy did not always guarantee sufficient reward for the effort made by a captain and his crew. Not infrequently, the expense incurred by captains in the process of capturing 'slavers' and waiting for the court to pass judgement exceeded the eventual bounty they received. The Government of Bombay noted the complaints submitted by Indian Navy officers about this.[33]

Bearing in mind the stereotypical image of the 'slaver' drawn from the Atlantic cases, one might doubt such complaints, since such 'slavers' always carried a large number of slaves, meaning the bounty would have been large. However, whereas the 'Voyages' project led by David Eltis and Martin Halbert created a rich database of the Atlantic slave trade based on ships' logs and a mass of other documents for at least two thirds of all voyages between 1514 and 1866,[34] there is nothing like a similar amount of data available for the western Indian Ocean trade. Even so, many agree that the size of each transport would have been smaller than the Atlantic. Gerald S. Graham, in his study of early nineteenth-century British supremacy in the Indian Ocean estimated that 100 slaves per ship was normal for the region.[35] However, in reality, the number might well have been much smaller than even that estimate. Table 3.2 is based on data collected by the current author on the number of slaves found at each rescue by the Indian Navy until 1860. According to the table, only two ships carried over 100 slaves (2.4% of all the ships in Table 3.2), while 81.5% of ships carried fewer than 50 slaves, with 23.5% carrying fewer than five.

The Other Cause: Resistance by the Transporters

The other important reason for the slow progress of suppression was the success of the transporters' efforts at resistance. The transporters went to great lengths—and showed much ingenuity—in their determination to continue their work. One method frequently seen in the records is camouflage. There were several ways to use camouflage, but the most common seems to have been camouflaging the slaves themselves.[36] George L. Sullivan, a Royal Navy Captain, described the situation on board a dhow carrying slaves:

> Twenty or thirty, perhaps are told off to represent part of the crew; the half-dozen Arabs, who are generally on board and concerned in the matter, dress up some of the women slaves, each representing one as his wife, and sometimes he is fortunate enough to have two; the remainder of the negroes, or as many as possible, are dressed up in Arab costumes, turbans, &c., and called passengers, and they too sometimes have their wives sitting by them … All these are usually arranged round the ship in dumb silence, which is sufficient alone to create suspicion in the experienced.[37]

Sometimes, such camouflage was used on a grand scale. One notable example is to be found in a report from 1837, actually before the naval campaign had started in earnest. The report states that one *nakhodha* (the one who has responsibility for the dhow's navigation and the management of its cargo while on board) and seven seamen kidnapped 233 girls from Barbara and carried them to al-Baṣra, Bandar-e Būshehr and other ports for sale. The girls were disguised as the seamen's wives just as in the above-quoted instance described by Sullivan.[38] In addition, while it was common to see African sailors on board ships in the Gulf of Oman and the Persian Gulf as well as on the route between these regions and East African coast, many naval officers would not have been familiar with local customs and manners, and thus would have been unable to communicate fluently enough in the local languages. Thus, officers frequently faced difficulties in distinguishing slave sailors, who were on the way to be sold, from free Africans who simply happened to be sailors.[39] For that reason, men who knew the local customs and manners and could act as interpreters were taken on board ship with the naval patrols,[40] but even then officers were often suspicious that the interpreters might have been in the pay of the slavers. William M. Coghlan, Political Resident and Commandant in Aden, acknowledged that 'common native interpreters, who, as a class, are open to bribery, and by no means disposed to discriminate between the real crew and the slaves who are often falsely represented to belong to it'.[41] Another common form of camouflage was the hoisting of a false flag, something which will be explored in Chap. 9.

The transporters had a huge advantage both in their highly skilled seamanship and the technical merit of their vessels.[42] The maximum speed of their dhows was usually about 11 knots in favourable conditions,[43] quite enough fast to give naval officers an unpleasant surprise.[44] Sometimes, transporters discovered new routes. For example, a Church Mission Society (CMS) missionary Johann L. Krapf, who surveyed the coastal region of East Africa between Mombasa and Cape Delgado in 1850, reported that many slaving dhows moved northward from Kilwa to head off the east coast of Zanzibar.[45] That was most probably because they could thereby avoid being seen by other ships—including patrolling naval vessels. If the dhows sailed along the west coast of Zanzibar where Stone Town was located they ran a far greater risk of detection. Other dhows selected Lamu as their ostensible destination, which was at the southern end of Bū Saʿīdi control. Rigby noted that these dhows originally carried slaves with permission from Bū Saʿīdi Sultan, then headed northward from this border port on the sly.[46] According to the treaties, by 1860, when Rigby was writing, slave transport was legal within East African Bū Saʿīdi territory. Thus, slaves were first transported to isolated locations such as banks with dense vegetation, small creeks or bays, and then embarked for a journey northwards.[47] A good number of slaves embarked at Mkokotoni on Zanzibar, some 35 km away from Stone Town, while Pemba Island was another frequent embarkation point. When they reached the Gulf of Oman and the Persian Gulf, the slaves were similarly disembarked at places British native agents or patrolling ships rarely visited, and from there transported to cities by land or in small boats.[48] The reason for using small boats was that they could run into shallow waters such as small inlets where patrol ships could not follow.[49] Other ships disembarked their slaves at locations on the Batīnah coast and returned to their home port, leaving the slaves to be transported separately.[50] Such a 'time lag' method was observed in the region of the Horn of Africa too.[51]

The transporters did not rely solely on their geographical knowledge and sailing skills. Another remarkable aspect of their resistance was that they watched the current methods of the anti-slave trade campaign very carefully. For example, when dhows carrying slaves began to be captured in the Gulf of Oman and the Persian Gulf, many began calling at Ṣūr at the entrance to the Gulf of Oman, in order to obtain the latest information about British patrols in the gulf.[52] The following phenomenon represents how carefully the transporters observed the progress of the legal restriction of slave trade. When the Hamerton Treaty came into effect in 1847, the price of slaves in Kilwa declined sharply. According to the observation by Loarer, who surveyed the East African coast during that period, the price fell by more than 25% in comparison with previous years because the transporters abided by the ban against entering Stone Town port, which was ordered immediately the treaty became effective.[53] In April 1847, at the end of the north-east monsoon season, the British Consul at Zanzibar reported there had been few slave dealings by vessels from the Gulf of Oman and the Persian Gulf throughout that season.[54] In another letter, he reported that 'not one-tenth of the number of slaves usually brought from the coast of Africa have arrived at Zanzibar'.[55] The calm continued likewise throughout the following north-east monsoon season. Nonetheless, once the transporters ascertained that the actual campaign had not become stricter in practice than before, slave trading along the East African coast revived in 1849.[56] The transporters did not always persist in carrying slaves, but rather carefully observed the current situation and did whatever they could to best operate their businesses.

Resistance by the transporters was radical enough for them to create the following method of plying their trade. In a letter dated 10 February 1848, the Consul at Zanzibar reported the following local situation in Persia: '[t]here is much talk amongst the people here relative to the refusal of the King of Persia to prohibit the importation of slaves into his ports'.[57] Just a month before that letter was sent from Zanzibar, Mollā Ḥusayn, British native agent in al-Shāriqah (Sharjah), wrote to Samuel Hennell, British Resident in the Persian Gulf (1838–1852):

> When the entire prohibition of the traffic was introduced by the British Government the Arabs of these countries were much distressed at heart but when they heard of the exemption claimed by the people of Lingah, as being the subjects of Mohamed Shah, over whom, the commands of the British Government had no force, then were they indeed rejoiced (to find) that ways and means are open to them for its prosecution.[58]

At that time, Britain had concluded treaties with almost all the polities surrounding the Gulf of Oman, as well as the Persian Gulf, to ban slave trading—except Qājār. This meant that only Qājārid ships could convey slaves without any treaty restrictions.[59] Therefore, if one could arrange for Qājārid ships to transport slaves, they would not be subjected to British interference.[60] So the slave transporters not only resisted physically, they were keenly aware of the complex and rapidly changing international situation regarding the legal restriction of the slave trade. As I have already mentioned, I have had to rely principally on British sources to describe various attempts at resistance by the transporters: British naval and consular officers noted each method of resistance as it occurred and subsequently took measures against it. The relationship they describe between themselves and the transporters emerges almost as a sort of never-ending 'hide and seek'.

Under such circumstances, in the early 1860s further progression in the methods of resistance was reported from Zanzibar as follows:

> A is a British Indian subject, the owner of a dhow, B is an Arab, who wants to run a cargo of slaves to Muscat, but fears to fall in with a cruiser if he runs coastwise. So B comes to A and says, 'I hear you want a crew to take your dhow to Bombay: you have lent me money on occasion; it would now be a pleasure to me to lend you a crew, with one of my Arab nakodas in command. I should not ask any remuneration, only when the dhow arrives at Bombay, just give the nakoda (captain) his discharge.' A thus gets his dhow run for nothing. B puts a crew—slaves—to the number of fifty on board, in charge of his nakoda. The dhow arrives at Bombay ...
>
> Presently the firm to whom the dhow is consigned, are about to run a bugalow to Muscat. 'Very well', says B, the nakoda, 'I must return to Zanzibar in any event. You have fed my people while in Bombay, I will run your bugalow to Muscat en route, no charge, only a "buckshish" for myself, if you are content with me and my crew, on discharge at Muscat.'[61]

In short, the report tells us that (a) an Arab who wanted to engage in slave dealings used dhows owned by an Indian resident in Zanzibar under the pretext of conveying only general items; (b) this transport was destined for Masqaṭ via Bombay; (c) slaves were disguised as seamen; and (d) the slaves who were eventually sold in Masqaṭ were employed as seamen until they got there. Those points can be interpreted as follows. First, the ostensible reason for sailing was to carry trade goods to Bombay, and the owner of the dhow was an Indian resident who could claim the rights of a British subject. Therefore, the dhow was able to obtain the proper certificates and permissions for sailing, enabling it to leave Zanzibar unhindered. There was another advantage in sailing via Bombay. In India, following the ban on slave imports to the Bombay

Presidency in 1805, the Bombay Government abolished the legal status of slaves in 1843, triggering the abolition of slavery throughout India.[62] Thus, in the middle of the nineteenth century, the security measures of the Indian Navy patrolling the ports of British India and off its coast turned out to be quite loose[63]; even if 'seamen' on board dhows were actually to be sold as 'slaves' at the end of their voyages, the ships could enter British-controlled ports relatively easily.

In addition, as mentioned earlier, from the beginning of the 1860s the suppression campaign in the western Indian Ocean came to be taken over by the Royal Navy and was focused on the East African coast. The Royal Navy's main target were the dhows sailing from the East African coast to the Gulf of Oman and the Persian Gulf. A memorandum dated 1 September 1864 by R. Lambert Playfair, Consul in Zanzibar from 1863 to 1866, suggests that, for effective suppression, between 1 September and the end of May ships should patrol in the area between Suqtrā Island and Cape Guardafui, since most vessels sailing between the two regions passed through there.[64] In fact, on the contrary, if the ships entered the Gulf of Oman via the Indian subcontinent they did not need to pass through there, for instead they could follow the coast of Kachchh and Makrān where British direct control had not yet reached and patrols were sporadic. That is, going via the Indian subcontinent allowed transporters to outwit British patrolling scheme entirely. It was only at the end of the 1860s that the campaign of suppression began to investigate that particular transport route.[65]

Conclusion

Transporters relied not only on their superior sailing techniques, their knowledge of the ocean and tricks such as disguising slaves in order to continue their business, but also exchanged between themselves the most up-to-date information they could compile. Physical resistance did occur, but it was only one of the methods the transporters used. Furthermore, they adapted adroitly as situations changed in the various polities and even used to their own advantage the very treaties originally intended for the suppression of their trade. In other words, transporters 'domesticated' suppression treaties effectively.

Notes

1. Ricks, 'Slave and Slave Traders in the Persian Gulf', 62–63.
2. Stephen M. Edwardes, *The Gazetteer of Bombay City and Island*, 3 vols, Bombay: Time Press, 1909, Vol. 2, 238, n. 4; Banaji, *Slavery in British India*, 301–304.
3. Kelly, *Britain and the Persian Gulf*, 419; Banaji, *Slavery in British India*, 73–78, 297–301, 344; William Adam, *Law and Custom of Slavery in British India, in A Series of Letters to Thomas Fowell Buxton, Esq.*, Boston: Weeks, Jordan and Co., 1840, 74–102; Andrea Major, *Slavery, Abolitionism and Empire in India, 1772–1843*, Liverpool: Liverpool University Press, 2012, 170–174.
4. For the process towards the abolition of the legal status of slaves in those parts of India under the East India Company's control, see Banaji, *Slavery in British India*. Saymour Drescher, *Abolition: A History of Slavery and Antislavery*, Cambridge: Cambridge University Press, 2009, 268–270. This shows the link between abolition in India and abolition movements in Britain and other British territories.
5. For the process towards the conclusion of this treaty, see Patricia R. Dubuisson, 'Qāsimī Piracy and the General Treaty of Peace (1820)', *Arabian Studies* 4 (1978); Hubert Moyse-Bartlett, *The Pirates of Trucial Oman*, London: Macdonald, 1966.
6. James Onley, 'Britain's Informal Empire in the Gulf, 1820–1971', *Journal of Social Affairs* 87 (2005), 39–40, 42–43.
7. Charles U. Aitchison, *A Collection of Treaties, Engagements and Sunnuds: Relating to India and Neighbouring Countries*, 8 vols, Culcutta: Savielle and Cranenburgh, 1862–1866, Vol. 7, 251.
8. For the text, see Aitchison, *A Collection of Treaties*, Vol. 7, 211–215.
9. Ibid., 213.
10. Ibid., 215.
11. Ibid., 226.
12. Beachey, *The Slave Trade*, 44.
13. For an overview of traditional concepts of jurisdiction at high seas in the western Indian Ocean, see Hassan S. Khalilieh, *Islamic Maritime Law: An Introduction*, Leiden: Brill, 1998, 136–138.
14. The treaty was concluded between Atkins Hamerton, the first British Consul at Zanzibar, on behalf of the Queen of the United Kingdom of Great Britain and Ireland and Sa'īd b. Sulṭān of the Bū Sa'īd in 1845, and became effective from the first day of 1847. It prohibited slave transport from the East African coast, which was controlled by the latter. However, it permitted the continued transport of slaves off the coast of the African territory controlled by the Bū Sa'īd, namely between Kilwa and Lamu. For the articles of this treaty see Aitchison, *A Collection of Treaties*, Vol. 7, 227–228.

15. Robert N. Lyne, *Zanzibar in Contemporary Times: A Short History of the Southern East in the Nineteenth Century*, New York: Negro Universities Press, 1969 (1st. 1905, London: Hurst and Blackett), 41. Lyne wrote the name of squadron as 'Cape of Good Hope and east coast of Africa squadron'; however, I could find no other reference mentioning this name.
16. John G. Lorimer, *Gazetteer of the Persian Gulf, 'Oman and Central Arabia*, London: Archive Editions, 1986 (1st. 1808–1815, Calcutta: Superintendent Government Printing), 2476–2484.
17. Lindsay Doulton, 'The Royal Navy's Anti–Slavery Campaign in the Western Indian Ocean, c. 1860–1890: Race, Empire and Identity' (Ph.D. dissertation, University of Hull, 2010), 29.
18. Low, *History of the Indian Navy*, Vol. 2, 98–111; Willem M. Floor, *Bandar Abbas: The Natural Trade Gateway of Southeast Iran*, Washington: Mage, 2011, 69–97.
19. *BPP*, Vol. 24, Class D, 27 [Kemball to Robertson, Karrak, 8 July 1842].
20. Gilbert, *Dhows and the Colonial Economy*, 60–61; Hopper, 'The African Presence in Arabia', 52; Moses D.E. Nwulia, *Britain and Slavery in East Africa*, Washington: Three Continents Press, 1975, 65–68.
21. Doulton, 'The Royal Navy's Anti-Slavery Campaign', 30.
22. Low, *History of the Indian Navy*, Vol. 2, 137.
23. Ibid., 577–584.
24. Ibid., Vol. 1, 410–473, Vol. 2, 140–160, 238–294.
25. Kelly, *Britain and the Persian Gulf*, 452–499.
26. See, for example, OIOC IOR/R/15/1/130/129–130 [Hamerton to Malet, Muscat, 1 June 1852]; OIOC IOR/R/15/1/168/5 [Mahomed Busheer to Jones, n.p., 24 Zilkaada 1275/26 June 1859]; OIOC IOR/R/15/1/171/175–176 [Fendall to Jones, Bushire Roads, 10 November 1859] and also Low, *History of the Indian Navy*, Vol. 1, 367–388.
27. OIOC IOR/R/15/1/127/20 [Hennell to Porter, Camp near Bushire, 26 June 1851]; OIOC IOR/R/15/1/157/227 [Ethersey to Jones, Bassadore, 24 July 1854]; OIOC IOR/R/15/1/168/34–35 [Jones to Anderson, Bushire, 25 April 1857].
28. OIOC IOR/R/15/1/143/367 [Extract Para 4 from a Despatch from the Honorable the Court of Directors dated the 1st March No. 1 of 1854]; OIOC IOR/R/15/1/157/19–37 [Jones to Anderson, Bushire, 26 May 1856]; OIOC IOR/R/15/1/168/46–47 [Jones to Jenkins, Amulgavine Roads, 30 April 1859]; OIOC IOR/R/15/1/171/63–65 [Extract paras: 28 @ 31 from a letter, from Brigadier W.M. Coghlan, in charge Muscat, Zanzibar Commission, dated 1st November 1860, No. 14].
29. Gilbert, *Dhows and the Colonial Economy*, 60–61; ZZBA AA3/20/364-365 [Rigby to Anderson, Zanzibar, 14 May 1861].
30. ZZBA AA3/20/364-365 [Rigby to Anderson, Zanzibar, 14 May 1861].

31. OIOC IOR R15/1/171/64 [Extract paras: 28 @ 31 from a letter, from Brigadier W.M. Coghlan, in charge Muscat, Zanzibar Commission, dated 1st November 1860, No. 14].
32. Ibid.; see also Gilbert, *Dhows and the Colonial Economy*, 60–61; Lyne, *Zanzibar in Contemporary Times*, 41; Sullivan, *Dhow Chasing*, 41, n. 2.
33. ZZBA AA3/20/364–365 [Rigby to Anderson, Zanzibar, 14 May 1861].
34. David Eltis, 'Construction of the Trans-Atlantic Slave Trade Database: Sources and Methods', available on http://www.slavevoyages.org/voyage/understanding-db/methodology-2 (last viewed 8 February 2017).
35. Graham, *Great Britain in the Indian Ocean*, 148.
36. Colomb, *Slave-Catching*, 59–60; Beachey, *The Slave Trade*, 54, 58; Kemball, 'Paper Relative to the Measures Adopted by the British Government', 651; Johann L. Krapf, *Travels, Researches and Missionary Labours during an Eighteen Years' Residence in Eastern Africa: together with Journeys to Jagga, Usambara, Ukambani, Shoa, Abessinia, and Khartum; and a Coasting Voyage from Mombaz to Cape Delgado*, London: Trubner, 1860, 424.
37. Sullivan, *Dhow Chasing*, 32–33.
38. MAHA PD/1837/78/854/393–400 [Hennell to Willoughby, Bushire, 24 September 1837].
39. Colomb, *Slave-Catching*, 59–60; Beachey, *The Slave Trade*, 54, 58; OIOC IOR/R/15/1/127/31 [Hennell to Malet, Bushire, 30 October 1851]; *BPP*, Vol. 44, Class A, 151 [Trotter to the Secretary to the Admiralty, Simon's Bay, 5 April 1857]; OIOC IOR/R/15/1/171/64 [Extract from paras: 28 to 31, from a letter, from Brigadier W.M. Coghlan, in charge Muscat, Zanzibar Commission, dated 1st November 1860, No. 14].
40. In his memoir, Colomb dedicated a whole chapter on his interpreter, called 'Bin Moosa' (Colomb, *Slave-Catching*, 104–111). He was born in Nzwani (Johanna) Island and engaged in commerce, including slave dealings, in Mozambique Channel in his early days. When his dhow was captured by British patrol, he became an interpreter. He was fluent in Kiswahili and Arabic, and he also picked up a few words of English and Portuguese as well as Malagasy. According to Colomb, he was 'the only honest one connected with Her Majesty's navy on the East India Station at that time' (ibid., 104–105).
41. OIOC IOR/R/15/1/171/64 [Extract paras: 28 to 31 from a letter, from Brigadier W.M. Coghlan, in charge Muscat, Zanzibar Commission, dated 1st November 1860, No. 14].
42. Their highly developed sailing skills were frequently mentioned. For example, ZZBA AA/12/29/85 [Hamerton to the Chief Secretary to Bombay Government, 25 October 1849].
43. Burton, *Zanzibar*, Vol. 1, 74.

44. Colomb, *Slave-Catching*, 44–45.
45. Krapf, *Travels, Researches and Missionary Labours*, 424.
46. MAHA PD/1860/159/830/194–195 [Rigby to Anderson, Zanzibar, 28 March 1860].
47. OIOC IOR/R/15/1/171/101–102 [Rigby to Anderson, Zanzibar, 13 September 1858]. See also, Beachey, *The Slave Trade*, 59.
48. OIOC IOR/R/15/1/123/19, 20 [Translated substance of a letter from Moollah Houssein Agent at Shargah to Lieutenant Colobel Hennell Resident in the Persian Gulf dated 25th Rujub or 6th June 1850]; OIOC IOR/R/15/1/143/304 [Kemball to Thomson, Bushire, 12 January 1854]; OIOC IOR/R/15/1/171/150 [Hajee Yacoob to Jones, s.l., 2 Moohurrum 1276]. OIOC IOR/R/15/1/127/23 [Mollah Houssein to Hennell, s.l., 13 June 1851] reported that the Sultan of Ras al-Khaymah ordered his subjects to take the land route rather than the sea route for transporting slaves.
49. OIOC IOR/R/15/1/127/56 [Taylor to Hennell, Basra, 16 September 1851]; OIOC IOR/R/15/1/130/292 [Kemball to Malet, Bushire, 12 November 1852]; OIOC IOR/R/15/1/168/109 [Jones to Forbes, Bushire, 2 September 1861]; Miles, *The Countries and Tribes*, 490. Along the East African coast, shallow-draft *mtepe* could often escape from patrolling ships (Devereux, *A Cruise in the 'Gorgon'*, 122).
50. OIOC IOR/R/15/1/127/18–19 [Moollah Houssein to Hennell, s.l., 17 May 1851].
51. OIOC IOR/R/20/A1A/318/85 [Memorandum for the guidance of Mr. Rutherford I.N. commanding HMS *Fanny*, 9 March 1861].
52. OIOC IOR/R/15/1/127/18 [Moollah Houssein to Hennell, s.l., 17 May 1851].
53. Centre des Archives d'Outre-Mer (hereafter CAOM) FM/SG/OIND/2/10(2)/n.p. [Travaux de M. Guillain, 1850 s, Ports au Sud de Zanguebar].
54. ZZBA AA12/29/77 [Hamerton to Secretary to Bombay Government, Zanzibar, 3 April 1847].
55. *BPP*, Vol. 36, Class B, 178 [Hamerton to Palmerston, Zanzibar, 10 February 1848].
56. *BPP*, Vol. 39, Class A, 197 [Hennell to Malet, Bushire, 9 October 1849]; ZZBA AA12/29/85 [Hamerton to the Chief Secretary to Bombay Government, Zanzibar, 4 May 1849].
57. *BPP*, Vol. 36, Class B, 178 [Hamerton to Palmerston, Zanzibar, 10 February 1848]. See also ZZBA AA12/29/81 [Hamerton to Secretary to Bombay Government, Zanzibar, 7 March 1848]; ibid., [Hamerton to Secretary to Bombay Government, Zanzibar, 10 May 1848].
58. NAUK FO84/737/86–87 [Extract of a letter from Mollah Hoossein, Agent at Shargah to Major Hennell, 6 January 1848].

59. ZZBA AA12/29/81 [Hamerton to Secretary to Bombay Government, Zanzibar, 7 March 1848].
60. See also OIOC IOR/R/15/1/134/1 [Hennell to Taylor, Bushire, 6 February 1852]. The Qājār accepted the British request in June of the same year, and ordered a ban on importing and exporting Africans by sea. However, what is remarkable is a document written by Moḥammad Shāh Qājār (r. 1808–1848) to his Ṣadr-e A'aḍam (Prime Minister) Ḥajj Mīrzā Āqāsī on the matter: 'Your Excellency the Hajee (sic.), let them not bring any negroes (sic.) by sea, let them be brought by land' ('Translation of an Autograph Note from His Majesty the Shah to Hajee Mirza Aghassee, June 12th 1848', in Aitchison, *A Collection of Treaties*, Vol. 7, 144). See also, ibid., 144–147, for the reaction of the Qājārid side.
61. NAUK FO800/234/95 [Pelly to Stewart, Zanzibar, 10 July 1862]. The same document is reproduced in Colomb, *Slave-Catching*, 97–98.
62. Banaji, *Slavery in British India*, 403; Beachey, *The Slave Trade*, 40.
63. Colomb, *Slave-Catching*, 99–101; Kemball, 'Paper Relative to the Measures Adopted by the British Government', 651–652; Lyne, *Zanzibar in Contemporary Times*, 41–42.
64. *BPP*, Vol. 50, Class B, 45. A suggestion to station a fleet near water supply points for the dhows is also found in OIOC IOR/L/P&S/9/42/352 [Merewhether to Secretary to Bombay Government, Aden, 17 May 1865].
65. *BPP*, Vol. 51, Class B, 133–134 [the Commodore commanding the Indian Division of the Royal Navy to the Governor of Bombay, Bombay, 6 February 1867]; ibid., 134 [Bedingfeld to the Commodore commanding the Indian Division of the Royal Navy, Zanzibar, 1 December 1866]; ibid., 135 [Wedderburn to the Commissioner of Police, Bombay and the Commissioner of Customs, Bombay, Bombay Castle, 25 February 1867]. However, at the end of investigation, the chief of police in Bombay judged that crew members on board dhows owned or captained by Arabs were not slaves (MAHA PD/1867/126/286/55–56 [Souter to Secretary to Bombay Government, Bombay, 6 March 1867]. The same document is available in *BPP*, Vol. 51, Class B, 135–136).

CHAPTER 4

"They are Raising the Devil with the Trading Dows:" Reconsidering the Royal Navy's Anti-Slave Trade Campaign from the Slave Trader Perspective

Introduction

The campaign of suppression in the western Indian Ocean was transformed when the Royal Navy became fully committed to it in 1860—quite simply their achievement in terms of the number of slaves they rescued was outstanding. However, considering the inseparable nature of slave transport from other cargo transport in those waters, the navy's activities significantly affected other maritime trade. Another issue which will be explored in this chapter is the background to the Royal Navy's success. Why were they successful when the Indian Navy failed? As Lindsay Doulton claims, the methods of the Royal Navy's campaign were more or less same as those of the Indian Navy, and the suppression of the slave trade was never regarded as a high priority among their various tasks.[1] If that is true, what explains the Royal Navy's result? This chapter will grapple with these questions, and will grasp at a hidden connection between the slave trades of the Atlantic and the western Indian Ocean by looking at the suppression campaign of the Royal Navy from the point of view of the transporters.

Participation of the Royal Navy: The 1860s Onward

After 1860, the Cape of Good Hope squadron of the Royal Navy joined the anti-slave trade campaign in the western Indian Ocean in full force,[2] with its main task the patrolling of East African coastal waters.

H. Suzuki, *Slave Trade Profiteers in the Western Indian Ocean*, Palgrave Series in Indian Ocean World Studies,
DOI 10.1007/978-3-319-59803-1_4

There were several reasons for the focus on that particular area. One was that the East African coast had become the largest market for slaves around the western Indian Ocean in response to the steep rise in the economic importance of plantation production. Another reason is apparent from a letter from Christopher P. Rigby, British Consul in Zanzibar, to the Chief Secretary to the Government of Bombay, in which he wrote:

> A further reason in favour of making the chief efforts for the suppression of this traffic on the coast of Africa instead of on the coast of Arabia, or in the Persian Gulf, is the suffering and mortality among the slaves before they reach the latter coast.[3]

The Royal Navy's campaign was much more successful than that of the Indian Navy. Between 1865 and 1869 around 3000 slaves were rescued by Royal Navy ships in the western Indian Ocean and sent to the port of Aden,[4] over 17 times the total number rescued by the Indian Navy between 1852 and the end of June 1858, as shown in Table 3.1 of Chap. 3. We do not know for certain the total number of slaves rescued by the Royal Navy in entirety of the 1860s. At the time of the report written by the Civil Commissioner of Seychelles in July 1869 there was no order regarding the captured dhows, but generally slaves rescued from ships seized north of the equator were sent to Aden while those rescued south of the equator were sent to the Seychelles.[5] In addition to the Seychelles, Bombay, Natal, Cape Town and Mauritius were known as ports at which rescued slaves were disembarked, as were Masqaṭ and Zanzibar, where the Prize Court was located.[6] Thus, we need to expect further number of slaves were rescued by the Royal Navy between 1865 and 1869.

We could present various explanations for such a remarkable difference in the number of slaves rescued by the Royal Navy and the Indian Navy; for instance, the quality and number of the former's ships. However, the Royal Navy's ships were obsolete and slow,[7] and there were too few of them.[8] So much so that the British Consul in Zanzibar claimed the poor quality of the squadron sent by the Admiralty 'was a common cause of joking'[9] among the non-British on the island. He continued:

> [T]here was the 'Sidon', an old tub. That any dhow on the coast could beat; there was the 'Gorgon', that took 40 days to do 800 miles, and vessels of that class, perfectly useless for any other service.[10]

Obviously then, an improved standard of equipment and increased number of ships deployed were not the reasons for the difference in the respective operational achievements of the Royal and Indian Navies. What about the difference in the areas patrolled? Until the 1850s, the Indian Navy had patrolled mainly in the Gulf of Oman and the Persian Gulf, but the Royal Navy mainly targeted the sea lanes off the East African coast. Table 4.1, featuring the number of slaves on board dhows seized by the Royal Navy, shows that vessels carrying over 100 slaves amounted to 17.3% of the total.

The proportion of ships with fewer than five slaves on board was 50%, which means that when the Royal Navy switched operations to focus on the East African coast they had more luck than the Indian Navy in intercepting both large- and small-scale slave transports.

Under the Indian Navy regulations there was little profit to be made from intercepting small-scale slave transports. Indeed, it was not uncommon for the expense incurred by Indian Naval officers in arresting small slavers to exceed the bounty they eventually received for them. On the other hand, Table 4.1 shows that half the ships captured by the Royal Navy were carrying fewer than five slaves. That it was worth the Royal Navy's while arresting the smaller traffic is explained by the difference in how bounties were regulated. The Royal Navy offered the same bounty per head as the Indian Navy, but offered an additional bounty which was dependent on the tonnage of the captured ship (£1 10 *S.* per ton).[11] Even if there were no slaves on board, the captain and crews would still be awarded £4 per ton.[12] Furthermore, after 1866, when a Prize Court was established in Zanzibar, which was close to their area of operations, the Royal Navy was able to submit cases to that court, which helped both to speed the process up and simplify it.[13] Moreover, in contrast to the Indian Navy, Royal Navy regulations allowed officers to destroy captured ships if they judged them to be unseaworthy; thus, officers could submit multiple cases to the court at the same time after the one patrol.[14] Such incentives meant that the Royal Navy officers were much more highly motivated to capture 'slavers' and much more easily able to pocket a decent bounty than could their colleagues in the Indian Navy.[15]

In particular, that they were allowed to destroy any vessel they deemed unseaworthy was a great advantage for officers of the Royal Navy, because in the western Indian Ocean, slave transportation, like that of other cargo, was scheduled in accordance with the monsoon season.[16] The anti-slave trade campaign was therefore obliged to follow the

Table 4.1 Number of slaves on board ships confiscated by Royal Navy patrols, 1860–1880, featuring 246 dhows

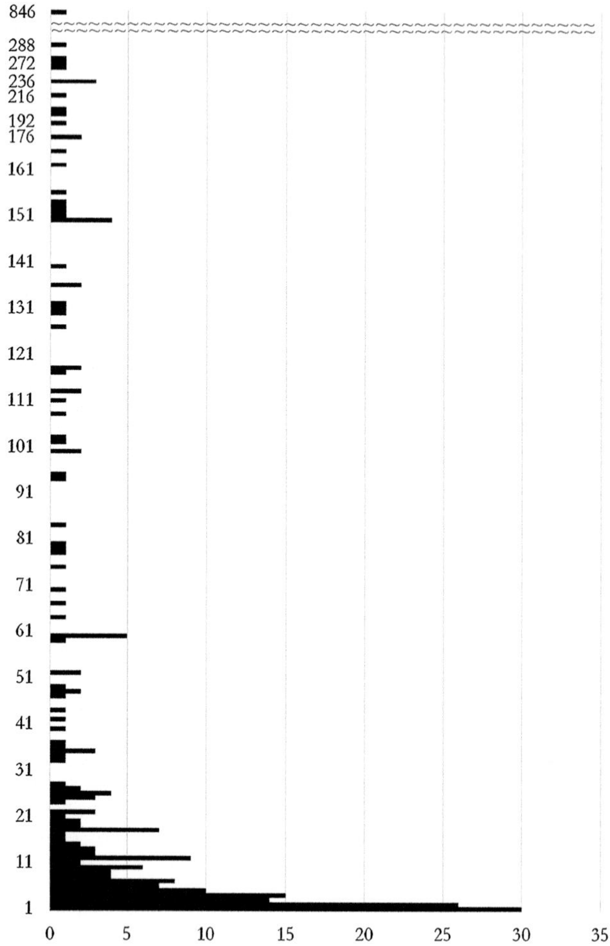

(*Source* BPP, Slave Trade, Vol. 48, Class A, 12–13, 29–31, 164; ibid., Vol. 49, Class A, 42–43, 188, Class B, 73, Class C, 64–65, 68, 180, Class D, 120, 125; ibid., Vol. 50, Class A, 15, 17–18, 91, 99–100, 102, 104–105; ibid., Vol. 51, Class A, 10, 68, 71; ibid., Vol. 52, Class A, 86; ibid., Vol. 91, 138, 187–189, 198–199, 203, 488; MAHA PD/1864/54/704/279; MAHA PD/1864/54/942/14; MAHA PD/1865/52/780/13; MAHA PD/1877/149/689/66; NAUK ADM123/179/n.d.; NAUK FO84/1224/205; NAUK FO84/1245/189; NAUK FO84/1325/166; NAUK FO84/1344/139; NAUK FO800/234/66, 93; NAUK FO881/1703/3, 6; NAUK FO881/3342/5-7; OIOC IOR L/P&S/9/42/349-351; OIOC IOR/L/P&S/18/B84/65, 72, 81; OIOC IOR/R/20/A1A/285/77; OIOC IOR R/20/A1A/318/90-91, 143; ZZBA AA12/2/9-10.)

seasons in the same way, so it was always a race against time for everyone. For example, if officers captured a 'slaver' near Aden, Indian Navy regulations required them to sail at once to Bombay, a voyage of roughly 18 days one way; otherwise, they would have to sail with the captured vessel while searching for other 'slavers'. By contrast, the Royal Navy's regulations enabled officers to save time and meant they could operate more effectively. Furthermore, as Erik Gilbert argues, the calculations made to determine the tonnage of the 'slaver', and hence the value of the prize, were sometimes of dubious accuracy, with the weight often exaggerated.[17] Once the dhow in question had been destroyed, there was little hope of verifying claims.[18]

Royal Navy captains could submit cases to the Prize Court, and if their claims were approved and the captured vessels recognized as 'slavers', the ship's officers could be awarded a bounty regardless of whether there were actually any slaves on board the supposed 'slavers' or not. For instance, the Zanzibar National Archives hold records for 77 cases between 1867 and 1869 which were adjudicated at the Prize Court in Zanzibar. Forty-nine of the cases (63.64%) concerned 'slavers' with no slaves on board at the time they were captured.[19] The presence on board of large jars and water tanks was sufficient reason for arresting officers to call seized vessels 'slavers'.[20]

Bounty was shared among the officers according to rank, with higher-ranking officers naturally receiving more than lower-ranking ones.[21] However, as W. Cope Devereux has noted, some of the more junior officers were able to further line their pockets. Devereux wrote one of the earliest memoirs by the officers engaged in the anti-slave trade campaign in the western Indian Ocean entitled *A Cruise in the 'Gorgon'*. In it he vividly described the behaviour of junior shipboard ranks once they had captured a 'slaver'. About an anonymous crew member named 'Jack' he wrote:

> Having undergone all the dangers and vicissitudes of boat-work, he thinks he should be allowed to keep all loot, whether money or jewellery, &c., collected during the cruise—honestly or dishonestly.
>
> This irregular manner of looting is very disgraceful, and, unchecked, will lead to some dire results. As soon as a prize is taken, Jack's first thought is 'loot'; if once he smells it, like the bloodhound, he must take it; and to gain it, everything is sacrificed. 'Honest Jack', too often becomes the dishonest brute,—the worst of the Tower Hill genus. Leaving his officer and

> a few *conscientious* men to clew up the capture, he sneaks below, breaks open doors and boxes, pounces upon money and jewellery, and to gain which he often perpetrates deeds that the man-vulture on the deadly field of battle would be ashamed of. The sex to whom he is naturally so gallant, is not only disrespected, but roughly handled.[22]

The Anti-slave Trade Campaign and Criticism by the Merchant Community

So far in this chapter the blanket term 'slaver' has been used, for the chief reason explained in Chap. 2, which is related to the particular circumstances of slave transport in the western Indian Ocean. However, there are other reasons in this chapter to use this general term, one being that the vessels captured by the Royal Navy included ships which, although they were actually carrying slaves, were operating within the limits for slave transport permitted by the Hamerton Treaty.[23] The second and more important reason is that, regardless of this, naval officers often destroyed ships as 'slavers' despite there being insufficient grounds for doing so. In the light of the favourable bounty terms offered to Royal Navy officers, it is entirely conceivable that their activities were no different from those of bounty hunters operating under their own rules, or privateers. The effect of the navy's activities on shipping in general should not be ignored. For example, in 1869 Francis R. Webb, an American merchant in Zanzibar, wrote to a colleague of his anxieties, claiming that Royal Navy ships engaged in the anti-slave trade campaign:

> are raising the devil with the trading Dows on the coast and will ruin trade if they keep on. Not less than 70 have been destroyed by them the past year and there is no doubt that a great proportion of them were harmless traders with no slaves on board except their crews, which seem to be sufficient now to cause their destruction.[24]

Local rulers and merchants in the western Indian Ocean region often petitioned the British Consul in Zanzibar to demand that proper control be exerted over the Royal Navy's activities because, they complained, the destruction of local ships by the navy in the name of the anti-slave trade campaign was harming commerce.[25] In March 1863, a number of European and American companies based in Zanzibar protested strongly in similar terms against the conduct of the Royal Navy,[26] and even

Johann L. Krapf, a CMS missionary who had settled near Mombasa, sent similar criticism to the British Consul in Zanzibar.[27] Even within the Royal Navy itself there was criticism. Devereux wrote in his memoirs that:

> [M]any captains have gone to extremes when prize-money has been the sole motive, and captured every dhow with even a shadow of a slave on board, thus doing as much damage as good—destroying legitimate trade, which we should of course endeavour to encourage.[28]

However, such criticisms, accusations and petitions were insufficient to deter the Royal Navy from hunting for bounty.

General antipathy to the conduct of the navy seems to have been shared by people living throughout the western Indian Ocean region. For example, British Consul in Zanzibar Rigby wrote that the *Lyra*, a Royal Navy ship engaged in suppression campaign, was locally called 'El Sheetan', which literally means 'the Satan'.[29] Another example can be found in a report on 10 January 1862 by Lewis Pelly, another British Consul in Zanzibar:

> A gentleman who for personal reasons begs me not to divulge his name (but whose name I transmit in a private communication to His Excellency) informs me that having just sailed down the Arabian and African Coast he was surprised and astonished to find the people every where infuriated against the English Consul at Zanzibar. This rage pervades Makalla, 'and at Ras al Kheima they said openly that they had planned the murder of the English Consul at Zanzibar; but had postponed the execution till they should see whether the Consul was not repudiated in England'.[30]

Experience in the Atlantic and Reality in the Western Indian Ocean: Dissociation

The Royal Navy's campaign then amounted to '"slaver" hunting', and indeed 'raised the devil' with the dhows sailing in the western Indian Ocean. Given European and American merchants' businesses were inseparable from these dhow activities, it is not difficult to imagine how the Royal Navy's campaign affected them. Not a few of the vessels caught and destroyed by the Royal Navy were, of course, entirely 'sinless merchant ships'.[31] Devereux stated that the campaign contributed directly to 'destroying legitimate trade'.[32] That the Royal Navy should encourage legitimate trade was, in fact, a point made emphatically to its officers, and repeated on various occasions including in the *Instructions for the Suppression of the Slave Trade*,[33] a text circulated to all officers engaged in the campaign.

Why did the Royal Navy persist with such tactics when they were so disadvantageous to legitimate trade? The lure of bounty certainly played a part, but so too did the difference between what the officers had experienced in the Atlantic campaign and what they encountered in the western Indian Ocean. When the Royal Navy began its operations in the western Indian Ocean, they drew on their experience in the Atlantic. As Philip H. Colomb, another Royal Navy Captain engaged in the suppression campaign in the western Indian Ocean, stated in his memoirs:

> There is no 'Hand-book' to the East African slave trade, and he must acquire his knowledge of it chiefly by experience. Information respecting his powers of dealing with the slave trade in general, and instructions more or less minute, are however supplied to him in an octavo volume, the growth of many years' West Coast practice, under the title of 'Instructions for the Suppression of the Slave Trade'.[34]

This set of instructions, which included details of agreements with other nations, related to the Atlantic slave trade and, according to Colomb, had 'very little indeed [...] to do with the East African slave trade'.[35] Another part of his memoirs listed certain features of slavers, which were communicated by headquarters to officers patrolling the western Indian Ocean.[36] They were, in fact, the same as those described in the ordinance for the suppression of the Atlantic slave trade (enacted in 1839, 2 and 3 Victoria, *Cap.* 73),[37] and indeed as those given for the same purpose in the treaty with France in 1833.[38] Almost identical content was repeated in the agreements and treaties concluded with other European and South and Central American states.[39]

Furthermore, even officers experienced in operating in the western Indian Ocean found it difficult to distinguish, simply by their appearance, between vessels with normal cargo and those used to transport slaves.[40] Henry A. Churchill, British Consul in Zanzibar in the 1860s, declared that there was no significant structural difference between slave-transport ships and other vessels, and criticized the practice of random seizure.[41] The experience gained in the Atlantic suppression was simply not at all applicable to western Indian Ocean. Dhows were plainly not the sort of vessel normally described as 'slavers', not only in terms of structure and appearance, but also in terms of their function in regional trade, and contemporary reports and dispatches relating to the western Indian Ocean frequently noted that ships transporting slaves carried other merchandise too.[42] Colomb mentioned that 'many of those [materials] present in the Arab slaver will also be present in the legal trader'.[43] Mangrove poles were frequently mentioned in documents as merchandise transported, along with slaves, from the East African coast to the Gulf of Oman and the Persian Gulf, while salt and salted dried fish were noted as merchandise brought by 'slavers' to the East African coast.

It was not only between the East African coast and the coast of the Gulf of Oman and the Persian Gulf that slave transport coexisted with other more general cargo transport. The same was true of shipping in the Red Sea.[44] The *Soobloo Salam* of 226 tons, constructed in 1851 and owned by Ḥajj 'Abd al-Karīm 'Ambar Dāwūd, was an example of a Red Sea vessel. She was detained at Maṣṣawa' in May 1859 by the local British Resident for having transported three slaves. Ḥajj 'Abd al-Karīm 'Ambar Dāwūd, who was not only the owner of the vessel but also its *nakhodha*, was eventually sentenced at Aden to 3 years hard labour. Among the documents relating to the case is a shipping manifest which showed that the vessel was carrying 365 bags of rice (valued at 1873.14 Indian rupees) which were the property of the *nakhodha*,[45] along with building materials such as squared timbers and rafters. Then, the list of cargo included sugar, candied fruit, cardamom, drugs and glassware which belonged to four other persons.[46]

These commodities carried by 'slavers' were fundamental to the maintenance of communications between remote regions of the western Indian Ocean. It was the demand for those items that was the major driving force connecting such regions with each other and underpinned the historical cohesion in the area. Given that it must be clear that suppressing the slave trade was inseparable from damaging local trade in general, the British campaign of suppression was a serious attack on the cohesion so long and carefully constructed in the western Indian Ocean region.

Because of the difficulty in distinguishing between ships carrying slaves from others, in the late 1860s the British Consulate at Zanzibar tried to enforce a new regulation requiring all ships sailing along the

East African coast to carry a certificate issued at Zanzibar, written in both Arabic and English. However, the plan came to naught when it was discovered that many vessels did not call at Zanzibar and sailed only between minor ports along the coast.[47] As their experience and knowledge of the slave trade in the western Indian Ocean grew, the symbiotic nature of the trade and the region's stability and prosperity dawned on the British. The Royal Navy tried to find a method of telling the difference between 'harmful' and 'harmless' traffic, but in the end it proved impossible. Some of the British Consuls in Zanzibar even suspected that, in fact, all dhows carried slaves.[48]

Conclusion

As is confirmed by the octavo volume mentioned in Colomb's memoirs, when the Royal Navy began to take part in the anti-slave trade campaign, its officers naturally brought with them their experience in the Atlantic, and because they had been successful there they began their campaign in the western Indian Ocean in the same way. However, they discovered that the reality of slave transport in the West Indian Ocean was very different from what they had seen in the Atlantic. Furthermore, Royal Navy regulations, which awarded officers a bounty that depended on the weight of a captured vessel even if there was no slaves on board, and also allowed them to destroy it as unseaworthy, gave individual captains effective *carte blanche* in their pursuit of 'slavers'. As a result, many 'harmless' traders were affected. Although the humanitarian motivation to push the suppression campaign forward is often emphasized, the personally grasping character of the campaign in individual confrontations at sea must not be ignored. Given the condition of general shipping in the region, with slave cargoes forming only a modest component of the total cargo, we can fairly assume that the seizure and destruction of ships—even if at the time they did happen to be transporting slaves—adversely affected the transport of other commodities. The effects of the British campaign were not limited to local merchants, shipowners, and crews, for as the strong protests by European and American companies based in Zanzibar showed, they too were affected, and through them the western Indian Ocean's links with the rest of the world. In other words, the influence of 'slaver' hunting spread far beyond the geographical limit of the western Indian Ocean.

We have recognized that the western Indian Ocean slave trade was a non-specialist undertaking and re-examined the anti-slave trade campaign there in that context; this has allowed us to illuminate a particular and important aspect of the campaign to hunt down 'slavers'. By separating the anti-slave trade campaign from its dichotomous relationship with the slave trade and viewing it in a much wider perspective we can see clearly revealed the gap between the blueprint for the campaign the Royal Navy brought with them from the Atlantic and the reality they faced in the western Indian Ocean. Their approach ultimately had a deleterious effect on legitimate trade, which they should have been endeavouring to encourage.

Notes

1. Doulton, 'The Royal Navy's Anti-Slavery Campaign', 27–29.
2. Gilbert, *Dhows and the Colonial Economy*, 61. The Royal Navy already had bases located around the western Indian Ocean prior to this period. However, they concentrated mostly on patrolling East Asian waters to protect the free traders who emerged after the East India Company's monopoly was abolished in 1833 (Katsuhiko Yokoi, *Ajia no umi no dai-ei-teikoku: 19seiki kaiyō shihai no kōzō*, Tokyo: Kōdansha, 2004 (1st. 1988, Tokyo: Dōbunkan), 200–210). As to the Royal Navy's operations around Mozambique prior to the 1860s, see Lloyd, *The Navy and the Slave Trade*, 229–242. The Cape of Good Hope squadron joined the East India squadron in 1865 (ibid., 250).
3. *BPP*, Vol. 47, Class B, 84 [Rigby to Russell, Zanzibar, 14 May 1861].
4. OIOC IOR/L/P&S/18/B84/69 [Memorandum of Number of Slaves landed and liberated at Aden, and how disposed of, Aden Residency written by W.R. Goodfellow, 13 July 1869].
5. NAUK FO881/1703/8 [the Civil Commissioner of Seychelles to H. Barkly, s.l., 6 May 1869]. In addition, according to standing orders in 1873, those slaves rescued near Zanzibar were to be sent to the Seychelles while those in the Mozambique Channel were to go to Natal (Hopper, 'The African Presence in Arabia', 76).
6. Colomb, *Slave-Catching*, 73; Lloyd, *The Navy and the Slave Trade*, 253; Hopper, *Slaves of One Master*, 171.
7. Hopper, 'The African Presence in Arabia', 52–53; Lloyd, *The Navy and the Slave Trade*, 242–243.
8. Sullivan, *Dhow Chasing*, 40–41; Lloyd, *The Navy and Slave Trade*, 250.
9. HCPP: Report from the Select Committee on Slave Trade (east coast of Africa); together with the Proceedings of the Committee, Minutes of Evidence, Appendix and Index, 1871 (420), XII, 68.
10. Ibid.

11. Colomb, *Slave-Catching*, 78.
12. Ibid., The captor could opt for a bounty of £4 per ton instead of a bounty per head if there were few slaves on board.
13. Gilbert, *Dhows and the Colonial Economy*, 61.
14. ZZBA AA3/20/365 [Rigby to Anderson, Zanzibar, 14 May 1861]; Colomb, *Slave-Catching*, 73–74; Gilbert, *Dhows and the Colonial Economy*, 61.
15. The Indian Navy changed its regulations in the 1860s. The 'Memorandum for the guidance of Mr. Rutherford I.N. Commanding H.M.S. *Fanny*', written by R. Lambert Playfair on 9 March 1861, stated that the captor would be paid a bounty of £5 per each rescued slave, and it also instructed captains, when they found ships conveying slaves, to rescue the slaves and continue their patrols without seizing the vessel (OIOC IOR/R/20/A1A/318/86).
16. For example, the instructions distributed to captains engaged in the anti-slave trade campaign in the western Indian Ocean mentioned the movement of dhows in detail. They described how the dhows from the Gulf of Oman and the Persian Gulf came to Zanzibar for slaves between December and February; by the end of March they had obtained their slaves, either by purchasing or kidnapping them. They would then set sail from Zanzibar between 10 and 20 March when the direction of the wind changed (NAUK ADM123/179/n.p. [Report called for by the Instructions for the Suppression of the Slave Trade, Page 7, Article 7]).
17. Gilbert, *Dhows and the Colonial Economy*, 61–62.
18. There are a few exceptions. See the case of *Sidon*'s mistake introduced in Chap. 9.
19. ZZBA AA7/2-3.
20. ZZBA AA7/2-3. See also ZZBA AA2/4/n.p. [List of Dhows taken by HMS *Nymphe* in the Slave Trade Now and Before].
21. Colomb, *Slave-Catching*, 82–83.
22. Devereux, *A Cruise in the 'Gorgon'*, 129.
23. It is claimed that between 1860 and 1862 the Royal Navy destroyed over forty ships which should not have been targeted according to the Hamerton Treaty (NAUK FO800/234/85 [Pelly to Forbes, Zanzibar, 12 February 1862]). See also ibid., 76–77 [Pelly to Oldfield, Zanzibar, 22 November 1861].
24. Philips Library, Peabody Essex Museum (hereafter PPEM) MH201/3 [F.R. Webb to E.D. Ropes, Zanzibar, 13 April 1869].
25. For these petitions see MAHA PD/1867/127/97/46-47 [Mājid to Seward, s.l., 9 Shawwāl 1283 (15 February 1867)]; NAUK FO800/234/75 [Pelly to Forbes, Zanzibar, 30 October 1861]; ibid., 76–77 [Pelly to Oldfield, Zanzibar, 22 November 1861]; NAUK

FO84/1261/298-303 [Seward to Gonne, Zanzibar, 9 September 1866]; OIOC IOR/L/P&S/18/B84/76 [Pelly to Secretary to Bombay Government, Bushire, 24 April 1869]; ibid., 76–77 [Sheikh Sultan to Miraza Mahmood, s.l., n.d.]; NAUK FO881/1703/10 [Otway to the Secretary to the Admiralty, Foreign Office, 21 July 1869]; Gilbert, *Dhows and the Colonial Economy*, 64–65.

26. NAUK FO84/1204/352-353 [Copy of resolution passed by the European and American merchants at Zanzibar at a meeting held on the evening of 6 March 1863].
27. NAUK FO800/234/97 [Statement of facts relative to the proceedings which took place in the harbour of Mombas, on the 8th and 9th of April 1862, between a party of Arab soldiers and two English boats, belonging to Captain Oldfield's slave cruising squadron].
28. Devereux, *A Cruise in the 'Gorgon'*, 343.
29. Mrs Charles E.B. Russell, *General Rigby, Zanzibar and the Slave Trade: With Journals, Dispatches, etc.*, London: Allen & Unwin, 1935, 183.
30. NAUK FO800/234/81 [Pelly to Forbes, Zanzibar, 10 January 1862]. In the same document, Pelly complained that the extreme behaviour of the officers of the Royal Navy had not been ordered by him, and in another dispatch to the Bombay Government he bitterly criticized the anti-slave trade campaign by the Royal Navy and its disregard for the Hamerton Treaty (ibid., 205–209 [Memo: submitted to the Government of Bombay dated 12th November 1862]). Furthermore, he claimed that patrolling ships calling at Zanzibar increased the vulnerability of British Consulate (ibid., 90 [Pelly to Oldfield, Zanzibar, 26 March 1862]).
31. PPEM MH201/3 [F.R. Webb to E.D. Ropes, Zanzibar, 13 April 1869].
32. Devereux, *A Cruise in the 'Gorgon'*, 343.
33. Admiralty, *Instructions for the Guidance of Her Majesty's Naval Officers employed in the Suppression of the Slave Trade*, London: T.R. Harrison, 1844, 6.
34. Colomb, *Slave-Catching*, 62.
35. Ibid.
36. Ibid., 71–72.
37. Admiralty, *Instructions for the Guidance*, 221–222.
38. Ibid., 309–310.
39. According to the Admiralty's *Instructions for the Guidance*, treaties had been concluded with Spain in 1835 (ibid., 343–344), Uruguay in 1839 (ibid., 460–461), Venezuela in 1839 (ibid., 418–419), Argentina in 1839 (ibid., 431–432), Chile in 1839 (ibid., 386–388), Bolivia in 1840 (ibid., 503–504), Russia, Prussia, France and Austria in 1841 (ibid., 574–575), Portugal in 1842 (ibid., 603–604), Texas in 1842 (ibid., 534–535) and Mexico in 1842 (ibid., 534–535).

40. OIOC IOR/L/P&S/18/B84/85-86 [Memorandum by Mr Churchill respecting Slave Trade on the east coast of Africa, s.l., n.d.]; ZZBA AA12/2/112 [Rigby to Bombay Government, s.l., 18 April 1861].
41. OIOC IOR/L/P&S/18/B84/85-86 [Memorandum by Mr Churchill respecting slave trade on the east coast of Africa, s.l., n.d.].
42. In addition to several quotes in Chap. 2, see *BPP*, Vol. 51, Class B, 124 [Extracts from Lieutenant-Colonel Disbrowe's Diary of his Journey (overland) from Muscat, Capital of the Sultan of Muscat's Dominions, to Ras-el-Khymah, Capital of the Joasmee Chief's Dominions, Extract 3, Murrayr, 15 April 1865]; NAUK ADM123/179/n.p. [Extract from Rear Admiral Baldwin Walker's letter to the Secretary of the Admiralty No. 239 of 7 November 1863]; NAUK FO84/1279/83-84 [Mājid to Seward, s.l., 9 Shawāl 1283]; NAUK FO800/234/84 [Pelly to Forbes, Zanzibar, 12 February 1862]; OIOC IOR/R/15/1/143/319 [Montrion to Clarke, Aden, 3 March 1854]; OIOC IOR/R/15/1/157/208 [Jones to Anderson, Bushire, 28 August 1856]; OIOC IOR/R/20/A1A/285/39 [Rigby to Coghlan, Zanzibar, 23 March 1860].
43. Colomb, *Slave-Catching*, 73.
44. Janet J. Ewald, 'The Nile Valley System and the Red Sea Slave Trade 1820–1880', in Clarence-Smith (ed.), *The Economics of the Indian Ocean Slave Trade*, 80.
45. OIOC IOR/R/20/A1A/255/83 [Cash account of receipts and expenditure on account of the ship *Soobloo Salaam*].
46. OIOC IOR/R/20/A1A/255/84 [Memorandum of Cargo said to be on board the prize ship *Sabaloo Salaam* belonging to parties other than the owner of said ship, Aden, 22 August 1859]. For a similar case, see also NAUK FO881/1703/19-26 [Report by Mr Rothery respecting Dhows lately captured by Her Majesty's ships 'Peterel' and 'Nymphe'].
47. OIOC IOR/L/P&S/B84/85-86 [Memorandum by Mr Churchill respecting Slave Trade on the east coast of Africa, s.l., n.d.].
48. NAUK FO84/1261/343 [Playfair to Stanley, 8 James Street, 19 December 1866].

CHAPTER 5

Chains of Reselling: Reconsidering Slave Dealings Based on Slaves' Own Voices

Introduction

This chapter reconsiders the slave trade from the micro-perspective, as, by examining individual experiences, we can challenge the conventional view of the trade. So, how can we reconstruct individual experiences or, more precisely, what sort of materials are available? Observations found in contemporary travelogues and official reports have been used in many previous studies to describe and investigate the actual conditions of the slave trade.[1] However, what such observations reveal is only a small part of a much bigger process. By using accounts provided by slaves or former slaves and people who participated in trading them we can show the whole process and also reveal the conditions of the trade most vividly. It would be natural to presume that the most reliable sources would be accounts by the persons directly concerned, but in fact those accounts vary a great deal. Although autobiographies and oral life histories of ex-slaves have been collected and published by Christian missionaries in the past and modern scholars today,[2] this chapter does not principally rely on them for two reasons. First, it seems that they were typically edited by Christian propagandists—with regard to portraying missionaries' efforts in a wholly positive light—and, second, because of the time lapse between when the correspondents were in slavery and when their experiences were documented. The contemporary nature of sources is important due to the implicit bias arising when people narrate their own stories from memory. In addition, an individual's experiences between emancipation and

H. Suzuki, *Slave Trade Profiteers in the Western Indian Ocean*, Palgrave Series in Indian Ocean World Studies,
DOI 10.1007/978-3-319-59803-1_5

the documentation of their account of their slavery might well influence what they say. For those reasons some circumspection is required in considering private accounts such as life histories or autobiographical sources.

The main sources for this chapter are the accounts given by rescued slaves and recorded by British officers at the time of rescue. While naval forces were ill-prepared to deal with slave vessels, information about newly arrived slaves reached the officers at ports around the western Indian Ocean all the time via their local intelligence networks. Cases of slaves from the Indian subcontinent were usually not overseen by officers, because those slaves were regarded as being under British jurisdiction, so action on them could be taken more readily than with those recognized as under other jurisdictions. Even though the navy could not exercise legal force until the relevant treaties were concluded, when information was received about slave dealings involving people from the Indian subcontinent, consular staff—depending upon how strongly each individual officer tried to combat slavery and the slave trade—quickly investigated, recorded and reported the details as fully as possible in order to be able to release the slaves. The first five accounts considered in this chapter are by girls from India who were saved from slavery. The Consuls and the local agencies in ports around the rim of the western Indian Ocean, such as Masqaṭ, Zanzibar, Bandar-e Būshehr, had their own reliable local intelligence networks, so as soon as they came across a case they recorded and reported it after a series of interviews with not only the slaves but sometimes with their owners and the dealers. Such accounts were recorded not for public propaganda, but for noting the actual conditions of slave dealings and to enable enquiries to be made of higher officials in Bombay or London about appropriate procedures. These documents are more reliable than general 'autobiographies' not only because they are contemporary but because they are more objective. Of course, there still remains the question of what details each narrator included or excluded as well as each recorder recorded or omitted. Also, as Alpers and Hopper point out, these accounts are brief comparing with accounts from the Atlantic slave trade. In addition, even these from the western Indian Ocean slave trade were not written by slaves, thus the issues on transcription, translation, or representation which were emerged during the production process of accounts makes analysis complicated.[3] Nevertheless, as Alpers and Hopper also admit,[4] the accounts recorded by British officers are still the most reliable available sources for discovering the actual conditions of slave dealings in any detail.

The different accounts introduced in this chapter reveal a common thread, and we shall follow that thread to discover both where it came from and where it leads.

Experience

Case 1 (for summary see Table 5.1)

In this case a native agent at Masqaṭ became aware that an Indian slave girl had been sold at the local market in 1841. He engaged several persons to procure information about her.[5] Based on information received, he contacted her buyer, Banjoli Beloochee, who had bought her from a broker named Moosulein bin Budeo. While the girl was kept in the agent's house, the agent summoned the person who had entrusted her to the broker for sale, and arranged for him to return the money he had received from Banjoli. After the money was returned to Banjoli, he thought the girl might express a desire to go along with him, and asked the agent to bring her to him. The girl claimed that she did not love Banjoli and that she would not return to him. The agent then asked her

Table 5.1 Summary for case 1

	Purchaser	*Transaction type*	*Place of transaction*	*Length of possession*	*Notes*
1	Two Arabs	Kidnap	Yadgeer	Unknown	
2	Hubeen Ibrahim	Purchase	Hyderabad	Unknown	
3	Moobaruk	Purchase	Hyderabad	More than 2 months	
4	Unbar	Purchase	Moculla (al-Mukallāh)	Unknown	
5	Meroo	Purchase	Muserah (Masīra Island)	8–9 months	
6	Peroo	Purchase	Mutrah	4–5 months	
7	Purdan	Purchase	Mutrah	5 months	He served the same master as 6
8	Banjoli	Purchase at market via broker	Muscat (Masqaṭ)	—	

Source BPP, Vol. 25, Class A, 401 [Rubil bin Uslan to Hennell, 13 Ramaẓān 1257/27 October 1841]

'how she came to be removed from her native country and brought to Muscat, and requested her to speak the truth'. This account is her reply:

> My native country is Yadgeer, under the jurisdiction of Nasir ood Dowla; I and two other girls, each of us eight or nine years old, were one day playing in the street, when two Arabs came to us and asked us to go along with them, promising to give us food and money. One Arab took me along with him, and the other two were thus separated. I was then taken to Hyderabad, and sold to one Hubeeb Ibrahim, from whom I was purchased by an Arab named Moobaruk. The Arab brought me down to Bombay, where I stayed for upwards of two months, he then took me to Moculla, and after a few days sold me to Unbar, a native of Soor, who carried me to the Island of Muserah, and sold me to Meroo, a Latia of Muttrah.[6] I lived with Meroo for two months in Muserah, and then went with him to Muttrah, where I lived in his house for three months; meanwhile I had a quarrel with his wife, in consequence of which Meroo took me back to Muserah. Three or four months after, a servant came to him from his wife, along with whom Meroo sent me to his wife in Muttrah, where, after a few days, he himself returned, and sold me to Peroo, a Latia of Bombay. After four or five months Peroo returned to Bombay, leaving me behind in the house of Purdan Latia, both being servants of Seit Nubeeb Ibrahim, a Latia, residing in Bombay. Five months after, being tired of me, Purdan, two days before the 1st of Ramazan, took all my things from me, and having given me some tattered clothes, brought me in a boat to Muscat, and entrusted me to Mooseleim bin Budeo, a broker, from whom Banjoli Beloochee purchased me.

Case 2 (for summary see Table 5.2)

Eight days after the events of Case 1, the same agent again received information that a wheat merchant named Hajee Mahomed Mughrabee was holding a female Indian slave.[7] He investigated further and realized that she had been sold to him by one Unbar. The agent asked Hajee Mahomed to hand her over to him. At first Hajee Mahomed refused, but finally brought her to the agent. When the girl, who was about 12 years old, appeared, she was in tears and asked him to allow her to return to Hajee Mahomed. The agent kept her for a while in order to ascertain if she really wanted to return to Mahomed or not. For his part, Hajee Mahomed claimed that he intended to marry the girl, but the agent had received information that he had in fact offered her for sale. After the girl had calmed down, she admitted to the agent that she had been forced to say that she loved Mahomed, but that really she would rather stay with

Table 5.2 Summary for case 2

	Purchaser	*Transaction type*	*Place of transaction*	*Length of possession*	*Notes*
1	An Arab	Kidnap	Calcutta	Unknown	
2	Mahomed	Purchase	Hyderabad	Unknown	
3	Zakoot	Purchase	Hyderabad	Unknown	
4	Hajee Ibrahim	Purchase	Busra (al-Baṣra)	Unknown	
5	Hajee Hoosain	Purchase	Busra	Unknown	
6	Hajee Suleman	Purchase	Busra	Unknown	Friend of 5
7	Umbar	Purchase	Muscat	Unknown	Servant of 5
8	Hajee Mahomed	Purchase via broker	Muscat	Unknown	—

Source BPP, Vol. 25, Class A, 401–402 [Rubil bin Uslan to Hennell, 13 Ramaẓān 1257/27 October 1841]

the agent. According to the agent, she also told him that she could not bear to look Mahomed in the face. On 24 Ramaẓān (9 November), the agent asked her to tell him all her particulars. This account is her reply:

> My native country is Cawnpore, whence my parents afterwards removed themselves to Calcutta, on account of the scarcity of rain there. One day when I was playing in the street, an Arab came to me, and asked me to go along with him, promising to give me sweetmeats. Having thus wheedled me, he took me along with him to Hyderabad, in the Deccan. When I began to cry on the road, he told me that my parents were at Hyderabad, and that he intended to take me to them. I was at that time seven or eight years old. He then sold me to one Mahomed, with whom I stopped for some time. At that time there were two persons in Hyderabad engaged in the purchase of slaves; one of them, an Abyssinian, by name Zakoot,[8] a servant of a merchant in Judda; he had married an Indian women with him. The other was Shaik Mahomed Ameer, a native of Medina. He had an Abyssinian woman with him; both of them lived together. Zakoot purchased eight girls, including myself, and the Shaik bought two girls and one boy. Both of them then went to Aurungabad, where Zakoot sold two girls to a dancing-woman. They thence proceeded to Bombay, and on their arrival at Panwell they halted in a mosque. Zakoot, accompanied by his wife and two girls, came to Bombay, where, on being questioned regarding his companions, he replied that one of them was his wife, and the remaining two his daughters. He took up his lodgings in a house situated in the market street. Next day Shaik Mahomed Ameer also came to Bombay in a

similar manner. Zakoot afterwards brought over to Bombay the remaining slaves, under cover of similar pretences, and sold three of them there. Zakoot and the Shaik then embarked for Muscat, whence they went to Muttrah. Sometime after, the Shaik proceeded to Bussora, where he sold his three slaves. Zakoot, after selling one slave to his Highness the Imaum, embarked for Bussora, and had only two slaves with him; one of them was purchased by an Indian, and the other, that is myself, by Hajee Ibrahim of Turkey, who kept me in the house of Hajee Suleman, an Abyssinian inhabitant of Surat. Hajee Ibrahim afterwards sold me to Hajee Hoosain, who was friend of Hajee Suleman, and lived with him. When Hajee Hoosain was preparing himself to embark for Bagdad, Hajee Suleman persuaded me to cry, and express my disinclination to go to Bagdad, on which Hajee Hoossain sold me to Hajee Suleman, who brought me to Muscat, and sold me to Umbar, a servant of Hajee Ibrahim of Turkey, from whom I was afterwards purchased by Hajee Mahomed Mughrubee for 37 rials, through a broker, without being brought to the market.

Case 3 (for summary see Table 5.3)

The native agent at Masqaṭ heard of yet another case in which an Indian female slave was held by one man and sold in the market. On further investigation, the agent got to know Zakoot Wallee Latia, who had brought her to Masqaṭ. Because Zakoot was planning to leave Masqaṭ, the agent immediately sent some persons with a subpoena to prevent his departure. The following morning, Zakoot came to the agent and the agent asked him how he had obtained the girl, and threatened to inform the government. Frightened by this, Zakoot told him that

Table 5.3 Summary for case 3

	Purchaser	*Transaction type*	*Place of transaction*	*Notes*
1	Zakoot Wallee Latia	Purchase via middleman	Mulkee	(paid 60Rps) [40.0–56.1%]
2	Issa bin Khaffan Latia	Purchase	Muscat	42MT$ [4.8%]
3	Moosalin bin Budeo	Purchase	Muscat	44MT$ [77.3%]
4	Mahomed Buharranee	Purchase at market	Muscat	78MT$

Source BPP, Vol. 25, Class A, 402 [Rubil bin Uslan to Hennell, 28 Ramaẓān 1257/13 November 1841]; ibid., 427 [Reuben Aslan to Hennell, n.p., 27 Ramaẓān/12 November 1841], * [] shows the purchaser's profit margin

about three years before he had left Manglore on board a bugla called *Mahomoadi*, and gone over to Mulkee, where he purchased the slave in question for 60 rupees. Since then, she had lived with him before he put her up for sale at Masqaṭ. According to him, prior to coming to Masqaṭ he had sailed to Zanzibar with the girl to try to sell her there. At Masqaṭ, he sold her for 42 rials to Issa bin Khaffan Latia, from whom she was purchased for 44 rials by Moosalin bin Budeo, a broker who, after a few days, again offered her for sale at the market. Finally a pastry maker named Mahomed Buharranee bought her for 78 rials.[9]

Following their interview, the agent asked Zakoot to deposit 42 rials with him in order to resolve the financial angle, and then sent for the persons whom Zakoot had mentioned: they confirmed that they had indeed bought and sold the girl as described. After the agent had resolved the financial matters among these persons and procured the release of the girl, he asked her to tell him herself the details of her case. Her account confirmed that of Zakoot:

> I am a native of Banglore, and my father's house is situated near the market. My father only is alive, and has married another wife since the death of my mother. He is a butler in the service of a European. One Madden, a great friend of my stepmother, came one day to our house, accompanied by Koonjee Mahomed, a broker, and Zakoot Wallee, and having shown me to them, and conversed with them for a while, went away. In the night they returned, excepting Zakoot, when my father was not at home. My stepmother having desired me to go along with them, I did so, and those two persons took me to a boat through the fish-market street, and having put me on board, the boat returned. The boatmen carried me to the bugla, and delivered me over to Zakoot Wallee, who was on board the bugla, which sailed the next morning.[10]

Case 4 (for summary see Table 5.4)

In 1860, Christopher P. Rigby, British Consul in Zanzibar (1858–1861), discovered that a native of India was living in Zanzibar as a slave:

> a girl about 18 years of age, who states that she was stolen whilst playing near the sea at Bombay, she does not remember her parents and has no wish to return to India. She was brought to Lamoo and there sold to a person who afterwards sold her here to a Frenchman by name Bérard; after residing with him some time he sold her to a Banian by name Ramjee Bhanjee who is now in Cutch.[11]

Table 5.4 Summary for case 4

	Purchaser	*Transaction type*	*Place of transaction*
1	Unknown	Kidnap	Bombay
2	Unknown	Purchase	Lamoo (Lamu)
3	Bérard	Purchase	Zanzibar
4	Ramjee Bhanjee	Purchase	Zanzibar

Source MAHA PD/1860/159/830/271 [Rigby to Anderson, Zanzibar, 14 September 1860]

Case 5 (for summary see Table 5.5)

John Kirk, a British Consul in Zanzibar, reported another case of an Indian girl in 1871:

> I have the honor to report for the information of His Excellency the Governor in Council that yesterday it came to my knowledge that an Indian girl was being offered for sale by the Slave Auctioneer and taken round along with Georgian females at night to the houses of the wealthy Arabs and that $250 had already been offered for her.
>
> I at once applied for assistance to his Highness Seyd Burgash who on finding that the Slave had been taken back to her former master from the hands of the Auctioneer on it being known that the case had attracted my attention had her removed from the Harem and brought to my house.

Table 5.5 Summary for case 5

	Name	*Transaction Type*	*Place of Transaction*	*Notes*
1	Own father	—	—	
2	One man	Purchase	Bombay	
3	One Sooroor	?	Hyderabad	
4	A man of eastern Africa	Purchase	Makulla (al-Mukallāh)	
5	Saeed Anter	Purchase	Lamo (Lamu)	'the notorious Slave dealer'
6	One of the Kadis (*Qāḍī*)	Purchase	Zanzibar	
7	A young Persian	Purchase	Zanzibar	Bringing the girl to market for sale
8	A wealthy Arab	Purchase via a slave auctioneer	Zanzibar	250MT$

Source MAHA PD/1871/143/963/86-87 [Kirk to Wedderburn, Zanzibar, 8 April 1871]

> I found her a woman obviously of Indian countenance and manner who spoke Hindostanee fluently and other languages most imperfectly and whose tale was as follows, known in India by the name of Fatima and in the Harem where she now was by that of Marieum, she had when young been sold in Bombay by her father Mohammed, a Jemadar in the Service of the Bombay Government, to a man who took her to Hyderabad in the Deccan, there she remained a long time when she was taken by one Sooroor to Makulla in Arabia and there sold to a man of eastern Africa, at Lamo she fell into the hands of the notorious Slave dealer Saeed Anter an Arab of Sheher who sold her, I am told, to one of the Kadis here, afterwards she passed to the hands of her present owner a young Persian who to make a profit put her in the market.
>
> In this examination I availed myself of the assistance of some Patans to which tribe she is said originally to have belonged and called in Tariabhay Topin the leading Khoja Merchant here.[12] As there remained no doubt that the woman was from India and her story appeared true and as she herself desired to be sent back to Bombay. I asked Tariabhay Topin to keep her in his house until a Dhow could be found to take her away.
>
> Whatever the exact law on such a subject may be the case was obviously a disgrace to the British Indian Community and I did not hesitate to follow the course I have stated hearing the Sultan and his Slave dealing Subjects to arrange the matter of compensation or loss as best they may among themselves.
>
> The woman will be heard of at the house of Jaffer Taria Bombay, agent of Tariabhay Topin of Zanzibar and Bombay, and I beg that enquiry may be made and if it be found that the father was guilty of selling his child that he may be disrated or punished as he deserves[13]

Chains of Reselling

So a number of interwoven threads emerge from the accounts quoted. First, it is clear that individuals whose principal occupation was not in the slave trade, such as a grain merchant, a pastry maker and a *qāḍī* (magistrate), dealt in slaves within the circle of their personal acquaintances. Second, their transactions did not necessarily pass through 'professional' hands like brokers or via the slave market. Third, the purchasers tended not to keep slaves for very long, or at least generally they did not wish to do so, instead trading them relatively quickly. In short, the accounts given above bring to light a chain of private onward sale, a chain of reselling.

We have no detailed information about how each of their owners actually employed any of these girls, but there can be little doubt that it would have been in the domestic sphere. Nonetheless, an important fact is that the chain of reselling links not only cases of the Indian girls but also those of numerous young African males, some of whom were not used as domestic servants. An example is a boy who was taken into protection near Masqaṭ in 1878.

Case 6 (for summary see Table 5.6)

> My present name is Marjan.[14] My former name was Almas. I do not know the name of my parents. I am about 12 years of age. I am a native of Jimma in Abyssinia. One day when I was very young, I with a few of my village children went out to play, our parents being absent from home. While we were engaged in playing some Arabs came and caught about twenty of us. We were taken by them to Hodeida where I was sold to a Turk named Hoossein Effendi. The Turk took me to Sana in Yemen where he resided. After sometime the Turk took me to Mecca where he sold me to an Arab named Shaikh Suleman Bahreini. This Arab took me in a steamer to Muscat. Before our landing some men of the British Political Agent, and the Consul at that port came on board the vessel and seized me. At the same time two other slaves (one girl and one boy) were also seized by them, but the former shortly afterwards died at Muscat. When I was stolen from my native country my father was dead. I do not wish to return to Abyssinia, I am willing to remain in Bombay and to serve any gentleman who would be kind to me. The name of Marjan was given to me by the Turk.

Table 5.6 Summary for case 6

	Name	*Transaction type*	*Place of transaction*	*Notes*
1	Some Arabs	Kidnap	Near his village	
2	Hoossein Effendi	Purchase	Hodeida (al-Ḥudayda)	He brought the boy to Hodeida where he lived
3	Shaikh Suleman Bahreini	Purchase	Mecca (Makka)	He tried to bring the boy to Muscat

Source MAHA PD/1878/135/83/n.p. [Statement of Marjan, Bombay, 16 November 1878]

Another case was that of Khamsini, who was rescued from his master Kanoo Munjee, a British subject in Zanzibar. In February 1860, Rigby, the British Consul in Zanzibar, found that Kanoo had recently purchased slaves, though Rigby had frequently warned him of the heavy penalties he would incur if he ever again engaged in either the purchase or sale of them. He arrested Kanoo, and discovered that he had 69 slaves in his possession. Rigby procured a legal certificate of emancipation from *qāḍī* for each slave and also made Kanoo pay a sum of 10 dollars to each of the slaves for their present support. Rigby also interviewed each slave to collect their particulars and then sent accounts of them to the Government of Bombay. The account given below was recorded following one such interview[15].

Case 7 (for summary see Table 5.7)

> 'Khamsini' a Male African, age 24 of the Yao tribe,[16] deposes as follows. About three years ago my tribe was attacked by another tribe and I was taken prisoner. I was taken a journey of two months to Mangao [Mgau] on the sea coast, and was there sold to an Arab by name 'Masaood' I was with him two years. About nine or ten months ago my present master Kanoo Banian came to Mangao and purchased me of the Arab. A few days after Kanoo had bought me he shipped me in a Dow and brought me to Zanzibar. Besides myself Kanoo brought seven slaves with him from Mangao to Zanzibar, of these three were females, and two were young boys, of whom one has since died. Since I have been in Zanzibar I have worked for my master in the town, conveying goods to and from the Custom House &c.[17]

Table 5.7 Summary for case 7

	Name	*Transaction type*	*Place of transaction*	*Notes*
1	Neighbouring tribe	Capture	His village	
2	Masaood	Purchase	Mgau	The boy stayed with him for 2 years
3	Kanoo Munjee	Purchase	Mgau	He brought the boy to Zanzibar

Source MAHA PD/1860/159/830/231-232 [Depositions of various male and female African slaves found in the possession of Kanoo Munjee, a Banian, residing at Zanzibar, British Consular court, Zanzibar, 5 February 1860]

Table 5.8 Summary for case 8

	Name	*Transaction type*	*Place of transaction*	*Length of possession*	*Notes*
1	Own father				
2	An Arab merchant	Purchase	Unknown	3 years	He stayed with the boy in Kilwa
3	Unknown	Purchase	Kilwa	1 year	He stayed with the boy in Zanzibar
4	Unknown	Purchase	Zanzibar		He tried to bring him to Muscat

Source Philip H. Colomb, *Slave-catching in the Indian Ocean: A record of naval experiences*, New York: Negro Universities Press, 1873, 28–30

Case 8

This is from Colomb's memoirs, in which he reported the narratives of seven former slaves who were manumitted off the Arabian coast in 1869.[18] Six of the seven had experience of a chain of reselling, while the one who had been sold in Zanzibar had later been kidnapped. One of the six who experienced chain of reselling was Frejara from the Yao, who told Colomb that he had been sold by his father to an Arab merchant, and that he then lived in Kilwa for 3 years. After that he was sold again to a new owner, who brought him to Zanzibar. After a year there he was resold to a new owner, and on the way to Masqaṭ with this person, he was rescued and placed under the protection of the authorities. (for summary, see Table 5.8)

Case 9 (for summary, see 5.9)

The chain of reselling was also a feature of the African interior. William C. Harris, an engineer of the East India Company, interrogated slaves about their life histories during his 18-month stay in Ethiopia, the following account being narrated by a native of the village of Suppa in Enarea. He was named Dibbo, the son of Betta.

> When about twenty years of age, being one day engaged in tending my father's flocks, an armed band of the Ooma Galla, with whom my tribe had long been in enmity, swept suddenly down, and took myself, with

Table 5.9 Summary for case 9

	Owner	*Transaction type*	*Place of transaction*	*Length of possession*	*Notes*
1	Ooma Galla	Tribal war	His native place	5 days	
2	Toomee Galla	Purchase at market	Sundaffo	1 day(?)	Paid 30 amolee (= 6s. 3p.)
3	Muslim rover	Purchase	Sundaffo	(1 ~ 7 + 2) days	
4	Nono Galla	Purchase	Unknown	6 weeks	A few ells of blue calico
5	Agumcho Galla	Purchase at market	Meegra	Unknown	40 amolee (= 8s. 4p.) [75%]
6	Soddo Galla	Purchase at market	Plain of Hawash	Unknown	70 amolee (= 14s. 7p.) [42.9%]
7	?	Purchase	Roque	Unknown	100 amolee (= 20s.) [150%]
8	Muslim subject of Sahela Selassie	Purchase at market	Alio Amba	3 months	12 MT$
9	Sahela Selassie	Confiscated from 8	—	—	

Source BPP, Vol. 25, Class A, 440 [Harris to the Secretary to Bombay Government, Ankober, 20 July 1842]

six other youths, prisoners, killing four more who resisted. Having been kept bound hand and foot during five days, I was sold to the Toome Galla, one of the nearest tribes, for thirty amoles (about six shillings and three pence sterling). The bargain was concluded in the Toomee market-place, called Sundáffo [Sendafa], where, in consequence of the dearness of salt, two male slaves are commonly sold for one dollar; and after nightfall the Mahomedan rover who had purchased me, came and took me away. Having been kept bound in his house another week, I was taken two days' journey with a large slave caravan, and sold privately to the Non[o] Galla for a few ells of calico; My companions in captivity were assorted according to their age and size, and walked in double file, the stout and able-bodied only, whereof I was one, having their hands tied behind them. In the market-place of Nono, called Mugra [Mīgra], I was, after six weeks' confinement, sold by public auction to the Agame[c]ho Galla for forty pieces of

> salt (value eight shillings and four-pence), thence I was taken to the market-place, which is beyond Segualo [Segalat'], on the plain of the Hawash, and sold for seventy pieces of salt to the Soddo Galla, and immediately afterwards to Roqué [Rogē], the great slave-mart in the Tener [Yerer] district, where I was sold for one hundred amoles (20s.). From Roqué, I was driven to Aia Amba [Aliyu Amba], in Shoa, where a Mahomedan subject of Sehela Selassie purchased me in the market for twelve dollars; but after three months, my master falling into disgrace, the whole of his property was confiscated, and I became the slave of the Negus, which I still am, though permitted to reside with my family at Angollolla [Angolala], and only called upon to plough, reap, and carry wood. Exclusive of halts, the journey from my native village occupied 15 days; I was tolerably fed, and not maltreated. All the merchants through whose hands I passed were Mahomedans, and until within a few stages of Alia Amba, I was invariably bound at night, and found no opportunity to escape. Prior to my own enslavement, I had been extensively engaged as a kidnapper; and in this capacity had made party in three great slave hunts into the country of the Doko negroes, beyond Caffa, in the course of which 4,000 individuals of both sexes were secured.[19]

The above cases confirm that the chain of reselling applied not only to Indian slaves nor only to female slaves, but were experienced by many young people around the western Indian Ocean[20].

Background to the Chain of Reselling: Contemporary Context

Short periods of possession and frequent resale by owners imply that slaves were items of merchandise for owners, notwithstanding that the Prophet Muḥammad allegedly stated that the 'seller of men is the worst of men'.[21]

In fact, there is a mountain of evidence confirming that slaves were regarded thus and sometimes used for exchange and as payment in kind. For example, a report in 1860 of slave-holding among Indian inhabitants along the East African coast states that:

> The Banian, Khojahs, and Bhorahs, who reside at all the towns and villages on the coast, are chiefly retail traders and shopkeepers, and readily take young children in payment for their goods, and they thus encourage the Deewans or petty Chiefs to get up slave hunts in the hills in the

> neighbourhood, and give them cotton cloths, muskets, gunpowder &c. in return for the children they kidnap. They also take young slaves in pawn for money or goods advanced. They keep these children until a convenient opportunity occurs for disposing of them to Arab slave dealers to be brought to the market here, or shipped off to foreign countries.[22]

It has not been ascertained whether the frequent resale of slaves took place earlier than the nineteenth century, although there are some indications that it did, such as in a story allegedly narrated by a king of Zanj, who was sold into and freed from slavery in a tenth-century collection of sailors' stories entitled *'Ajā'ib al-hind* (*The Wonder of India*).[23]

Various circumstances in the nineteenth-century Indian Ocean region might induce owners to avoid longer-term holdings of newly purchased slaves and also encourage the utilization of them as merchandise or simply as a reflection of wealth and power, rather than as a labour force.

First, the region was prone to repeated serious epidemics. Several plague outbreaks took place from the early nineteenth century onwards,[24] while a cholera pandemic around the Persian Gulf and the Gulf of Oman in 1821 was the first of many:[25] between 1831 and 1865 the whole Indian Ocean region was affected.[26] Many slaves lost their lives in such epidemics like the 1858 cholera epidemic that swept southwards from the Red Sea with the north-east monsoon, affecting cities like Baraawe (Brava), Mogadishu and Mombasa. By the end of 1858 the cholera finally reached Zanzibar, and between January and February of the following year it was recorded that each day 200 people died on the island.[27] Most probably because of the lack of immunity, most of the victims were either African or Comorian, they being jointly the main body of the slave population on Zanzibar.[28] Another example of the effect of infectious disease concerned a dhow carrying 277 slaves which left Kilwa in the middle of May 1870. When she arrived in Zanzibar, after just 3 days' sailing from Kilwa, 90 slaves had died of cholera.[29]

Apart from plague and cholera, there were other diseases common in the western Indian Ocean region such as malaria and smallpox, smallpox being especially common among slaves brought to the Persian Gulf.[30] Thus, such 'property' was high risk. Many reports from consulates and a number of travelogues estimated an exceptionally high annual mortality rate of slaves of over 20%.[31]

Another thing to take into account is the gradual strengthening of the British anti-slave trade campaign. A series of treaties had been concluded between Britain and local polities in the region before the end of the 1840s, and an 'informal' branch of the British Empire was established in the Persian Gulf in the 1820s. Despite the inadequacy of the available naval force, a new series of arrests began, fines were imposed on slave dealings and slaves compulsorily released.[32] Indian residents in particular found it difficult to purchase or own slaves, as we shall see in Chap. 8. From the 1840s onwards when the suppression campaign was activated, the purchase of slaves and even the holding of them became a rather dangerous activity in the western Indian Ocean region. Even if a slave owner managed to purchase and keep a slave secretly, there was still the possibility of losing the 'property' to disease. Furthermore, the progress of the anti-slave trade campaign certainly affected the slave market and prices became unstable. For example, John G. Taylor, Agent for the East India Company and the British Vice-Consul at al-Baṣra from 1851 to 1858, wrote to Kemball about the situation there: 'the prohibition has materially enhanced the prices, and at the present day the price of a healthy slave adult ranges from 150 to 200 Shamis, which in former years could have been procured for 40 or 50'.[33]

Therefore, in order to avoid the risks associated with longer-term possession and to extract a profit from slaves, owners considered shorter-term possession more efficient. Whilst British anti-slave trade activities imposed certain limits on slave trading, monitoring the details of individual slave dealings, especially if conducted secretly and privately, was virtually impossible.

In fact, slave dealing still promised and produced high profits. Traders could receive intermediate margins from slave transactions, which we can see in the summary for cases 3 (Tables 5.3 and 5.9). Notes on Table 5.3 show the prices at which each purchaser bought the slave according to the account of Zakoot Wallee Latia. Referring to those figures, he paid 60 Rupees (Rps) on his purchase. According to William G. Milburn and Burton,[34] the exchange rate between Maria Theresia Thaler (MT$) and Rps in the first half of the nineteenth century was 1 MT$ = 2 – 2.23 Rps, thus, 60 Rps was equal to 26.91 – 30MT$. Because Zakoot Wallee Latia resold this slave at Masqaṭ for 42 MT$, his profit margin was 40–56.1%. The purchaser of the slave from Zakoot Wallee Latia then resold to someone else for 44 MT$, and finally the slave was sold in a market for 78 MT$, a further significant mark-up. Dibbo from case 9 was traded mainly in *Amoles*, salt-bars, which Harris converted at 2*s* 1*d* per Amole. Table 5.9 shows the number of Amoles paid by each purchaser, and the equivalent amount in pounds sterling,[35] revealing the profit of some of the purchasers. Case 9 also clearly indicates that the prices of slaves increased with resale.[36] Therefore, while repeated epidemics and the increasing pressure of British anti-slave trade activities did make it troublesome for owners to keep slaves long term, the resale of slaves still more or less guaranteed a secure profit in monetary terms, at least.

Background to the Chain of Reselling: Cultural Context

The former slaves whose narratives are referred to in this chapter were typically young, certainly no more than 20, and we could not find a single case in which a slave over 30 was the main target for a chain of reselling. It is well known that young people were preferred as slaves in the western Indian Ocean region,[37] partly because they were easily captured and more easily subdued than adults. Another reason emerges from a report on the slave trade in the Persian Gulf by Arnold B. Kemball in 1842:

> The slaves of either sex, whether Hubshee or African, of an age exceeding twenty years, on their first sale, are of less comparative value, from their being at that mature age less tractable, and taking less kindly to the language, religion, and customs of their masters.[38]

Indeed, the prices which Kemball gave in the same report were 7–15MT$ for a boy aged from 7 to 10, 15–30MT$ for a boy aged 10–20, and, for over the age of 20, 17–20MT$.[39] So, according to Kemball, youths aged between 10 and 20 were the most valued male slaves. Similarly, another observer stated that from what he himself saw in the Persian Gulf the most frequently purchased slaves ranged between 10 and 14 years old regardless of gender, while few slaves over 30 were sold.[40]

A preference was found on the East African coast too where the most favoured were *muwallad* or *mzalia*—slaves born from slave parents—because they shared the owners' language and customs.[41] Children newly brought from the interior were prized also, as they were easily adaptable. By contrast, Richard Burton found that adults from the interior were less highly prized both because they were much less docile and naturally found it more difficult to learn a new language and seamlessly adopt the unfamiliar customs of their owners. Similar analysis was done by Charles New, who travelled throughout East Africa as a missionary in the early

1860s.[42] Those observations by Burton and New correspond with several of the Swahili proverbs collected by William E. Taylor, a CMS missionary in East Africa during the second half of the nineteenth century. Among his collection of proverbs is 'mtumwa mwenyi busara ni Azawao ("Born-here" is the sensible slave)'.[43] Taylor explains 'an "*mzalia*", i.e. a slave of the first or second generation, gets accustomed to the ways of the coast; in contrast to the *mshenzi*, the bumpkin from the interior, that never quite loses his clumsiness'.[44]

However, despite such convincing evidence that the most valuable slaves were born slaves, selling them was regarded as disgraceful behaviour by their owners.[45] Realistically then, newly enslaved young people were the most valuable slaves whom the owners could sell. Their ability to assimilate with the owners and their potential when they reached physical maturity added to their value. The chain of reselling allowed the realization of a slave's value based on his or her relative immaturity and innocence, but acknowledging their potential up to a certain age.

Conclusion

For this qualitative approach to the slave trade in the nineteenth-century western Indian Ocean, the experiences of slaves and dealers as recorded by British officers make a useful contribution. Although the accounts which have been used for this chapter are neither numerous nor were recorded and preserved systematically, nonetheless they provide important details of slave dealings from the parties directly concerned. The contemporary nature of these accounts, and the officers' resultant substantiation, tend to corroborate the details, and thus offer a reliable source for research about the actual condition of slave dealings.

We have also revealed the significance of the existence of a chain of reselling. Slaves were sold privately or in secret, so the whole process might easily have been overlooked if reference had been made only to other contemporary materials like travelogues or the general reports of officers, even if based on their own observations. Such conventional source materials have always allowed only a limited view of all the slave dealings that actually went on. The chain of reselling was revealed as applying to both Indian females and African males: common elements were the short-term nature of dealings and the relatively young ages of the slaves traded.

This chapter has examined the contemporary background to the chain of reselling, focusing on the time cycle of slave-holding and the greater value attached to young slaves. It is unclear how common such frequent reselling of slaves was before the nineteenth century, but two main circumstances encouraged it in the nineteenth-century western Indian Ocean context. One was the increasing pressure of the anti-slave trade campaign, and the other was the prevalence of repeated epidemics. The former made it difficult for owners to purchase and retain new slaves. Furthermore, for owners, particularly Indians, it turned to be difficult even to make good use of the slaves they already owned. However, British patrols were not able to pay close enough attention to the finer details of individual slave dealings, which left owners still able to make good profits from trading in slaves if they cared to accept the risks—the chain of reselling was the result. Even if buyers managed to obtain and keep slaves secretly under the eye of the British, they risked the loss of their property to epidemics, so selling them on quickly became the best chance of making a profit.

The stories of the slaves which this chapter has examined have been limited to those told by relatively young people. While there might have been slaves older than 30 years who experienced frequent reselling it was overwhelmingly the younger slaves whom owners prized, because younger people are more easily assimilated and have the potential to become better specimens as they reach physical maturity.

Notes

1. See Abdussamad H. Ahmad, 'Ethiopian Slave Exports at Matamma, Massawa and Tajura, c.1830–1885', in Clarence-Smith (ed.), *The Economics of the Indian Ocean Slave Trade*; Edward A. Alpers, 'The Other Middle Passage: The African Slave Trade in the Indian Ocean', in Emma Christopher, Cassandra Pybus and Marcus Rediker (eds.), *Many Middle Passages: Forced Migration and the Making of the Modern World*, Berkley, Los Angeles and London: University of California Press, 2007; Beachey, *The Slave Trade*, 11–66; Lloyd, *The Navy and the Slave Trade*, 248–257; Iain McCalman, 'The East African Middle Passage: David Livingstone, the Zambezi Expedition and Lake Nyassa, 1858–1866', in Christopher, Pybus and Rediker (eds.), *Many Middle Passages.*
2. For studies on slavery based on autobiographies and interviews with ex-slaves in East Africa, see Sarah Mirza and Margaret Strobel (eds.), *Three Swahili Women: Life Histories from Mombasa, Kenya*, Bloomington and Indianapolis: Indiana University Press, 1989; Margaret Strobel, 'Women and Slavery on the East African Coast', in Chizuko Tominaga (ed.),

Rethinking African History from Women's/Gender Perspectives: Slavery, Colonial Experience, Nationalist Movement and After, Osaka: National Museum of Ethnology, 2004; Marcia Wright, *Strategies of Slaves and Women: Life-Histories from East/Central Africa*, New York: Lillian Barber Press, 1993.

3. Edward A. Alpers and Matthew S. Hopper, 'Parler en son nom? Comprendre les témoignages d'esclaves africains originaires de l'océan Indien (1850–1930)' *Annales* 63, 4 (2008), 799–828.
4. Ibid.
5. *BPP*, Vol. 25, Class A, 401 [Rubil bin Uslan to Hennell, 13 Ramaẓān 1257/27 October 1841].
6. 'Luti' derives from 'lūtī', 'lūtītā', 'lūtīwālā' in Hindu or 'lutaru', 'lutaro' in Gujarati, or in Arabic and Persian 'lūtī', which mean 'a plunderer', 'a blackguard', 'a robber' and 'a pederast'. See also Yule and Burnell, *Hobson-Jobson*, 520–521, s.v. Looty, Lootiewalla, and 'luti' in the nineteenth century Persian context, see Vanessa Martin, *The Qajar Pact: Bargaining, Protest and the State in Nineteenth-Century Persia*, London and New York: I.B. Tauris, 2005, 113–128.
7. *BPP*, Vol. 25, Class A, 401–402 [Rubil bin Uslan to Hennell, 13 Ramaẓān 1257/27 October 1841]. A shorter version of this case is in *BPP*, Vol. 25, Class A, 427 [Reuben Aslan to Captain Hennell, 27 Ramaẓān 1257/12 October 1842].
8. Omar Khalidi, 'The Habshis of Hyderabad', in Kenneth X. Robbins and John McLeod (eds.), *African Elites in India*, 247–248, quotes a document in Mahārāshtra State Archives revealing that a freed slave named 'Yacoob' served a merchant in Jidda and dealt in slaves in Hyderabad in early 1840s. There are similarities between 'Zakoot' in the above quotation and the 'Yacoob' mentioned in Khalidi's chapter: both of them served a Jidda merchant and worked in Hyderabad; both were described as 'Habshi' and both of them took a wife in Hyderabad. Moreover, contemporary British documents often take the initial 'z' for 'y', and 't' for 'b' as a final consonant. Thus, I have identified the two figures as the same man. For further information on this figure, see *BPP*, Vol. 25, Class A, 427 [Reuben Aslan to Hennell, 27 Ramaẓān/12 November 1841].
9. *BPP*, Vol. 25, Class A, 402 [Rubil bin Uslan to Hennell, 28 Ramaẓān 1257/13 November 1841]; ibid., 427 [Reuben Aslan to Hennell, n.p., 27 Ramaẓān/12 November 1841].
10. *BPP*, Vol. 25, Class A, 402 [Rubil bin Uslan to Hennell, 28 Ramaẓān 1257/13 November 1841].
11. MAHA PD/1860/159/830/271 [Rigby to Anderson, Zanzibar, 14 September 1860]. The same document is found also in ZZBA AA/12/2/57.

12. This figure can be identified with Taria Topin, since 'bhay' is a title for a male in Gujarati.
13. MAHA PD/1871/143/963/86-87 [Kirk to Wedderburn, Zanzibar, 8 April 1871].
14. MAHA PD/1878/135/83/n.p. [Statement of Marjan, Bombay, 16 November 1878].
15. MAHA PD/1860/159/830/231-232 [Depositions of various male and female African slaves found in the possession of Kanoo Munjee, a Banian, residing at Zanzibar, British Consular Court, Zanzibar, 5 February 1860].
16. Original spelling is 'Mizaw'. Identification is based on my research of the Rigby Manumission List, see Suzuki, 'Enslaved Population and Indian Owners', 217.
17. MAHA PD/1860/159/830/231-232 [Depositions of various male and female African slaves found in the possession of Kanoo Munjee a Banian, residing at Zanzibar, Zanzibar, 5 February 1860].
18. Colomb, *Slave-Catching*, 28–30.
19. *BPP*, Vol. 25, Class A, 440 [Harris to Secretary to Bombay Government, Ankober, 20 July 1842]. William C. Harris, *The Highlands of Æthiopia, described, during 18 months' residence of a British Embassy at Christian Court of Shoa*, 3 vols, London: Longman, Brown, Green, and Longmans, 1844, Vol. 3, 303–305, cited the same story with differing spelling of several place names. In Dibbo's case, he was circulated around the interior of Africa. However, the places to which he was taken were obviously along the slave route towards coastal ports such as Maṣṣawa' (see *BPP*, Vol. 25, Class A, 440–441 [Harris to Secretary to Bombay Government, Ankober, 20 July 1842]).
20. The chain of reselling is also confirmed in the following cases of several Indian girls on OIOC IOR/F/4/28499/12-14 [Extract of Fort St George Judicial Constitutions, n.p., 28 June 1825]; the cases of one boy and two girls from Abyssinia, who were protected in October 1857 off Maṣṣawa' (OIOC IOR/R/20/A1A/255/56-57 ['the statement of the three liberated slaves' compiled by R. Barrowiz, Massowah, 10 May 1857]); the case of an Englishman who bought a slave girl for the purpose of resale (Emilie Ruete, *An Arabian Princess between Two Worlds: Memoirs, Letters Home, Sequels to My Memories: Syrian Customs and Usages*, ed. and intro. E. van Donzel, Leiden: Brill, 1993, 329). Furthermore, Arthur C. Madan collected a series of stories written by students in Universities' Mission to the Central Africa Mission School in Kiungani, Zanzibar, who were rescued from slavery. These stories contain full details of resales (Arthur C. Madan, *Kiungani; or, Story and History from Central Africa*, London: George Bell and Sons, 1887, 23–26,

30–31, 34, 40–43, 46–47, 52, 56–8, 62, 67–72, 76–77). Fred Morton uses narratives in *Kiungani* and other missionary sources to analyze the experience of children in East African slave trade in the nineteenth century. In his work, he also points out frequent reselling (Fred Morton, 'Small Change: Children in the Nineteenth-Century East African Slave Trade', in Gwyn Campbell, Suzanne Miers and Joseph C. Miller (eds.), *Children in Slavery though the Ages*, Athens: Ohio University Press, 2009, 60). In addition, there are a couple of cases of Indian males who were resold frequently in OIOC IOR/R/15/1/229/19-21 [Narandas Jethanand Meghuvanai to the Secretary, 20 December 1925], while Mirzai, 'Slavery, the Abolition of the Slave Trade, and the Emancipation of Slaves', 72, 122, records the cases of an Abyssinian concubine in 1905 and of a Zanzibar-born woman in 1927. See also, cases analyzed in Alpers and Hopper, 'Parler en son nom?'. Above all, it is clear that the chain of reselling continued even in the first half of the twentieth century.

21. This phrase is quoted by various Islamic theologians in NAUK FO/84/692/30-32 [Question to various priests in Tehran regarding the slave trade], see also NAUK FO/84/737/77 [Rawlinson to Farrant, Baghdad, 15 January 1848] and Joseph Cooper, *The Lost Continent or Slavery and the Slave Trade in Africa 1875, with Observations on the Asiatic Slave Trade Carried on under the Name of Labour Traffic, and Some Other Subjects*, London: Frank Cass, 1968, 114–115; Kelly, *Britain and the Persian Gulf*, 595–598; Mirzai, 'Slavery, the Abolition of the Slave Trade, and the Emancipation of Slaves', 141– 146; William G. Clarence-Smith, *Islam and the Abolition of Slavery*, New York: Oxford University Press, 2006, 34–35. Hamilton A.R. Gibb, J.H. Kramers, E. Lévi-Provençal et al (eds.), *Encyclopaedia of Islām*, new ed., 12 vols, Leiden: E. J. Brill. 1960–2005, Vol. 1, s.v. 'Abd mentions that under Islamic law owners were unable to resell slaves without facing considerable sanctions.
22. MAHA PD/1860/159/830/271-272 [Rigby to Anderson, Zanzibar, 14 September1860].
23. Buzurg b. Shahriyār, Pieter A. van der Lith and L. Marcel Devic, *Livre des merveilles de l'Inde = Kitāb 'ajā'ib al-Hind*, Leiden: Brill, 1883–1886, 50–60.
24. Lorimer, *Gazetteer of the Persian Gulf*, 2530– 2534.
25. Ḥamīd ibn Muḥammad ibn Ruzayq, *Al-fataḥ al-mubīn fī sīra al-sāda al-bū sa'īdiyīn*, ed. 'Abd al-Mun'im 'Āmir and Muḥammad Mursī 'Abd Allāh, Masqaṭ: Wizāra al-turāth wa al-thaqāfa, 2001, 472; Christie, *Cholera Epidemics in East Africa*, 97–98. However, in Madagascar, a cholera outbreak occurred in 1819/20. It was brought in by an English frigate *La Topaze* from Calcutta and Ceylon in November 1819. See

Gwyn Campbell, 'Madagascar and Mozambique in the Slave Trade of the Western Indian Ocean, 1800–1861', in Clarence-Smith (ed.), *The Economics of the Indian Ocean Slave Trade*, 184–185; Bernard-Alex Gaüwère and Pierre Aubry, 'Histoire des épidémies et des endémoépidémies humaines dans le sud-ouest de l'océan Indien', *Médecine et Santé Tropicales* 23 (2013), 147– 148.

26. Christie, *Cholera Epidemics in East Africa*, 97–147; Lorimer, *Gazetteer of the Persian Gulf*, 2518–2530.
27. MAHA PD/1859/188/825/151-152 [Rigby to Anderson, Zanzibar, 18 March 1859].
28. MAHA PD/1859/188/825/152 [Rigby to Anderson, Zanzibar, 18 March 1859].
29. NAUK FO84/1325/166-167 [Kirk to Wedderburn, Zanzibar, 20 May 1870]. For another case in the Persian Gulf, see OIOC IOR/R/15/1/168/24 [Jones to Anderson, Bushire, 26 October 1858]; OIOC IOR/R/15/1/168/27 [Robinson to the Senior Naval Officer, Tigris, 26 October 1858].
30. For example, *BPP*, Vol. 24, Class D, 31 [Edwards to Kemball, Bushire, 9 July 1842]. See also Mirzai, 'Slavery, the Abolition of the Slave Trade, and the Emancipation of Slaves', 122–123.
31. For example, *BPP*, Vol. 27, Class D, 142 [Hamerton to the Earl of Aberdeen, Zanzibar, 2 January 1844]; Burton, *Zanzibar*, Vol. 1, 463.
32. For example, OIOC IOR/R/15/1/168/24 [Jones to Anderson, Bushire, 26 October 1858]; OIOC IOR/R/15/1/168/27 [Robinson to the Senior Naval Officer, Tigris, 26 October 1858].
33. 'Précis on Slave Trade in the Gulf of Oman and the Persian Gulf, 1873–1905 (With a Retrospect into Previous History from 1852)', in Jerome A. Saldanha (ed.), *The Persian Gulf Précis*, 8 vols, Gerrards Cross, Archive Editions, 1986 (1st. in 18 vols., 1903-1908, Calcutta and Simla), Vol. 3, 91.
34. William G. Milburn, *Oriental Commerce: Containing a Geographical Description of the Principal Places in the East Indies, China, and Japan, with their Produce, Manufactures, and Trade*, 2 vols, London: Black, Parry, and Co., 1813, Vol. 1, 116, 173–174, 198; Burton, *Zanzibar*, Vol. 1, 324–325, Vol. 2, 406, 418. See also Robert G. Landen, *Oman since 1856: Disruptive Modernization in a Traditional Arab Society*, Princeton: Princeton University Press, 1967, 128–131.
35. The rate was £1 = 20*s*. = 4.75MT$ (Burton, *Zanzibar*, Vol. 1, 324–325, Vol. 2, 406, 418; Milburn, *Oriental Commerce*, Vol. 1, 116, 173–174, 198; Landen 1967, 128–131).
36. Colomb, *Slave-Catching*, 55-6, mentions the profit from the resale.
37. For example, Campbell, 'Introduction', xxi; Clarence-Smith, 'The Economics', 14; Sheriff, *Slaves, Spices and Ivory*, 37. For example,

Richard P. Waters observed at Mozambique a couple of slavers embarking slaves 'mostly with children from 10 to 14 years of age' (PPEM MH14/4/1 [22 February 1837]).

38. *BPP*, Vol. 24, Class D, 26 [Kemball to Robertson, Karrak, 8 July 1848]. The same content is found in Kemball, 'Paper Relative to the Measures', 649.
39. *BPP*, Vol. 24, Class D, 26 [Kemball to Robertson, Karrak, 8 July 1848].
40. *BPP*, Vol. 24, Class D, 32 [Wilson to Government, n.p., 28 January 1831].
41. Hideaki Suzuki, 'Tracing their "Middle" Passages: Slave Accounts from the Nineteenth-Century Western Indian Ocean', in Alice Bellagamba, Sandra E. Greene and Martin A. Klein (eds.), *African Voices on Slavery and the Slave Trade*, Cambridge: Cambridge University Press, 2013, 311. Burton, *The Lake Regions of Central Africa*, Vol. 2, 310– 311.
42. Charles New, *Life, Wanderings and Labours in Eastern Africa: With an Account of the First Successful Ascent of the Equatorial Snow Mountain, Kilima Njaro, and Remarks upon East African Slavery*, London: Frank Cass, 1971 (1st. 1873, London: Hodder and Stoughton), 56–57. Modern scholars such as Fred J. Berg, 'Mombasa under the Busaidi Sultanate: The City and its Hinterlands in the Nineteenth Century' (PhD dissertation, University of Wisconsin, 1971), 170–171, and Jonathan Glassman, *Feasts and Riots: Revelry, Rebellion, and Popular Consciousness on the Swahili Cost: 1856–1888*, London: James Currey, 1995, 85–90, also accept this analysis.
43. William E. Taylor, *African Aphorisms; or, Saws from Swahili-land*, London: Society for Promoting Christian Knowledge, 1891, 78. For further examples, see ibid., 8, 71. Moreover, slave treatment in Persia corresponds to the East African case. See Mirzai, 'Slavery, the Abolition of the Slave Trade, and the Emancipation of Slaves', 114–122.
44. Taylor, *African Aphorisms*, 78.
45. Berg, 'Mombasa under the Busaidi Sultanate', 171.

CHAPTER 6

The Transformation of East African Coastal Urban Society with Regard to the Slave Distribution System

Introduction

Almost all the estimates agree that the peak of the East African slave trade occurred in the nineteenth century. For example, Paul E. Lovejoy estimated the number of the slaves exported from East African coast then as 882,000,[1] more than double an estimate of 400,000 for the previous century.[2] In the system of slave distribution in the western Indian Ocean region, the East African coastal urban society played two well-recognized roles: as emporium of slaves brought from the interior and exported to markets overseas, and as itself a creator of demand for slaves. After the 1830s when Zanzibar rushed headlong into what Abdul Sheriff has called 'clove mania', the demand for slaves rose notably. However, another role which the coastal society began to play seems to be largely ignored thus far: it was a slave ground, and it became one almost at the same time as it created its own demand for slaves. This chapter will clarify the process by which that happened and will explore the background to it.

The Growing Demand for Slaves on the East African Coast

The three roles mentioned above can be understood as a causal chain, and in this section I shall clarify how the first two developed. The coastal region had played the role of exporter for long time, but a rapid increase

H. Suzuki, *Slave Trade Profiteers in the Western Indian Ocean*, Palgrave Series in Indian Ocean World Studies,
DOI 10.1007/978-3-319-59803-1_6

in slave exports began in the last quarter of the eighteenth century, corresponding with the increase in demand for slaves in the Mascarene and Caribbean Islands as their plantation economies grew.[3] The coastal area and its immediate hinterland initially met that demand,[4] but at the start of the nineteenth century local sources of slaves began to be depleted. Slaves were then brought from further into the interior; Alpers, for example, points out that at that time a large number of Yao slaves are recorded in Mozambique Island.[5] In fact, according to the French trader Épidariste Colin who visited that part of the coast in 1804, he found more slaves from the Yao than from the Makua, who generally lived much closer to the island. He even saw slaves from the Maravi, whose homeland was much farther away than that of the Yao.[6] James Prior, a surgeon on board the Royal Navy ship *Nisus*, also noticed the depopulation of the hinterland of Kilwa when he visited in 1811.[7]

The coastal region developed a large appetite for slaves in the first half of the nineteenth century, largely because of the rise of a plantation-based economy in that area, particularly north of Kilwa. Cash crops produced on plantations, such as cloves, sesame seeds or sugar, required close connections to the world market to be forged.[8] Economic dependency on plantation products followed the success of clove and coconut cultivation on Zanzibar and later on Pemba Island[9]; after that, it was only a matter of time before other products became important export commodities, with the plantation economy even spreading to the opposite coast of Zanzibar and Pemba.[10] For example, Rigby reported in 1860 that:

> [d]uring the last few years the cultivation of sesamum and rice on the opposite coast has much increased and these articles are now exported from Mombass and Lamoo to the amount of about two lacks [*sic.* lacs] of Rupees annually.[11]

Incidentally, all sesame seeds were exported to Marseilles.[12] The planting of grains, meanwhile, revived historical Malindi. As Esmond B. Martin explains, Mājid b. Saʿīd ordered the resettlement of Malindi, which began sometime around 1861 with the posting of a number of Baluchi soldiers to supervise resettlement and the cultivation of crops.[13] The plan appeared to succeed and crops were cultivated on a large scale around Malindi to provide foodstuffs for the cash crop cultivation centres, where arable lands for food crops were given over instead to cash crop production.[14] Similarly, along the Mrima Coast, the locals enjoyed prosperity with running 'large plantations of cereals and vegetables, with which they, or rather their slaves, supply the island of Zanzibar, and even the shores of Arabia'.[15] As such, not only Zanzibar and Pemba Islands but also several spots along the coast began to enjoy economic prosperity. Plantations required a large workforce of slave labour; for example, according to calculations by Sheriff, one slave could produce 60 lb of cloves annually.[16] Plantation owners bought more slaves with the profits generated by commercial crops. Indeed, in 1844 the British Consul reported an increase of population in Zanzibar where 'the people are growing rich, and able to buy more slaves to cultivate cloves'.[17]

Slaves were not only seen as a labour force creating profit for their owners; as Hamerton declared in 1842, 'a man's wealth and respectability in the dominions of the Imam of Muskat is always estimated by the number of African slaves he is said to possess'.[18] Ephraim A. Emmerton, a Salem merchant who regularly visited Zanzibar, observed in 1849 that '[s]laves are owned here because it is fashionable for to have them, not because it is profitable'.[19] Considering 'clove mania' had reached its peak by then, Emmerton's remark seems to imply that owning slaves for non-commercial purposes was widespread by that time; he went on in his diaries to mention that many slaves themselves owned slaves.[20] Furthermore, increasing numbers of Indian merchants wanted temporary wives while they were in Zanzibar, and since many Hindu communities prohibited females from going abroad, majority male Hindu communities in Zanzibar demanded female slaves, many of whom were then resold when their masters eventually left Zanzibar.[21] By the 1850s, East African coastal urban society included a large slave population.[22]

Further Depopulation of the Interior

As demand for slaves increased, the slave grounds extended further inland. Hamerton reported in 1842 the existence around Kilwa of a barter trade involving slaves and muskets, gunpowder and cotton clothes from America (called *merikani*).[23] An unknown contemporary Indian observer who had lived in Kilwa for many years reported to Rigby that it was sometime around the late 1840s that Arab slave merchants began to go deeper into the interior, accompanied by large numbers of armed men, and that the local chiefs, who desperately wanted the trade goods mentioned started attacking each other.[24] Considering the dates, it would be fair to suspect some relationship exists between this serious depopulation of the hinterland of Kilwa and the 'clove mania' and related events as mentioned in the previous section which produced a large demand of slaves. In other words, significant population movement towards coastal urban area including adjascent plantation has been occurred in East African region-wide.

Depopulation of the interior was reported from other regions besides Kilwa. For instance, a missionary of CMS, Johannes Rebmann, observed in 1848 that in Jagga, at the foot of Kilimanjaro, local people waged war against each other to obtain captives who would be sent to the coast.[25] In addition, there is a report about the region of the Sagara, west of Uluguru Mountains, quite similar to that Rigby reported about Kilwa[26]; Krapf revealed that the Kamba overpowered the Kwavi and as a result of it, the Kamba carried away a large number of children of the Kwavi—of both genders—because slave dealers preferred their appearance.[27]

Rigby made following interesting observations about the extension of the slave ground into the interior. When he undertook to set free slaves owned by Indians resident along East African coast at the beginning of the 1860s, he noticed a significant difference between those who had been held for a long time and those who were newly enslaved: the majority of the former had come from the Mrima Coast and its immediate hinterland, while many of the latter were from the Yao or the Nyasa tribes, who lived further inland.[28] He estimated the number of slaves brought to Zanzibar during the north-east monsoon season in 1860 at 19,000: 4000 from the Mrima Coast and its immediate hinterland and 15,000 from the region around Lake Nyasa, which is about 40 days' journey from Kilwa.[29] As the reason for the change in the area of supply from the coast to inland regions, he pointed to the extensive depopulation of the Mrima Coast and its hinterland.[30] Serious depopulation was observed around Kilwa too, where, by 1860, the previously densely populated area—roughly, ten to 12 days' distance inland from Kilwa—had become totally depopulated.[31] Rigby's observation corresponded to the list of slaves of Indian owners along the East African coast freed by the Consul in 1860.[32] For example, the slaves from the inland were, on average, younger than those from the regions much closer to the coast.

Depopulation brought with it a number of side effects. The Yao had previously cultivated a large amount of cotton, but after the slave ground was extended to cover their region they stopped doing so.[33] Furthermore, the wars carried on for the purpose of procuring captives made caravan routes unsafe.[34]

Becoming a Slave Ground: Kidnap and Plunder in the East African Coastal Urban Society

After the British anti-slave trade patrol became active in the western Indian Ocean in the 1850s, testimonies like those quoted below could be found in the consulate documents:

> I gave myself up to the Agent at Lingar [*sic.* = Bander-e Lengeh] and claimed protection. I was born at Marema [*sic.* = Mrima] near Zanzibar and was taken quite young to Zanzibar, where I was sold to an Indian man who belonged to Surat, I remained at Zanzibar. I was about thirteen of years old when my master died and I obtained my liberty and remained at Zanzibar free. Until a few months ago when I went to a dance, and on returning I was met by Feroze bin Samied who had at other three men with him and as soon as my sister and myself had passed these men, they turned and caught us and dragged us to their Batel, who which they sent us and brought us to Ras el Khyma [*sic.* = Ras al-Khayma]. There was about twenty other slaves in this boat, all were landed at Ras el Khyma, I remained at Ras el khyma 6 days when Feroze brought three of us over to Lingar and sold me to Kummal a Busra man and he told me not to show myself outside the house, because the English Agent would see me, I met a slave girl in Lingar, who told me that to go to Busra but to go to Ahmed the Agent who would save me, which I did and he sent me to Bassadore [*sic.* = Basidu = Bandar-e 'Abbās].[35]

That statement was given by a 22-year-old woman named Khyzran, in Bandar-e Lengeh, 1856, while in the same year a boy of 13 named Meerjohu, who had come under the protection of a local agent at the same place, made a statement summarized as follows:

> [T]hese men had plenty of sweetmeats which they gave them every now and then and they [Meerjohu and his friends] followed these men to get these sweetmeats,[36] until they were a long way from their villages, when these men caught them and put them in a Boat and took them on board the Buggalow, this was near Zanzibar, there was a great number on board the Buggalow … hundred landed at Ras el Khyma, they were all landed there... of which he was one, was sold and brought to Linga, six remained with his master when he left Ras el Khyma, and all the others had been sent away to Busra in the Boats.[37]

Apart from those two cases, similar incidents were reported from Zanzibar, Pemba, Mombasa and Lamu.[38] In his despatch written on 13 September 1858, Rigby mentioned the general pattern of these raids:

> The Buggalows on their departure from Zanzibar or other ports put into some small Bay under the pretence of procuring fresh water and then the crew land in a body armed and carry off as many Negroes as they can seize from the neighbouring plantations. They also frequently have on an accomplice who conveys Negroes to a particular spot agreed upon for clandestine sale. Many are also kidnapped from the Town of Zanzibar and conveyed on board a Buggalow just as it is about to sail. Some time ago, the Arab commander of one of His Highness the Sultan's ships of war was thus kidnapped, released the next morning when they ascertained who he was.[39]

From the end of the 1850s the East African coastal urban society began to experience serious raiding. A letter of 28 March 1860 from the British Consul in Zanzibar to the Secretary to the Indian Government mentioned that during the early north–east monsoon season of 1859, 'a very unusual number' of boats visited from the Gulf of Oman and the Persian Gulf.[40] Several local dhows were attacked by these boats off Pemba Island, while at Mombasa the local inhabitants rose up against the crews who had stolen their slaves and children—a number of lives were lost during the ensuing melee.[41] The Consul continued his report:

> Zanzibar resembles a city with a hostile army encamped in its neighbourhood. Every person who is able to do so, sends his children and young slaves into the interior of the island for security, people are afraid to stir out of their houses after dark, reports are daily made of children and slaves kidnapped and in the suburbs of the town. They even enter the houses and take the children away by force.[42]

Kidnap victims included a boy who had been freed just a month earlier and was employed in the house of a Consulate, and the small daughter of a *havildar* (commandant) at the British Consulate[43]; all in all the raids 'inspired terror amongst all classes' in Zanzibar,[44] with foreign merchants and even Consuls no exception. Rigby complained that the officers and *jemadar* (military official) of the Bū Saʿīd were too cowardly to stop the raids and actually went in fear of the Northern Arabs.[45] Consequently, the raiders could be seen 'carrying kidnapped children though the public streets in large baskets during the day'.[46]

Similar incidents were recorded again in the next north–east monsoon season; this time the number of visitors from Oman and the Persian Gulf had increased from the previous season and there was much kidnapping.[47]

For example, on 14 July, five kidnapped slaves were found in the house of a man of the Qawāsim, and a certain Aḥmad b. Sulaymān from Ṣūr managed to kidnap 40 slaves in a single night.[48] At the beginning of the monsoon season, the Customs House at Stone Town was attacked, and on 9 March 1861 the American Consulate was occupied by raiders.[49] Some of the raiders were seen 'brandishing their swords and calling out that they would have the blood of a white man'[50]; they then surrounded the British Consulate and continued to threaten violence. Both consulates were relieved after Mājid paid 500 MT$ to the ringleader of the raiders.[51]

This 500 MT$ was not the first payment that the Northern Arabs received from Mājid. According to Rigby, they visited his palace every morning demanding money and food—and eventually they got it.[52] On another occasion they requested 5000 MT$ from Mājid and eventually received a half of this amount after a few days' negotiation.[53] Money they received on these occasions was immediately exchanged for slaves.[54] On the other hands, some of slave owners in Zanzibar chose to sell their slaves to the Northern Arabs, rather than risk losing them to the Arabs anyway via kidnap and plunder. As a result, a slave market operated every day in the suburbs of Stone Town, and Northern Arabs could buy slaves without interference.[55] It was no surprise then, when HMS *Lyra* arrived at Zanzibar on 19 March and captured a number of Northern Arab vessels which together held 250 slaves, 200 of whom had been purchased either in the slave market or privately.[56] Northern Arabs were in the habit of renting houses in Stone Town where they imprisoned slaves in darkened rooms, as reported by the British Consul.[57] He even noted that large numbers of slaves were quite openly forcibly embarked in ships beached just yards from the consulate's premises.[58] This situation continued even after the end of the north-east monsoon season.[59]

Since slaves made up a large proportion of the population in the East African coastal urban society as a result of its transformation into a lucrative plantation economy, the local populace themselves began to be targeted by kidnappers. There are no reliable sources that can be used to estimate the number of raids, and also the level of exploitation would have been much modest than interior areas such as the Shire River valley, but without doubt they had an enormous effect on the coastal urban society, as the cases above show. Moreover, the Omani historian Saʿīd

b. ʻAlī al-Mughayrī (1300–78 AH = 1882/3–1958/9 AD), the author of *Juhayna al-akhbār fī tārīkh Zanzibār*,[60] listed two main ways of enslaving people. First, there was the possibility of capturing them in war and taking them as plunder, or, second, one might simply kidnap them. *Juhayna*, with implicit disapproval, pointed out that although the latter was in fact much more likely, the former was the only permissible method under the law of Islam.[61] Sullivan mentioned in his memoir of anti-slave trade patrolling in Zanzibar's waters that one of the questions he had learned to ask in the Kiswahili language of slaves rescued at sea was whether they had been kidnapped or bought.[62]

Who Changed the East African Coastal Urban Area into a Slave Ground?

The question to be asked then is: 'Who turned the East African coastal urban society into a slave ground from the mid-1850s onwards?' To answer the question, we must consider the timing; in other words, 'why the mid-1850s?'

The contemporary records always refer to Northern Arabs as the raiders.[63] The term 'Northern Arabs' generally refers to sailors and merchants who visited the East African coastal towns from Oman and the Persian Gulf. They were infamous in the western Indian Ocean waters. For instance, in 1827, the brig *Ann* from Salem set sail from Ṣūr along the East African coast in consort with a dhow. Only later was *Ann*'s master told by another local captain that the Ṣūri dhow had intended to commit piracy against *Ann*.[64]

Northern Arabs had a similar reputation for infamy in the British documents too, but in fact they were not the only ones raiding coastal societies and kidnapping their peoples to enslave them. They worked with agents from within the coastal societies. The contemporary records report a number of raids masterminded by officers of the Sultan. For instance, Rigby reported that a Turkish jemadar admitted that he had sold 62 children to Northern Arabs despite the fact that his job was to patrol the coast against them.[65] Another case was unearthed by Rigby in August 1861. The Consul reported that several Arab mercenaries had kidnapped a large number of slaves and carried them away by ship.[66] Three days later, Rigby wrote another report stating that 12 kidnapped slaves had been found in the house of an Arab jemadar.[67]

However, simply identifying Northern Arabs and their local partners-in-crime as the culprits does not provide the full answer. Northern Arabs were by no means newcomers to East African coastal towns, yet we can find no trace of any great tendency to raiding and kidnapping by them at any time prior to the mid-1850s. That being so, we must consider what changed them so thoroughly in that period? The most important change going on in the mid-1850s was in the anti-slave trade policy of the Bū Saʿīd. Since the Moresby Treaty's conclusion in 1822, the British had repeatedly requested the sultans of Zanzibar to take strict measures against the slave trade.[68] During his reign, Saʿīd, who transferred his capital to Zanzibar in 1828, appealed in his *darbār* (royal court) as well as to 'the people of influence' not to sell slaves to Northern Arabs,[69] and prohibited the public sale of slaves.[70] He went further, even ordering the locals not to rent houses to Northern Arabs.[71] Nonetheless, the British Consul expressed doubt about whether those orders actually had any effect on slave dealings.[72] In fact, the Sultan was not truly cooperating with the British; according to Hamerton, Saʿīd's real intention was to keep slave dealing away from 'white people''s sights; thus the slave market was moved to the suburbs of the town.[73] Saʿīd's motivations can be explained: the income from the poll tax of slaves was an important revenue stream for him and he owned a large number of slaves himself and exported them. Probably to explain his position, he once remarked to Hamerton that the Qur'ān sanctioned the slave trade and the institution of slavery, and that Arabs enjoyed the right to enslave all infidels.[74]

By contrast, Mājid (r. 1856–1870), his successor, put in place much stricter measures. He prohibited all slave dealings during the north-east monsoon season 1859/60 and detailed his frigate called '*Piedmontese*' near the north end of Zanzibar and later moved it to the entrance of the Stone Town harbor to examine all passing dhows.[75] Furthermore, he closed slave market during the entire north-east monsoon season and ordered all dhows belonging to the people of the Qawāsim and from Ṣūr to drop anchor about six miles from Stone Town, whereupon their rudders would be confiscated.[76] However, these did not make any effect, as few were on board '*Piedmontese*' constantly and slave market was carried everyday just outside the town and Northern Arabs could purchase slaves freely.[77] In the following north-east monsoon season of 1860/61, partically owing to raidings of Northern Arabs, Royal Navy's *Lyra* and *Sidon* patrolled around the East African coast and captured 25 vessels and rescued slaves on board these vessels.[78] Finally, Mājid used his own force to arrest slave traders in 1862, and several of them were imprisoned, and his soldiers and Northern Arabs clashed each other and several Northern

Arabs lost their lives.[79] In the meeting with Playfair in May 1863, Mājid reported Playfair these events and his future plans for slave trade suppression.[80] Actually, the Annual Report of the British Consul at Zanzibar in 1864 revealed that the Sultan adopted following measures[81]:

1. Slave exporting from Kilwa port can be permitted only on ships belonging to the Sultan's subjects that had obtained special permission from Zanzibar Customs.
2. All slave transport was completely prohibited between 1 January and 1 May when the Northern Arabs visited East African coast.

Though these measures did not always work well to begin with, the policy became stricter afterwards.[82] According to a dispatch from Mājid to Churchill, the British Consul who succeeded Rigby at Zanzibar, on 10 Muḥarram 1285 AH (3 May 1868), Mājid had sent letters to the shaykhs of the Northern Arabs requesting them to prohibit their subjects from visiting Zanzibar, and he also warned them that he would impound and then burn any of ships which ignored this ban.[83] These actions of Mājid gradually came into effect and such progress was well-recognized by British and American Consuls.[84] Combined with the Royal Navy's eager campaign targetting East African waters, that action by Mājid certainly prevented the Northern Arabs from regular and formal slave dealings with Zanzibar and even stopped them entering Stone Town.[85] Under such circumstance, Playfair observed a certain transition of Northern Arab's behavior. He reported in his letter to Bombay on 26th August 1863 that '[t]he Gulf Arabs finding it difficult to obtain cargos of slaves by open purchase, have adopted the more economical expedient of kidnapping all on whom they can lay hands' and 'majority of the slaves belonged to residents at Zanzibar, and had either been decoyed into their captor's possession by temptation, or taken by force'.[86]

Conclusion: Ironic Reality

This chapter has traced the dynamic transformation of East African coastal urban society in the framework of slave distribution in the nineteenth century. Long-established slave entrepôts now took on a new role as themselves creators of demand for slaves after the plantation economy began to flourish. The first plantations led to the requirement for more plantations of different types: cash crop plantations required commodity plantations. In other words, East African coastal urban society transformed itself to operate a complex plantation economy with global links. The attendant demand for ever more labour was met by exploiting the East African interior as an extended slave ground. Wars over the capture of slaves made the region insecure and seriously depopulated the interior, while on the coast demand rose for more slaves not only for commercial wealth creation but also for enhancement of social status. Simultaneously, the upsurge in the anti-slave trade campaign in the western Indian Ocean coupled with the anti-slave trade stance taken by Mājid made it more difficult for overseas slave traders to obtain slaves in the same manner as before. Slave markets were often closed and even the vessels from the Persian Gulf and the Gulf of Oman were excluded from East Africa during the north-east monsoon season. As a consequence, in order to procure slaves, traders resorted to violence, and raiding of the coastal regions became rampant, adding to feelings of insecurity among populations there. Obviously, the coastal region began to play a new role in the slave distribution system—that of a slave ground.

It is somewhat simplistic to point to the so-called Northern Arabs as the actors who created the upheaval in the coastal societies, for although they might be seen as the agents for it, we find they had accomplices along the coast, such as the jemadars of the Sultan of Zanzibar. Furthermore, if we accept that the anti-slave trade policy of Mājid was effective in preventing Northern Arabs from purchasing slaves legally, then we must also acknowledge that the policy itself had an effect in creating insecurity, even if only indirectly and presumably unintentionally. Why did Mājid adopt a stricter policy against the slave trade compared with his father Saʿīd? The answer to that question will enable us to further explore the dynamic social transformation of East African coastal urban society in the slave distribution system. Moreover, it will bring the complex political scramble into our argument. Chapter 7 will address that question.

Notes

1. Lovejoy, *Transformations in Slavery*, 151–152.
2. Ibid., 45, 46.
3. Edward A. Alpers, *Ivory and Slaves: Changing Pattern of International Trade in East Central Africa to the Later Nineteenth Century*, Berkeley: University of California Press, 1975, 185–189; Cooper, *Plantation*

Slavery, 39–41; Patrick Manning, *Slavery and African Life: Occidental, Oriental, and African Slave Trades*, New York: Cambridge University Press, 1990, 52–53; Sheriff, *Slaves, Spices and Ivory*, 41–48; Allen, *European Slave Trading*, 23–24. For details of the trans-Atlantic slave trade from Mozambique, see José Capela, *O tráfico de escravos nos portos de Moçambique; 1733–1904*, Porto: Edições Afrontamento, 2002, 66–133. For East African slave trade in earlier period, see Thomas Vernet's works such as Thomas Vernet, 'Slave Trade and Slavery on the Swahili Coast (1500–1750)', in Behnaz A. Mirzai, Ismael Musah Montana and Paul E. Lovejoy (eds.), *Slavery, Islam and Diaspora*, Trenton: Africa World Press, 2009, 37–76; Thomas Vernet, 'The Deep Roots of the Plantation Economy on the Swahili Coast: Productive Functions and Social Functions of Slaves and Dependents, Circa 1580–1820', in Awet T. Weldemichael, Anthony A. Lee and Edward A. Alpers (eds.), *Changing Horizons of African History*, Trenton: Africa World Press, 2017, 51–100. And also Henri Medard, Marie-Laure Derat, Thomas Vernet et al (eds.), *Traites et esclavages en Afrique orientale et dans l'océan Indien*, Paris: Karthala, 2013 includes several chapters on earlier slave trade from East African coast.

4. Alpers, *Ivory and Slaves*, 152–153.
5. Ibid., 199.
6. Épidariste Colin, 'Notice sur Mozambique', *Annales des voyages, de la géographie et de l'histoire* 9 (1809), 321–322.
7. James Prior, *Voyage along the Eastern Coast of Africa to Mosambique, Johanna, and Quiloa: To St. Helena; to Rio de Janeiro, Bahia, and Pernambuco in Brazil in the Nisus Frigate*, London: Richard Phillips and Co., 1819, 75–77.
8. Cooper, *Plantation Slavery*, 47–79; Sheriff, *Slaves, Spices and Ivory*, 33–73; Lovejoy, *Transformations in Slavery*, 152.
9. Cooper, *Plantation Slavery*, 47–79; Sheriff, *Slaves, Spices and Ivory*, 48–60.
10. For example, NAUK FO84/540/177 [Hamerton to the Earl of Aberdeen, 2 January 1844]. The typed version is available in *BPP*, Vol. 27, Class D, 143. Cooper, *Plantation Slavery*, 56, n. 34, shows the reference NAUK FO54/6; however, during my research in July 2006, I found that the applicable section had been cut off.
11. MAHA PD/1860/159/830/225 [Rigby to Anderson, Zanzibar, 11 February 1860].
12. Ibid.
13. Esmond B. Martin, *The History of Malindi: A Geographical Analysis of an East African Coastal Town from the Portuguese Period to the Present*, Nairobi: East African Literature Bureau, 1973, 56–57. See also, Cooper, *Plantation Slavery*, 81–83.

14. Ahmed Salim, *The Swahili-Speaking Peoples of Kenya's Coast, 1895–1965*, Nairobi: East African Publishing House, 1973, 26; Cooper, *Plantation Slavery*, 81–97; Martin, *The History of Malindi*, 56–68. See also, Helge Kjekshus, *Ecology Control and Economic Development in East African History: The Case of Tanganyika 1850–1950*, London: Heinemann, 1977, 22.
15. Burton, *The Lake Regions of Central Africa*, Vol. 1, 25.
16. Sheriff, *Slaves, Spices and Ivory*, 64–65.
17. NAUK FO84/540/177 [Hamerton to the Earl of Aberdeen, 2 January 1844].
18. ZZBA AA12/29/43 [Hamerton to Secretary to Bombay Government, Zanzibar, 2 January 1842].
19. Bennett and Brooks, Jr (eds.), *New England Merchants*, 427 [A Visit to Eastern Africa, 1849]. Jeremy Prestholdt argues the process which slave owners used slaves as a sort of symbol to represent themselves, which he calls 'symbolic subjection'. For further details, see Jeremy Prestholdt, *Domesticating the World: African Consumerism and the Genealogies of Globalization*, Berkeley: University of California Press, 2008, 117–124.
20. Bennett and Brooks, Jr (eds.), *New England Merchants*, 427 [A Visit to Eastern Africa, 1849].
21. ZZBA AA12/29/91 [Outward letter by Hamerton to Bombay, 15 February 1850].
22. The fact that slaves made up a high proportion of the population is frequently mentioned in contemporary documents. See, for example, Colomb, *Slave-Catching*, 368; NAUK FO54/10/74 [Memorandum relative to British Indian subjects residing at Zanzibar, s.l., 29 January 1846]; and Cooper, *Plantation Slavery*, 56–57.
23. ZZBA AA12/29/45 [Hamerton to Secretary to Bombay Government, Zanzibar, 2 January 1842].
24. MAHA PD/1860/159/830/211-212 [Rigby to Anderson, Zanzibar, 21 March 1860]. See also MAHA PD/1860/159/830/272 [Rigby to Anderson, Zanzibar, 14 September 1860].
25. Main Library, University of Birmingham (hereafter MLUB) CMS/CA5/O24/52B/n.p.; Krapf, *Travels, Researches and Missionary Labours*, 196.
26. NAUK FO84/1120/226 [Coghlan to Anderson, Aden, 1 November 1860].
27. PPEM MH14/2/3 [Krapf to Waters, Mombasa, 17 February 1845].
28. MAHA PD/1860/159/830/210 [Rigby to Anderson, Zanzibar, 21 March 1860].
29. MAHA PD/1860/159/1500/291-293 [Rigby to Anderson, Zanzibar, 1 June 1860].
30. MAHA PD/1860/159/830/210 [Rigby to Anderson, Zanzibar, 21 March 1860]; MAHA PD/1860/159/1500/292 [Rigby to Anderson, Zanzibar, 1 June 1860].

31. MAHA PD/1860/159/830/212 [Rigby to Anderson, Zanzibar, 21 March 1860].
32. Suzuki, 'Enslaved Population and Indian Owners', 222–223.
33. MAHA PD/1860/159/830/210-211 [Rigby to Anderson, Zanzibar, 21 March 1860].
34. PPEM MH14/2/3 [Krapf to Waters, Mombasa, 17 February 1845].
35. OIOC IOR/R/15/1/157/230 [Statement of a Woman named Khyzran aged 22 seized by the Agent at Lingar as a slave].
36. It seems to have been quite a common method for kidnappers to use sweetmeats, as Charles New describes. According to New, who travelled through East Africa in the 1860s, the locals along the coast called the people who kidnapped children by luring them with sweetmeats 'tendehalua' or 'watendehalua' (New, *Life, Wanderings, and Labours*, 35). Moreover, several medieval Arab geographers noted the method in their descriptions of the East African coast (Vladimir Minorsky, *Sharaf al-Zamān Ṭāhir Marvazī on China, the Turks and India*, London: the Royal Asiatic Society, 1942, 47 [Arabic text]).
37. OIOC IOR/R/15/1/157/229 [Statement of a Boy named Meerjohu aged 13 seized by the Agent at Lingar as a slave].
38. ZZBA AA/12/29/35 [Hamerton to Secretary to Bombay Government, 13 July 1841]; ibid., 77 [Hamerton to Secretary to Bombay Government, 3 April 1847]; ibid., 78 [Hamerton to Secretary to Bombay Government, 29 April 1847]; ibid., 126 [Hamerton to Resident of Persian Gulf, 10 January 1854]; OIOC IOR/R/15/1/171/101 [Rigby to Anderson, 13 September 1858]; ZZBA AA/3/26/n.p. [Political Agent to Bombay Government, 15 April 1865]; MAHA PD/1865/52/780/24 [Playfair to Gonne, 17 April 1865].
39. OIOC IOR/R/15/1/171/101-102. The same content is also found in ZZBA AA/12/2/14-15, although there the dispatch date was given as 16 September 1858.
40. MAHA PD/1860/159/830/189 [Rigby to Anderson, Zanzibar, 28 March 1860].
41. MAHA PD/1860/159/830/189-190 [Rigby to Anderson, Zanzibar, 28 March 1860].
42. MAHA PD/1860/159/830/192 [Rigby to Anderson, Zanzibar, 28 March 1860].
43. MAHA PD/1860/159/830/192-193 [Rigby to Anderson, Zanzibar, 28 March 1860].
44. MAHA PD/1860/159/830/195 [Rigby to Anderson, 28 March 1860]. A similar case was reported on ZZBA AA/2/4/203 [Rigby to Walker, 9 April 1861].

45. MAHA PD/1860/159/830/195 [Rigby to Anderson, 28 March 1860]; ZZBA AA2/4/211 [Rigby to Crawford, Zanzibar, 2 May 1861]; Russell, *General Rigby*, 331.
46. MAHA PD/1860/159/830/193 [Rigby to Anderson, 28 March 1860].
47. ZZBA AA/12/2/108-110 [Rigby to Bombay Government, 18 April 1861]; Russell, *General Rigby*, 90–91. According to al-Mughayrī, in May of that year 'unseasonable Arabs from the Persian Gulf and Oman' rushed for Zanzibar to plunder (Saʿīd b. ʿAlī al-Mughayrī, *Juhayna al-akhbār fī tārīkh Zanjibār*, ed. ʿAbd al-Munʿim ʿĀmir, Masqaṭ: Wizāra al-turāth al-qawmī, 1979, 201). Al-Mughayrī obtained this information from Rigby's writing, but I have been unable to identify the precise document.
48. ZZBA AA/3/20/408 [Rigby to Forbes, 5 September 1861].
49. ZZBA AA/12/2/108 [Rigby to Bombay Government, Zanzibar, 18 April 1861]. Four servants in the American Consulate were seriously injured.
50. ZZBA AA/12/2/109 [Rigby to Bombay Government, Zanzibar, 18 April 1861].
51. Ibid.; Russell, *General Rigby*, 90.
52. ZZBA AA12/2/109 [Rigby to Bombay Government, Zanzibar, 18 April 1861].
53. Ibid.
54. ZZBA AA/12/2/109-110 [Rigby to Bombay Government, Zanzibar, 18 April 1861].
55. ZZBA AA12/2/110 [Rigby to Bombay Government, Zanzibar, 18 April 1861].
56. ZZBA AA12/2/112-113 [Rigby to Bombay Government, Zanzibar, 18 April 1861]. See also ZZBA AA12/2/12 [Rigby to Bombay Government, Zanzibar, 5 September 1861].
57. ZZBA AA12/2/109-110 [Rigby to Bombay Government, Zanzibar, 18 April 1861]. See also, Christie, *Cholera Epidemics in East Africa*, 412–413.
58. ZZBA AA12/2/109-110 [Rigby to Bombay Government, Zanzibar, 18 April 1861].
59. ZZBA AA/3/26/n.p. [Political Agent to Bombay Government, 15 April 1865].
60. Al-Mughayrī lived in Zanzibar and this material is a chronicle of the Bū Saʿīd dynasty in Zanzibar. He mentions that he started to write in 1357 AH (1938 AD) (al-Mughayrī, *Juhayna al-akhbār*, 4), but does not mention a date of completion.
61. Ibid., 185.
62. Sullivan, *Dhow Chasing*, 92.

63. Burton, *Zanzibar*, Vol. 1, 373–374; Russell, *General Rigby*, 80, 90; Bennett and Brooks, Jr, *New England Merchants*, 531 [Hines to Seward, Zanzibar, 25 October 1864]; New, *Life, Wanderings and Labours*, 35.
64. PPEM LOG 1827A3 B9F1 [11 November 1827].
65. MAHA PD/1860/159/830/193 [Rigby to Anderson, Zanzibar, 28 March 1860].
66. ZZBA AA/3/20/408.
67. ZZBA AA/3/20/408-409.
68. For example, see; ZZBA AA/12/29/91-92 [Outward letter by Hamerton to Bombay, 15 February 1850]; ibid., 92 [Hamerton to Wyvill, Zanizbar, 8 May 1850].
69. ZZBA AA/12/29/78 [Hamerton to Secretary to Bombay Government, 29 April 1847].
70. ZZBA AA/12/29/64 [Hamerton to Secret Committee, 19 March 1844]; ibid., 113–114 [Hamerton to Wyvill, 13 March 1851].
71. ZZBA AA/12/29/77 [Hamerton to Secretary to Bombay Government, 3 April 1947].
72. ZZBA AA/12/29/91 [Outward letter to Bombay on 15 February 1850]; ibid., 64–65 [Outward letter by Hamerton to Bombay, 19 March 1844].
73. ZZBA AA/12/29/65 [Hamerton to Secret Committee, 19 March 1844].
74. ZZBA AA/12/29/46 [Hamerton to Secretary to Bombay Government, 2 January 1842].
75. MAHA PD/1860/159/12/6-7 [Rigby to Anderson, Zanzibar, 30 November 1859]; ZZBA AA12/2/117 [Rigby to Bombay Government, Zanzibar, 14 May 1861].
76. MAHA PD/1860/159/12/7 [Rigby to Anderson, 30 November 1859].
77. ZZBA AA12/2/117 [Rigby to Bombay Government, Zanzibar, 14 May 1861].
78. Ibid.
79. *BPP*, Vol. 49, Class B., 72 [Playfair to Chief Secretary to the Government of Bombay, Zanzibar 23May 1863]; NAUK FO800/234/151 [Pelly to Stewart, Zanzibar, 8 March 1862]; *Ibid.*,151-152 [Pelly toStewart, Zanzibar, 14 March 1862].
80. *BPP*, Vol. 49, Class B., 72 [Playfair to Chief Secretary to the Government of Bombay, Zanzibar 23May 1863]
81. MAHA PD/1864/54/942/12-3 [Playfair to Havelock, Zanzibar, 1 May 1864].
82. ZZBA AA12/2/117 [Rigby to Bombay Government, Zanzibar, 14 May 1861].

83. ZZBA AA/12/9/5 [the Sultan of Zanzibar to Churchill, s.l., 3 May 1868].
84. NAUK FO800/234/151 [Pelly to Stewart, Zanzibar, 8 March 1862; NAUS RG84/Zanzibar/12/n.p.[Hines to Seward, Zanzibar, 31 March 1864]; Ibidem, n.p. [Hines to Seward, Zanzibar, 25 October 1864];OIOC IOR/L/P&S/9/41/245 [Playfair to Havelock, Zanzibar, 3 February 1864]. ZZBA AA12/9 contains aseries of proclamations issued by sultans of Zanzibar between 1863 and 1885.
85. However, Mājid's attitude to the Northern Arab was quite complex. As Rigby reported, Mājid paid a certain amount of money to the Northern Arabs annually. Rigby suspected, therefore, that Mājid expected them to support him when he needed their help (ZZBA AA12/2/82 [Rigby to Coghlan, Zanzibar, 5 October 1860 (Appendix B: Lieutenant Colonel Rigby's answer to the List of Queries marked A in Brigadier Coghlan's letter to his address, No.12 of 1860, dated 1 October 1860)]).
86. NAUK FO800/234/220 [Playfair to Chief Secretary to the Government of Bombay, Zanzibar, 26August 1863].

CHAPTER 7

Consulate Politics in the Scramble after Saʿīd: How Did the British Consulate Secure Superiority over the Sultan of Zanzibar?

Introduction

Barghash b. Saʿīd (1837–1888, r. 1870–1888) was more popular locally than either Saʿīd or Mājid. He was one of the sons of Saʿīd, who succeeded Mājid, and will be one of the leading characters in this chapter. Today, Barghash is renowned as the founder of modern Zanzibar; as Zanzibar-born historian Issa bin Nasser al-Ismaily states: 'Sayyid Barghash is a wise king and he looked far into the future. He did much to develop Zanzibar.'[1] He built Bayt al-ʿajā'ib, which today hosts the National Museum of History and Culture, and is known as being the first building on the African continent to be equipped with electricity. In addition, Barghash built the first water system for Stone Town and it was also during his reign that submarine telegraph cables were laid between Aden and Zanzibar. On the contrary, it is generally less well known that he once attempted a coup d'état in order to get sovereignty over his late father's East African territory and as a consequence found himself exiled to India for a time. Few seem to have realized that his attempted coup d'état was without doubt related to inconsistency among the political figures in Zanzibar, and that its failure contributed to the establishment of the solid superiority of the British Consulate over the political situation in Zanzibar. Given British superiority exerted great influence over Mājid's anti-slave trade policy, in this chapter we shall follow the progress of Barghash's coup and explore its background. We shall then look in detail at how the British Consulate came to take over the reins of Zanzibar politics.

H. Suzuki, *Slave Trade Profiteers in the Western Indian Ocean*, Palgrave Series in Indian Ocean World Studies,
DOI 10.1007/978-3-319-59803-1_7

The question of the succession to Saʿīd's sultanate received much attention at the time, and modern scholars still pay close attention to it, as Mohamed Reda Bhacker points out.[2] The succession proved to be a turning point for the so-called 'maritime empire' of the Bū Saʿīd, because it eventually led to a split between the Omani and East African branches of the family. The most detailed and influential studies on the situation were by Sheriff and Reda Bhacker apart from Reginald Coupland's classical but imperialistic description in his *The Exploitation of East Africa*, and all agree that it was then that Britain finally established a solid foundation to exercise its influence over the Bū Saʿīd as well as over the East African coast; I agree with them. What this chapter contributes to our understanding of the matter is a broadening of our perspective on it. The existing literature is rather short-sighted in that its focus is primarily on the relationship between the sultans and the British Consulate. Indeed, we learn from them that the British Consuls repeatedly and rather aggressively requested Mājid to take strict measures against the slave trade.[3] However, from the usual 'narrow' perspective it is difficult to understand Mājid's autonomy to cooperate with British anti-slave trade policy. From the wider perspective offered here, which will include consideration of the local powers and the French Consulate, Mājid's attitude will become more comprehensible. This chapter effectively re-examines the relationship between Mājid and British Consulate from that wider perspective.

The Post-Saʿīd Scramble

Saʿīd died at sea in 1856 on his way from Masqaṭ to Zanzibar.[4] Though he left no written will relating to his dominions,[5] he entrusted them to three of his sons, Thuwaynī, Mājid and Turkī. Thuwaynī, the eldest son, took responsibility in Oman, especially during his father's visit to Zanzibar, and at his father's death served as wālī of Masqaṭ,[6] Mājid ruled Zanzibar during Saʿīd's absence, especially after the death of his elder brother Khālid in 1854,[7] while Turkī was in possession of Suḥār.[8] Though Barghash, a still younger brother, was not entrusted with any of his father's land, and usually resided in Zanzibar, he did frequently accompany his father on his business.[9] (For sons of Saʿīd alive in 1855, see Table 7.1.[10])

On 5 November, six days after Saʿīd had died on board, the ship bearing his remains sailed into Zanzibar. He was interred the following day, and then on 10 November, after the due period of mourning, Mājid gathered together all the family, as well as other influential individuals,

Table 7.1 Sons of Sa'īd b. Sulṭān alive in March 1855

Name	*Age*
Thuwaynī b. Sa'īd	34
Muḥammad b. Sa'īd	29
Turkī b. Sa'īd	23
Mājid b. Sa'īd	20
Barghash b. Sa'īd	18
'Abd al-Wahhāb b. Sa'īd	15
'Abd Allāh b. Sa'īd	13
Jamshīd b. Sa'īd	12
Ḥamdān b. Sa'īd	10
'Abd al-Azīz b. Sa'īd	6

Source ZZBA AA12/29/133

and announced that he was now the successor to his father in his East African territories. Six days after that he sent letters to the British Consul and the Bombay Government, as well as to the French Government, to report the circumstances of his father's death and to ask those organizations to recognize his inheritance.[11] That is, it was only 12 days after the arrival of his late father's body that Mājid sent his letters to the foreign authorities and demanded that the rest of his family and all the influential figures on the island acknowledge his succession.[12] Arab chroniclers such as al-Mughayrī and Ibn Ruzayq described the circumstance of the Bū Sa'īd family immediately after the death of Sa'īd as follows. They reported that Mājid buried his father's corpse in the yard of his residence, and after the mourning period was over he was elected chief by his brothers in Zanzibar. Then, he promised all of those who had held important posts during his father's reign that they would keep these. Mājid then dispatched a ship to Masqaṭ to inform his brothers there of the death of their father.[13] Mājid had established himself in power and requested both the British and French authorities to recognize it before his other brothers in the Arabian Peninsula knew of Sa'īd's death. As both the French Consul and Sayyida Salma, one of Sa'īd's daughters, pointed out,[14] it was obvious that on Sa'īd's death there would be conflict over the succession to the East African territories, which were the foremost source of the Bū Sa'īds' wealth. The late Sa'īd himself had had a large number of children, but the family had no clear consensus for the successor.[15] Therefore, Mājid decided to take prompt action to forestall confusion, and at the end of March 1857 the Bombay Government sent a reply recognizing him as the new Sultan.[16]

The above description might give the impression that Mājid found it easy to form a firm foundation for his reign. However, Saʿīd's daughter Salma, who was living in the palace of Saʿīd at the time of his death, wrote of the following incident in her memoir.[17] Salma and the others in the palace naturally knew nothing of the death of Saʿīd and were waiting as normal for his arrival. Then, some fishermen returning from off-shore waters informed them that a fleet, supposedly Saʿīd's, was sailing towards the port at Stone Town. However, the fishermen could not approach due to rough weather. In the event their information proved to be unreliable and in fact, that fleet did not arrive. So, Mājid decided to visit the fleet in question and put to sea himself from Stone Town. However, he had not returned by the promised time, nor had the elusive fleet. Later, at midnight, Salma and those who were waiting with her in the palace suddenly realized that they were encircled by armed men. The soldiers gave no explanation for their action and Salma recollected that she realized she and her companions were in a critical situation. The next morning, about the time for prayer, they finally discovered that the fleet was dropping anchor in the harbour, with the flags hoisted for mourning. Several days later, they realized that it was Barghash, whom they supposed had been accompanying their now deceased father, who had ordered the soldiers to surround them. According to Salma, Barghash was displeased that Mājid wished to take the initiative in arranging their father's funeral, so he detached himself from the rest of the fleet and landed secretly, in the ship carrying his dead father, under cover of darkness. He then ordered the encircling of the palace and tried to arrest Mājid in order to prevent his brother's self-aggrandizing plans.[18]

Reda Bhacker suspects that Barghash acted with the intention of himself succeeding Saʿīd as ruler of Zanzibar.[19] It is difficult to deny this, because after this incident Barghash began receiving 700 MT$ a month from Mājid, which could be regarded as payment to appease him.[20] However, Barghash remained dissatisfied with Mājid's assumption of power and adopted an openly defiant attitude. He never attended a darbār (royal court) held by Mājid and never hid his aversion from those Consuls who did recognize Mājid's succession.[21] Rigby noted that on his own arrival at Zanzibar he had received no letter of welcome from Barghash, nor had he been favoured with a visit from him since that time.[22]

There was another obstacle in Zanzibar to Mājid stabilizing his new reign—the Ḥirth, who had as much influence in Zanzibar as the Bū

Saʿīd.[23] Burton mentioned them as a major group of al-Hinawī residing in Zanzibar.[24] Originating in the south-east of Oman, they had sporadically emigrated to East Africa since the eighteenth century. They were now scattered throughout East Africa, not only in Zanzibar but also coastal towns like Lindi. They had even reached the interior.[25] According to Burton, they numbered 300 in Zanzibar in 1857 just after the death of Saʿīd,[26] while Rigby reported in 1860 that there were 800 adult male Ḥirth.[27] As various studies have already pointed out, it had been a critically important for Saʿīd to reconcile with the Ḥirth in order to stabilize his reign.[28] Thus, Saʿīd appointed several influential figures of the Ḥirth to important posts in the early period of his own reign, thus they were often to be seen wielding political influence during the reign of Saʿīd. ʻAlī b. Nāṣir al-Ḥārithī was one such major figure,[29] having twice been dispatched to London by Saʿīd as special envoy.[30] He served also as *walī* (governor) of Mombasa. The British Consul adjudged him ʻa favourite chief of His Highness'.[31] When ʻAlī b. Nāṣir al-Ḥārithī died during an expedition to Siu of Lamu Archipelago,[32] the British Consul officially informed the Bombay Government of his death.[33] He had been important to the diplomatic relationship between Britain and the Bū Saʿīd. Another figure from the Ḥirth, ʻAbd Allāh b. Jumʿa b. ʻĀmir al-Barwānī, held the position of *walī* of Zanzibar until sometime in the early reign of Saʿīd.[34] His *nisba*, al-Barwānī, indicates membership of a junior group under al-Ḥirth. Simultaneously, his brother, Muḥammad b. Jumʿa, served as *walī* on Mafia Island.[35] The Ḥirth repaid their warm treatment. For example, if we can rely on an article by P. Dallons, a French slaving captain, in 1804, they were enthusiastic in their military support for Saʿīd.[36]

However, a report left by F. Albrand, who visited Zanzibar in 1819, shows that circumstances changed. While he introduced ʻAbd Allāh b. Jumʿa b. ʻĀmir al-Barwānī as a ʻvery rich and highly regarded' figure and mentioned that he practically controlled Kilwa, Albrand noted that he used to be the *walī* of Zanzibar.[37] Therefore, when Albrand met him, ʻAbd Allāh had resigned from this influential post. Although contemporary records do not reveal the reason for ʻAbd Allāh's removal, Christine N. Nicholls and other scholars have conjectured that Saʿīd gradually became anxious about the increased influence of the Ḥirth in East Africa, especially that of the Barwānī.[38] In any case, the important thing here is that at the time of Saʿīd's death the Ḥirth were being kept at a certain distance from front-line politics on the East African coast. For the Ḥirth, then, the death of Saʿīd and the political chaos that followed seemed to offer them a unique chance to return to the front line. That might indeed explain why 'Abd Allāh b. Sālim al-Barwānī,[39] one of the most influential not only among the Ḥirth but also in all Zanzibar, chose to visit the British Consul just after the death of Saʿīd had been announced. 'Abd Allāh b. Sālim al-Barwānī possessed a large amount of land and a large number of slaves,[40] and allegedly implied he could engineer a coup d'état to take over political supermacy over Zanzibar in front of British Consul on that occasion.[41] However, if he had such a plan he never put it into practice, although like Barghash, he declined to attend the *darbār* held by Mājid.[42] Despite this, Mājid paid 1200 MT$ every year to this influential member of the Ḥirth, and even—as the British Consul reported—allowed his cargoes to pass without charge through Stone Town Customs.[43] However, unlike Barghash, 'Abd Allāh b. Sālim al-Barwānī was not won over by Mājid.

When those two discontented parties eventually joined forces for a series of revolts in 1859, another individual who joined them was Thuwaynī b. Saʿīd. Thuwaynī was one of those who learned of the death of Saʿīd in Oman after Mājid had declared himself Sultan in Zanzibar. When Thuwaynī heard of the death, he immediately dispatched his nephew Muḥammad b. Sālim as his envoy to Zanzibar to negotiate the inheritance of his father with Mājid.[44] Since there was an obvious difference in revenue between Zanzibar and Masqaṭ, Thuwaynī was naturally unhappy with the idea of his brother occupying the wealthy East African territory.[45] According to correspondence from Ladislas Cochet, French Consul at Zanzibar (1844–1861) to the French Foreign Minister in Paris, based on handwritten will of Saʿīd which Thuwaynī claimed to have discovered, Thuwaynī sent a letter to Mājid, care of Muḥammad b. Sālim, in which he admitted his authority over the East African territory on condition that Mājid take advice from three figures, namely Muḥammad b. Sālim, Mājid's elder brother Muḥammad b. Saʿīd, and Sulaymān b. Aḥmad, the current *walī* of Zanzibar.[46] Muḥammad b. Sālim remained at Zanzibar until September that year,[47] and eventually it was said that Mājid had agreed to pay Thuwaynī 40,000 MT$ annually.[48] In addition, though the reply from Mājid is obscure, Thuwaynī required him to cede Mombasa to him.[49] Doubts about the validity of those two conditions subsequently triggered conflict between Mājid and Thuwaynī. Those doubts turned out to be crucial since the conditions were agreed only by five persons, including Mājid and the representatives nominated in the correspondence of Thuwaynī, mentioned above.[50] That is, there was no impartial observer. The position of British Consul was vacant at that time, and neither the French nor the American Consul had been present at the meeting, so we have no reliable direct third-party evidence for any agreement. Nonetheless, considering that the term *masaadeh*—correctly *musāʿada* in Arabic and *msaada* in Kiswahili, literally 'aid'—was repeatedly found in correspondence between Muḥammad b. Sālim and Ladha Dhamjī, Custom Master of Stone Town port and also the leading Kachchhī Bhatiyā merchant in Zanzibar at the time,[51] and that Rigby stated the same was being said in letters from Mājid to Ladha,[52] it is reasonable to suppose that an agreement by Mājid to supply some assistance to Thuwaynī had indeed been made at that time.

From a Series of Revolts in 1859 to the 'Canning Arbitration'

Although we do not know the exact amount of 'aid' promised by Mājid to Thuwaynī, however much it was, it must have been difficult for Mājid, with his immense debts,[53] to meet Thuwaynī's monetary demands while the cession of Mombasa never actually took place. In the end, in February 1859 Thuwaynī equipped a fleet which set sail from Masqaṭ for Zanzibar on the pretext that the agreements had not been fulfilled.[54] Interestingly, this plan had been already noticed in Zanzibar by 10 January—before Thuwaynī's fleet had left Masqaṭ—so Mājid prepared to fight back with American muskets and other equipment. The *walī* of Zanzibar visited Rigby and asked for advice as well as exchanging the latest information.[55] Trade was suspended as people from both the island's interior and the mainland gathered together and 'they were roaming on the streets and one did not hear except sound of random gunshot, and people got excited'.[56] Even local rulers who regarded themselves as under the suzerainty of the Zanzibari sultans were ready to defend Zanzibar. One of them was Saʿīd b. Muḥammad, the ruler of Mwali Island, part of the Comoro Islands, who arrived at Zanzibar with 150 men.[57] On the other hand, Barghash and some of the Ḥirth, including 'Abd Allāh b. Sālim, also became active. In *Juhayna* al-Mughayrī copied a letter written by Barghash to ask ʿAbd Allāh b. Sālim for loan of 2000 qirsh of French silver coin.[58] Also, what is remarkable, in another letter from Barghash to 'Abd Allāh b. Sālim dated 23 Shaʿbān 1275 AH (28 March 1859) the guarantor of the 2000 qirsh is revealed to be none other than Thuwaynī.[59] Furthermore, according to a dispatch from Rigby to the Bombay Government dated 16 March 1859, Mājid had 'recently' acknowledged the existence of a letter in which the major shaykhs of the Ḥirth had asked Thuwaynī to dethrone Mājid.[60] These show that the active resistance to Mājid which grew and consolidated in Zanzibar was triggered by the news of Thuwaynī's expedition there. Simultaneously, it should be remembered that Mājid was aware of bonding of discontended elements against him in Zanzibar with Thuwaynī, another discontended element outside of Zanzibar, by the middle of March. Such then were the circumstances when, in that month, Mājid sailed past the residence of Barghash on his way back from Stone Town to his palace—only for his ship to come under fire from Barghash's residence.[61]

Nevertheless, the fleet from Masqaṭ never appeared in the port of Stone Town, for just after it left Masqaṭ it was intercepted off Ras al-Ḥadd by the British steam frigate *Punjaub*, which had been dispatched by the Bombay Government. Thuwaynī was prevailed upon to return to Masqaṭ,[62] and news of this development reached Zanzibar by 21 March 1859. On the same day a French fleet arrived at Stone Town, as did one dispatched by the Bombay Government.[63] On 24 March, a dhow from Oman arrived in the port at Stone Town but its crew were immediately arrested.[64] Realizing that the fleet from Masqaṭ would not arrive, Barghash was confined to an upper floor of his residence and some shaykhs of the Ḥirth visited the palace daily to entreat Mājid to allow them to attend the *darbār*.[65]

It was the French Consul who stepped into mediate between Mājid and his opponents and to shield Barghash and the Ḥirth. Letters written by the French Consul reveal his anxiety as well as a sense of rivalry with Rigby, the new British Consul who was taking advantage of the confusion that had followed Saʿīd's death to extend his political influence over Zanzibar.[66] On the other hand, Rigby himself wondered if the real intention of the French Consul's intervention was to gain control either of the port at Stone Town or the port of Mombasa. Rigby also suspected that the French Consul was unhappy with the enthronement of Mājid, who had not been cooperating with the French demand for labour to be sent to Bourbon Island.[67] With regard to labour recruitment, Thuwaynī and Barghash would be much easier prospects for the French Consul to deal with than the new Sultan, Mājid. As already mentioned, the French Consul was the only foreign representative with whom Barghash had any friendly contact. Between the end of March and early April, the Consul, accompanied by the captains of the French naval vessels anchored in Stone Town's harbour, paid many visits to Mājid in order to ask for his indulgence for Barghash and the shaykhs of the Ḥirth.[68] From what Mājid told Rigby,[69] the French Consul's visits were a sort of threat backed by French naval power.[70] Rigby reported that the French Consul had been in repeated secret meetings with Barghash, 'Abd Allāh b. Sālim and Aḥmad b. Sālim, who arrived at Zanzibar on 19 April as the envoy of Thuwaynī.[71]

Here we can observe another confrontation in the post-Saʿīd scramble. As Beatrice Nicolini described in detail,[72] from the early nineteenth century rivalry between Britain and France over western Indian Ocean had escalated, and alliance with the Bū Saʿīd, the most influential political body in the region, was one of the critical factors in gaining control. In addition, the situation with the slave trade changed after Hamerton left Zanzibar. The position of British Consul at Zanzibar had remained vacant for 13 months between Hamerton's departure and the arrival of Rigby, and during that time the slave trade had been reactivated with the encouragement of French Consul, who was under orders to send labour to Bourbon Island.[73] This reactivation of the trade was something which Rigby needed to tackle, so he could not tolerate close cooperation among the French-backed forces ranged against Mājid. In other words, Rigby was effectively obliged to support Mājid.

The effort against Mājid now became much more active. Barghash gathered about 500 or so soldiers in front of his residence and they performed Arab war dances and fired their muskets well into the night, while Rigby reported signs of armed risings among the Ḥirth.[74] On one occasion French support actually saved the day for Barghash, when on Friday 17 June, on the occasion of the weekly visit by his Zanzibar-based sons to Saʿīd's grave, Mājid decided to arrest him. However, the plan was discovered by the French Consul whose warning allowed Barghash to avoid capture.[75] While French Consul and Mājid's opponents kept in close contact, Mājid for his part came increasingly to rely on the British Consul. Eventually, on 7 July, Mājid arrested and detained five of the leading shaykhs of the Ḥirth and compelled Barghash to leave Zanzibar as soon as possible.[76]

Close to the end of the south-west monsoon sailing season, Rigby reported that Zanzibar had become quieter.[77] Indeed, a series of events that had occurred since early July had been enough to convince the British Consul that control of the island had been restored. One such event was the arrival of the news from Masqaṭ that Thuwaynī had confiscated several ships of the Ḥirth, including a newly built one actually at Masqaṭ, after it had come to his attention that the Ḥirth had been embezzling money from the funds he had dedicated to assist the opposition effort against Mājid. That information was brought to Zanzibar in a number of letters from Masqaṭ, and when the Arabs in Zanzibar learned of it the faith of the Ḥirth in Thuwaynī rapidly weakened.[78] At about the same time, two of the five Ḥirth shaykhs referred to above were released.[79] This prompted some of the Ḥirth to claim they had surrendered to Mājid, which Rigby reported.[80] Thuwaynī's envoy, Aḥmad b. Sālim, left Zanzibar on 11 September to return to Masqaṭ.[81] In addition, three weeks prior to his departure, the French Consul attended the *darbār* of Mājid and declared in front of Aḥmad that from then on he would not receive visits from Aḥmad.[82] For Rigby, that series of events seemed to amount to a clear indication of corruption among the forces opposing Mājid.[83]

However, once again there were further developments when Mājid asked Barghash to leave Zanzibar a second time.[84] Barghash initially agreed, but postponed his departure with various excuses while he gathered the younger sons of his late father—and their mothers—in his residence. Simultaneously he collected several barrels of gunpowder and declared his intention to stage a do-or-die resistance.[85] Mājid ordered the frigate *Piedmontes* to anchor in front of Barghash's residence, and early the following morning his men surrounded the residence and cut off the water supply.[86] Barghash thereupon dispatched an envoy to Rigby to ask his advice, but Rigby replied that he supported Mājid.[87] Mājid then dispatched Ladha Damjī as envoy to Barghash. Mājid commanded the envoys to ask his brother once again to leave Zanzibar, and eventually Barghash agreed to leave within one month and go to al-Mukallāh.[88] Finally, the date of departure was fixed as after Friday prayers on 10 Rabīʿ I (7 October).[89]

Nevertheless, the situation changed yet again. In the night of the sixth evening to the seventh morning of October, the expected day of departure, Barghash sneaked away from Stone Town towards his plantation, named Marseilles. From there he dispatched a letter demanding that he be allowed to leave quietly—not from Stone Town but from Bububu, six miles away.[90] While Mājid and his followers were wondering what to do about this development, no doubt following plans already laid Barghash had coconut trees cut down to make a barricade around his plantation and piled up stones for extra fortification.[91] Barghash was certainly well financed, having, for example, received 14,000 MT$ from Mājid to cover his expenses for leaving, a sum agreed when they had fixed the date of departure to al-Mukallāh.[92] Moreover, Barghash had been receiving financial assistance from the Ḥirth as well as from Thuwaynī, so he had easily been able to afford the provisions he had stored in the plantation called Marseilles. In fact, he had even employed men from the Gulf of Oman and the Persian Gulf as mercenaries.[93] All but a few Ḥirth armed themselves and joined him in Marseilles, along with the slaves from the plantation.[94] Mājid twice sent envoys to negotiate with the Ḥirth, but the talks failed and on the 12th, when he realized that negotiations with the Ḥirth could go no further, Mājid led his 5000 soldiers and major vassals to set up camp in a suburb of Stone Town.[95] The following day, when the news reached Stone Town that Barghash and his followers had begun plundering on a large scale and were cutting down clove trees on the plantations, shops were closed and those who could do so took ship and left for the mainland with their families.[96] In the evening, Stone Town descended into chaos: at least one Indian died and another was seriously injured.[97]

Just then, quite by accident, the Royal Navy steam sloop *Lynx* called at Stone Town on its way from Nzwani Island in the Comoro Islands. Rigby visited Mājid's camp along with the commanders of both *Lynx* and *Assaye* as well as many of the officers under their command.[98] Mājid had not yet decided his strategy, and Rigby strongly urged him to proceed against Barghash as the current situation was creating a great deal of danger for the inhabitants, among them British subjects.[99] Mājid decided on an all-out attack and asked the naval officers Rigby had brought with him if they would support the operation.[100] Mājid went into action on the 14th, but found that Barghash's fortifications remained steadfast. Mājid therefore requested additional support from Rigby,[101] who, the following morning, dispatched a force of 112 officers and seamen with one 12-lb howitzer and a few rockets, with the intention of overpowering the installations at Marseilles.[102]

While operations progressed Rigby returned to Stone Town for more supplies, and there he received an anonymous report from one of the Ḥirth that Barghash was actually in hiding in his residence in Stone Town and the Ḥirth under siege in Marseilles had decided to surrender after facing repeated attacks.[103] Immediately after receiving the report, Rigby had the town residence of Barghash surrounded and asked Mājid to dispatch a task force to capture Barghash.[104] Finally, on the morning of 16 October, under observation by Mājid's representative, Barghash surrendered.[105] It subsequently emerged that in his residence he had assembled enough weapons for 800 soldiers as well as a cannon, while another 400 muskets were found in the residence of ʻAbd Allāh b. Sālim, who by that time was in prison.[106]

In midday on the 16th, on his return to Stone Town, Mājid held an emergency *darbār* to discuss the disposal of Barghash. The unanimous view was that Rigby should decide his fate because Barghash had practically surrendered to him.[107] Rigby thereupon summoned Barghash to the *darbār* and proposed that Mājid should forgive Barghash on condition that he leave Zanzibar forever and forever afterward follow the instructions of the British Government.[108] Barghash declared that he would follow Rigby's advice.[109] The following day, another *darbār* was held, and Barghash signed an agreement accepting Rigby's proposal in front of the captains of *Lynx* and *Assaye* and other naval officers, and Rigby himself. Barghash also swore an oath on the Qur'ān.[110] Finally, he promised never to obey any orders from either the French Consul or the Ḥirth, but only from the British Government.[111] Barghash left Zanzibar in the early morning of 21 October on board *Assaye*, bound for Bombay via Masqaṭ.[112]

Following that outcome, the Bombay Government deputed an investigation into the complicated relationship between Zanzibar and Masqaṭ to William M. Coghlan, then Political Resident at Aden.[113] As the result of his investigation,[114] Coghlan recognized Mājid's claims to sovereignty. Soon after that, Charles Canning, Viceroy of India (r. 1858–1862), addressed a communication known as the 'Canning Arbitration' jointly to Thuwaynī and Mājid, by which was recognized not only the sovereignty of Mājid over Zanzibar and the African territory of the late Saʻīd, but the right of Thuwaynī to receive an annual subsidy from Mājid.[115] As a result of the 'Canning Arbitration' a new political order was created for these two successors of the Bū Saʻīd. The arrangements made by the British were accepted by the French too when they signed the 'Declaration between Great Britain and France, engaging reciprocally to respect the independence of the Sultans of Muscat and Zanzibar'; which they did at Paris in 1862.[116] Mājid had finally cemented his position as the successor of his father's rich territories on the East African coast, although, of course, his success had depended on the British and his reign continued under the shadow of their influence.

Britain continued to act as protector for the sultans of Zanzibar even after Mājid died. The Indian government began to pay the annual subsidy to Omani sultans in stead of Sultan of Zanzibar since 1873 as Sultan of Zanzibar was already behind from his payment.[117] This was because the annual subsidy was the former's main income, thus, if not paid, Zanzibar was in danger of being attacked by Oman.[118] In addition, it was 1873 when the Sultan of Zanzibar formally agreed to abolish slave trade in his territory.[119] The Sultan at that time was none other than Barghash.[120]

Conclusion

The fact that the East African coastal area became a slave ground is inseparable from the post-Saʿīd political scramble in Zanzibar. It is not possible to identify with certainty the mercenaries from the Persian Gulf and the Gulf of Oman led by Barghash in October 1859 as the same raiders who had been active during the north-east monsoon season in 1859/60. However, as even Mājid paid annual tribute to Northern Arabs so that he might expect their support in times of emergency, other politically influential figures in Zanzibar treated the Northern Arabs with respect and tried to make alliances with them in order to themselves survive after Saʿīd. Eventually, wealth poured into the hands of the Northern Arabs and their violence precipitated the slave dealing seen in Zanzibar.[121] Slaves were sold by owners who feared the outright loss of their 'property' to raids and kidnappings by the Northern Arabs. Consequently, the political scramble after Saʿīd's death, which ultimately involved the whole Ḥirth tribe and the British and French Consulates, can be recognized—even if only indirectly—as a reason why the East African coastal urban society became a slave ground.

If we look even more closely, we can draw the following conclusions. In the scramble for power after Saʿīd's death it appeared that every party around Mājid was his enemy, as Thuwaynī, Barghash and the Ḥirth tribe gradually united against him and even the French Consul joined in. It was only the political and military support of the British that Mājid could rely on, and which enabled him to become his father's successor on the East African coast. Not only that, but thanks to the British he managed to gain international acceptance too. Mājid's reliance on the British Consul is proved by the fact that he entrusted the decision over what to do with Barghash to Rigby. Mājid relied on British support in the political scramble, and eventually even to stabilize his reign, and it meant he had no choice other than to agree with the British anti-slave trade policy. The Northern Arabs, excluded from their 'legitimate' dealing in slaves due to Mājid's anti-slave trade policy, began to rely on violence to obtain slaves, with their adoption of raiding parties and kidnap.[122] Thus, Mājid's heavy reliance on the British also contributed to the new role of the East African coastal society in the slave distribution system.[123]

Notes

1. Issa bin Nasser al-Ismaily, *Zanzibar: Kinyang'anyiro na utumwa*, Rūwī: Issa bin Nasser al-Ismaily, 1999, 14.
2. Mohamed Reda Bhacker, *Trade and Empire in Muscat and Zanzibar: Roots of British Domination*, London: Routledge, 1992, 179.
3. Some of the contemporary sources clarify the aggressive request from the British Consul to the Sulṭān See. For example, ZZBA AA/12/2/11 [Rigby to Bombay Government, 5 September 1861].
4. NAUK FO54/17/37 [Hamerton to Clarendon, 10 November 1856].
5. ZZBA AA12/2/67 [Rigby to Coghlan, Zanzibar, 5 October 1860 (Appendix B: Lieutenant Colonel Rigby's answer to the List of Queries marked A in Brigadier Coghlan's letter to his address, No.12 of 1860, dated 1 October 1860)]. However, he admitted a certain degree of governance of Oman by Thuwaynī and that of African territory by Khālid in several documents (for instance, NAUK FO54/6/21-22 [Imam of Muskat to the Earl of Aberdeen, Zanzibar, 23 July 1844 (6 Rajab 1260)]). In addition, Rigby suspected that Barghash disposed of any letters written by Sa'īd on board the ship when Sa'īd died (ZZBA AA12/2/67 [Rigby to Coghlan, Zanzibar, 5 October 1860 (Appendix B: Lieutenant Colonel Rigby's answer to the List of Queries marked A in Brigadier Coghlan's letter to his address, No.12 of 1860, dated 1 October 1860)]). See also OIOC IOR/L/P&S/18/B150a [Précis of Correspondence Relating to Zanzibar Affairs, from 1856 to 1872, prepared by Captain P. D. Henderson].
6. Guillain, *Documents*, Part 2, Vol. 1, 229; Ruete, *An Arabian Princess*, 263; al-Mughayrī, *Juhayna al-akhbār*, 191.
7. NAUK FO54/17/38 [Hamerton to the Earl of Clarendon, Zanzibar, 10 November 1856]. Reda Bhacker points out that despite Mājid's the de facto rule over Zanzibar, his father had never appointed him as *walī* (governor) or *nā'ib* (deputy) of Zanzibar (Mohammad Reda Bhacker, 'Family Strife and Foreign Intervention: Causes in the Separation of Zanzibar from Oman: A Reappraisal', *Bulletin of the School of Oriental and African Studies* 54, 2 (1991), 274).
8. Miles, *The Countries and Tribes*, 352.
9. Reda Bhacker, *Trade and Empire*, 179. According to Ruete, *An Arabian Princess*, 237, Barghash accompanied his father on Sa'īd's last voyage.

10. There is no firm information about the number of Sa'īd's sons. For example, in his detailed account of the family, al-Fārsī claims that Sa'īd fathered 120 children, but at the time of his death, only 36 were living; more than half of them were female and 22 of the 36 were in zanzibar ('Abd Allāh b. Ṣāliḥ al-Farsī, *Al-Bū sa'īdiyūn: Ḥukkām zanjibār*, Masqaṭ: Wizāra al-turāth wa al-thaqāfa, 2005, 15).
11. Archives de Ministère des Affaires Etrangères (hereafter AMAE) CP/Zanzibar/1/100-101 [Traduction de la letter de l'Imam de Mascate]; NAUK FO54/17/41 [Mājid b. Sa'īd to Lārd Klārindan, s.l., 6 Rabī' al-awwal 1273]. See also, AMAE CP/Zanzibar/1/96 [Cochet to MAE, Zanzibar, 27 novembre 1856].
12. The above-mentioned dates vary according to the sources; however, here all the dates follow those mentioned in a letter by Mājid (AMAE CP/Zanzibar/1/100-101 [Traduction de la lettre de l'Imam de Mascate, 16 novembre 1856]). Therefore, for example, on 2 November 1856, which Reda Bhacker identified as the date of Mājid's enthronement (Reda Bhacker, *Trade and Empire*, 182), Mājid was unaware of his father's death. Reda Bhacker referred to the work by 'Abd Allāh b. Ṣāliḥ al-Fārsī for this date, but al-Fārsī does not show the source according to my reference to the reprinted version published in 2005 (al-Farsī, *Al-Bū sa'īdiyūn*, 21. The original was published in 1942 and Reda Bhacker referred to page 17).
13. Ibn Ruzayq, *Al-fataḥ al-mubīn*, 406; al-Mughayrī, *Juhayna al-akhbār*, 192.
14. AMAE CP/Zanzibar/1/98 [Cochet to MAE, Zanzibar, 27 november 1856]; Ruete, *An Arabian Princess*, 238, 241.
15. ZZBA AA12/2/67, 69 [Rigby to Coghlan, Zanzibar, 5 October 1860 (Appendix B: Lieutenant Colonel Rigby's answer to the List of Queries marked A in Brigadier Coghlan's letter to his address, No.12 of 1860, dated 1 October 1860)]; Reda Bhacker, *Trade and Empire*, 181; Sheriff, *Slaves, Spices and Ivory*, 210.
16. NAUK FO54/17/55-56 [The Earl of Clarendon to Prince Majid b. Saiid, s.l., 31 March 1857]. However, it took a long time for Mājid to receive this letter. Thus, Mājid sent another letter as a reminder (ibid., 59–60 [Mājid b. Sa'īd to Lārd Klārindan, s.l., 3 Dhu al-Ḥijja 1273/25 July 1857]).
17. Ruete, *An Arabian Princess*, 235–238.
18. This attempt by Barghash is recorded in ZZBA AA12/2/67-68 [Rigby to Coghlan, Zanzibar, 5 October 1860 (Appendix B: Lieutenant Colonel Rigby's answer to the List of Queries marked A in Brigadier Coghlan's letter to his address, No.12 of 1860, dated 1 October 1860)]. According to that, Barghash landed in the middle of the night and tried

to occupy a fort in Zanzibar; however, the Baluchi garrison repulsed him. Later, Barghash obtained heavy guns and a quantity of gunpowder and gathered a party of soldiers. Most probably, that party was the same one which surrounded the palace.

19. Reda Bhacker, *Trade and Empire*, 182. He raised two reasons why Barghash disagreed with the succession of Mājid; one is that Mājid had epilepsy, and the other is that Barghash had not been given any position by Saʿīd. The latter reason might be possible; however, there is no document confirming Mājid's epilepsy.
20. This continued until March 1859 (ZZBA AA12/2/20 [Rigby to Bombay Government, Zanzibar, 16 March 1859]; ibid., 4 [Sayyid Burghash to Lord Elphinstone, 31 March 1860]).
21. AMAE CP/Zanzibar/1/230 [Cochet to Monsieur le minister des affaires étranger, Zanzibar, 13 avril 1859]; ZZBA AA12/2/19 [Rigby to Bombay Government, Zanzibar, 18 March 1859]; al-Mughayrī, *Juhayna al-akhbār*, 197.
22. ZZBA AA12/2/19 [Rigby to Bombay Government, Zanzibar, 18 March 1859].
23. Fortuné Albrand, 'Extrait d'une mémoire sur Zanzibar et Quiloa', *Bulletin de la société de géographie* 2, 10 (1838), 78; Norman R. Bennett, *A History of the Arab State of Zanzibar*, London: Methuen, 1978, 37–38; G.S.P. Freeman-Grenville, *The East African Coast: Selected Documents from the First to the Earlier Nineteenth Century*, Oxford: Oxford University Press, 1962, 199; al-Mughayrī, *Juhayna al-akhbār*, 19; Bradford G. Martin, *Muslim Brotherhoods in Nineteenth Century Africa*, New York: Cambridge University Press, 2003 (1st. 1976), 160; John C. Wilkinson, *The Imamate Tradition of Oman*, London: Cambridge University Press, 1987, 55–56. They are known in East African coast as 'el-Harthi' and the above-mentioned references often use that spelling. The name indicates not only this immigrant group from Oman, but also those who had lived in the region for much longer and identified as 'el-Harthi', for example, a group in Pangani introduced by H.C. Baxter, 'Pangani: The Trade Centre of Ancient History', *Tanganyika Notes and Records* 17 (1944), 19. See also, Nicholls, *The Swahili Coast*, 72, 267.
24. Burton, *Zanzibar*, Vol. 1, 372.
25. Reda Bhacker, *Trade and Empire*, 94–95; Wilkinson, *The Imamate Tradition*, 55–56.
26. Burton, *Zanzibar*, Vol. 1, 372.
27. ZZBA AA12/2/75 [Rigby to Coghlan, Zanzibar, 5 October 1860 (Appendix B: Lieutenant Colonel Rigby's answer to the List of Queries

marked A in Brigadier Coghlan's letter to his address, No.12 of 1860, dated 1 October 1860)].

28. Nicholls, *The Swahili Coast*, 266–267; Sheriff, *Slaves, Spices and Ivory*, 50.
29. For this figure, see Richard F. Burton, 'Zanzibar, and Two Months in East Africa', *Blackwood's Edinburgh Magazine* 133 (1858), 223; Burton, *Zanzibar*, Vol. 2, 100. He died at the battle of Siu of Lamu Archipelago in 1843 (ZZBA AA12/29/72 [Hamerton to Secretary to Bombay Government, Zanzibar, 14 April 1845]). Following his death, 'Alī b. Nāir al-Bū Sa'īdī was appointed as *walī* of Mombasa as well as Malindi. For this 'Alī, see al-Mughayrī, *Juhayna al-akhbār*, 244; New, *Life, Wanderings and Labours*, 54. Al-Mughayrī mentioned that 'Alī b. Nāir al-Bū Sa'īdī concurrently served as both *walī* of Mombasa and of Malindi, and built a mosque in stone. Berg confused these two 'Alīs (Berg, 'Mombasa under the Busaidi Sultanate', 94, 334).
30. He was dispatched twice to Britain. The date of his first visit is unknown, but the second visit occurred in January 1842 (Bennett and Brooks, Jr (eds.), *New England Merchants*, 236 [Waters to Waters, Zanzibar, 1 January 1842]). Burton mentioned him as 'H.H. the Imaum of Muscat's Envoy Extraordinary to H.B. Majesty' (Burton, 'Zanzibar, and Two Months in East Africa', 233; Burton, *Zanzibar*, Vol. 2, 100). See also Nicholls, *The Swahili Coast*, 309.
31. ZZBA AA12/29/65 [Hamerton to Secretary to Bombay Government, Zanzibar, 20 March 1845].
32. Al-Mughayrī, *Juhayna al-akhbār*, 151. The Siu expedition, which operated from 1843 to the following year, has been mentioned as the most heroic defeat for Sa'īd b. Sulṭān. See Marguerite H. Ylvisaker, 'The Political and Economic Relationship of the Lamu Archipelago to the Adjacent Kenya Coast in the Nineteenth Century' (PhD dissertation, Boston University, 1975), 134–135.
33. ZZBA AA12/29/65 [Hamerton to Secretary to Bombay Government, Zanzibar, 20 March 1845]; ibid., 72 [Hamerton to Secretary to Bombay Government, Zanzibar, 14 April 1845].
34. Al-Mughayrī, *Juhayna al-akhbār*, 138.
35. CAOM FM/SG/OIND/2/10 (2)/n.d. [Note sur la côte orientale Afrique]; al-Mughayrī, *Juhayna al-akhbār*, 138. Loarer wrote that raiders from Madagascar attacked the island during the time when both of these served as *walī*, though he did not give any exact date (CAOM FM/SG/OIND/2/10 (2)/n.d. [Note sur la côte orientale Afrique]). According to al-Mughayrī, the raiders from Madagascar occupied Chole (this author has used another name for it, al-Shūla) on the island, and then 'Abd Allāh came to the rescue (al-Mughayrī, *Juhayna al-akhbār*,

138). That raid is identified with the raids by the Betsimisaraka in Nicholls, *The Swahili Coast*, 130. Furthermore, the raid was remembered along with those two names into the early twentieth century in the oral tradition (Amur Omar Saadi, 'Mafia: History and Traditions', tr. D.W.I. Piggott, *Tanganyika Notes and Records* 12 (1941), 25). For further information on the Ḥirth, particularly the Barwānī, see Norman R. Bennett, *Arab versus European: Diplomacy and War in Nineteenth-Century East Central Africa*, New York and London: Holmes and Meier, 1986, 33; Freeman-Grenville, *The East African Coast*, 228; Martin, *Muslim Brotherhoods*, 169–170.

36. Freeman-Grenville, *The East African Coast*, 199.
37. Albrand, 'Extrait d'une mémoire', 78.
38. Nicholls, *The Swahili Coast*, 131; Randall L. Pouwels, *Horn and Crescent: Cultural Change and Traditional Islam on the East African Coast, 800–1900*, Cambridge: Cambridge University Press, 1987, 105; Reda Bhacker, *Trade and Empire*, 96–97.
39. He accompanied Saʿīd on his last voyage. Rigby suspected that Saʿīd intended to prevent a coup d'état by the Ḥirth, including the Barwānī, in Zanzibar during his absence by going with him (ZZBA AA12/2/75 [Rigby to Coghlan, Zanzibar, 5 October 1860 (Appendix B: Lieutenant Colonel Rigby's answer to the List of Queries marked A in Brigadier Coghlan's letter to his address, No.12 of 1860, 1 October 1860)].
40. He possessed 1500 armed slaves (ZZBA AA12/2/19 [Rigby to Bombay Government, Zanzibar, 16 March 1859]).
41. ZZBA AA12/2/68 [Rigby to Coghlan, Zanzibar, 5 October 1860 (Appendix B: Lieutenant Colonel Rigby's answer to the List of Queries marked A in Brigadier Coghlan's letter to his address, No.12 of 1860, 1 October 1860)].
42. ZZBA AA12/2/19 [Rigby to Bombay Government, Zanzibar, 16 March 1859].
43. Ibid.; ZZBA AA12/2/74 [Rigby to Coghlan, Zanzibar, 5 October 1860 (Appendix B: Lieutenant Colonel Rigby's answer to the List of Queries marked A in Brigadier Coghlan's letter to his address, No.12 of 1860, 1 October 1860)]. Reda Bhacker states the annual stipend as 12,000 MT$, referring to a letter from Rigby to the Bombay Government in ZZBA AA12/2 (Reda Bhacker, 'Family Strife and Foreign Intervention', 275), which might be a copyist's error, although I could not identify its source. According to ZZBA AA12/2/74 [Rigby to Coghlan, Zanzibar, 5 October 1860 (Appendix B: Lieutenant Colonel Rigby's answer to the List of Queries marked A in Brigadier Coghlan's letter to his address, No.12 of 1860, 1 October 1860)], Sulaymān b. Aḥmad received the highest sum annually, 5000 MT$.

44. AMAE CP/Zanzibar/1/107-108 [Cochet to Monsieur le minister des affaires étranger, Zanzibar, 6 mars 1857].
45. OIOC IOR/L/P&S/18/B150a/10 [Précis of Correspondence Relating to Zanzibar Affairs, from 1856 to 1872, prepared by Captain P. D. Henderson].
46. AMAE CP/Zanzibar/1/107-108 [Cochet to Monsieur le minister des affaires étranger, Zanzibar, 6 mars 1857]; ZZBA AA12/2/77 [Rigby to Coghlan, Zanzibar, 5 October 1860 (Appendix B: Lieutenant Colonel Rigby's answer to the List of Queries marked A in Brigadier Coghlan's letter to his address, No.12 of 1860, 1 October 1860)]. Despite that, both al-Mughayrī and Reda Bhacker stated one Hamad b. Sālim was Thuwaynī's envoy (al-Mughayrī, *Juhayna al-akhbār*, 201–202; Reda Bhacker, *Trade and Empire*, 183).
47. AMAE CP/Zanzibar/1/107-108 [Cochet to Monsieur le minister des affaires étranger, Zanzibar, 6 mars 1857], 119–120 [Cochet to Monsieur le ministre des affaires étranger, Zanzibar, 18 septembre 1857].
48. ZZBA AA12/2/77 [Rigby to Coghlan, Zanzibar, 5 October 1860 (Appendix B: Lieutenant Colonel Rigby's answer to the List of Queries marked A in Brigadier Coghlan's letter to his address, No.12 of 1860, 1 October 1860)].
49. ZZBA AA12/2/79 [Rigby to Coghlan, Zanzibar, 5 October 1860 (Appendix B: Lieutenant Colonel Rigby's answer to the List of Queries marked A in Brigadier Coghlan's letter to his address, No.12 of 1860, 1 October 1860)].
50. ZZBA AA12/2/77 [Rigby to Coghlan, Zanzibar, 5 October 1860 (Appendix B: Lieutenant Colonel Rigby's answer to the List of Queries marked A in Brigadier Coghlan's letter to him, No.12 of 1860, 1 October 1860)].
51. It is a fairly long-standing and widespread tradition throughout the Indian Ocean world that the ruler of a port gave the right to tax at the port to those who could pay a certain amount of money. Shāh Bandar in sixteenth-century Malacca is a well-known example. The Bū Sa'īd introduced the system very early, and according to Reda Bhacker, it was already in place in the early nineteenth century. The Customs Master in Masqaṭ was a Banyan merchant (Reda Bhacker, *Trade and Empire*, 71–72). Vincento Maurizi, who first visited in Masqaṭ in 1819 and later served as commander to Sa'īd, also stated that the Customs of Masqaṭ were run by 'a rich Beniani' (Vincento Maurizi, *History of Seyd Said, Sultan of Muscat; together with an Account of the Countries and People on the Shores of the Persian Gulf, particularly of the Wahabees*, London: John Booth, 1819, 29). In Zanzibar, the position of Customs Master already existed in the early nineteenth century. A French slaving captain, P.

Dallons, stated that Customs were run by 'a Banyan or an Arab whose rich estates in Muscat guarantee his fidelity to the Prince' (Freeman-Grenville, *The East African Coast*, 198). Nicholls, *The Swahili Coast*, 78, and Sheriff, *Slaves, Spices and Ivory*, 126, indicate this source in referring to the early history of Indian Custom Masters in Zanzibar. On this island, the tenure of the position was 3 to 5 years, and it was auctioned. For example, in the second article of the will of Ladha Damjī, it is stated that he was contracted to do the job for 5 years (MAHA PD/1872/200/646/n.p. [Kirk to Wedderburn, Zanzibar, 9 December 1871]. See also, National Archives of the United States (hereafter NAUS) RG84/Zanzibar/100/n.p. [Waters to Forsyth, Zanzibar, 6 May 1837]; Bennett and Brooks, Jr (eds.), *New England Merchants*, 355 [Ward to State Department, Zanzibar, 21 February 1846].

52. ZZBA AA12/2/77 [Rigby to Coghlan, Zanzibar, 5 October 1860 (Appendix B: Lieutenant Colonel Rigby's answer to the List of Queries marked A in Brigadier Coghlan's letter to his address, No.12 of 1860, 1 October 1860)].
53. For the details of Mājid's financial situation, see Reda Bhacker, *Trade and Empire*, 176–178, 183.
54. OIOC IOR/R/15/1/163/n.p. [Rigby to Anderson, Zanzibar, 17 March 1859]; ZZBA AA12/2/3 [Cruttenden to Rigby, Muscat, 29 September 1859].
55. Russell, *General Rigby*, 78; ZZBA AA12/2/16 [Rigby to Bombay Government, Zanzibar, 17 February 1859].
56. Al-Mughayrī, *Juhayna al-akhbār*, 200.
57. Reda Bhacker, 'Family Strife and Foreign Intervention', 276. See also, ZZBA AA12/2/73 [Rigby to Coghlan, Zanzibar, 5 October 1860 (Appendix B: Lieutenant Colonel Rigby's answer to the List of Queries marked A in Brigadier Coghlan's letter to him, No.12 of 1860, 1 October 1860)].
58. Al-Mughayrī, *Juhayna al-akhbār*, 200.
59. Ibid.
60. ZZBA AA12/2/19 [Rigby to Bombay Government, Zanzibar, 16 March 1859].
61. Ibid.
62. Kelly, *Britain and the Persian Gulf*, 535; Reda Bhacker, *Trade and Empire*, 184–185.
63. ZZBA AA12/2/20 [Rigby to Bombay Government, Zanzibar, 16 March 1859].
64. Russell, *General Rigby*, 79. In addition, a part of Thuwaynī's fleet arrived at Lamu. However, cholera and smallpox were prevalent on board, and local inhabitants prevented the crew from taking on water

(OIOC IOR/R/15/1/163/n.p. [Rigby to Anderson, Zanzibar, 22 March 1859]), thus, some violence occurred.

65. ZZBA AA12/2/20 [Rigby to Bombay Government, Zanzibar, 16 March 1859].
66. AMAE CP/Zanzibar/1/229-232 [Cochet to Monsieur le ministre des affaires étranger, Zanzibar, 13 avril 1859].
67. NAUK FO54/17/210-211 [Rigby to India Office, received 22 March 1860]; ZZBA AA12/2/78-80 [Rigby to Coghlan, Zanzibar, 5 October 1860 (Appendix B: Lieutenant Colonel Rigby's answer to the List of Queries marked A in Brigadier Coghlan's letter to him, No.12 of 1860, 1 October 1860)]. In fact, in 1858, the Governor of Bourbon dispatched two battleships to Zanzibar, and urged the Sultan to deliver the labour force (NAUK FO84/1120/193 [Rigby to Bart, Zanzibar, 16 April 1860]). Later, when a French schooner anchored at Zanzibar to transport 300 children to Bourbon, the Sultan protested in the strongest terms (ibid.).
68. AMAE CP/Zanzibar/1/230-232 [Cochet to Monsieur le ministre des affaires étranger, Zanzibar, 13 avril 1859]; ZZBA AA12/2/20-21 [Rigby to Bombay Government, Zanzibar, 16 March 1859].
69. ZZBA AA12/2/20; ibid., 79 [Rigby to Coghlan, Zanzibar, 5 October 1860 (Appendix B: Lieutenant Colonel Rigby's answer to the List of Queries marked A in Brigadier Coghlan's letter to his address, No.12 of 1860, 1 October 1860)].
70. ZZBA AA12/2/20 [Rigby to Bombay Government, Zanzibar, 16 March 1859] recorded that *L'Estafette*, with six cannon, arrived at Stone Town port on 21 March and on 29th, *Cordélière*, with 20 cannon, arrived too.
71. MAHA PD/1859/189/193/39 [Rigby to Anderson, Zanzibar, 18 June 1859]; ibid., 71 [Rigby to Anderson, Zanzibar, 12 September 1859]; ZZBA AA12/2/21 [Rigby to Bombay Government, Zanzibar, 16 March 1859]. See also, AMAE CP/Zanzibar/1/259 [Thuwaynī b. Saʿīd b. Sulṭān to Kūsāy, s.l., 28 Rajab 1275].
72. Beatrice Nicolini, *Il Sultanato di Zanzibar nel XIX secolo: Traffici commerciali e relazioni internazionali*, Torino: l'Harmattan Italia, 2002, 78–117.
73. ZZBA AA2/4/267 [Rigby to Russell, Zanzibar, 1 July 1861] claimed that the slave trade was reactivated because, during the 13-month absence of British Consul, the French made public the fact that Britain never sent a Consul to Zanzibar after their defeat in the Indian Rebellion of 1857. The same document is available at ZZBA AA12/2/28. See also Russell, *General Rigby*, 139.

74. MAHA PD/1859/189/193/39-40 [Rigby to Anderson, Zanzibar, 18 June 1859].
75. MAHA PD/1859/189/193/40-41 [Rigby to Anderson, Zanzibar, 18 June 1859]. Under the unstable conditions of the series of events above mentioned, commercial activity in Stone Town temporarily stopped (ibid., 39).
76. MAHA PD/1859/189/193/58-61 [Rigby to Anderson, Zanzibar, 26 July 1859]. The Ḥirth gathered slaves in Stone Town from their plantations and demonstrated for the release of jailed shaykhs. However, when they realized that Mājid had no intention of releasing them, they immediately dispersed (ibid., 60).
77. MAHA PD/1859/189/193/70 [Rigby to Anderson, Zanzibar, 12 September 1859].
78. MAHA PD/1859/189/193/70-71 [Rigby to Anderson, Zanzibar, 12 September 1859].
79. MAHA PD/1859/189/193/70 [Rigby to Anderson, Zanzibar, 12 September 1859].
80. MAHA PD/1859/189/193/71 [Rigby to Anderson, Zanzibar, 12 September 1859].
81. Ibid.
82. MAHA PD/1859/189/193/71-72 [Rigby to Anderson, Zanzibar, 12 September 1859]. A few days after this incident at *darbār*, Amad won an Albanian *jamadār* over by bribery and attempted to assassinate Mājid, but failed (ibid., 72–73).
83. MAHA PD/1859/189/193/74 [Rigby to Anderson, Zanzibar, 12 September 1859].
84. MAHA PD/1859/189/193/96 [Rigby to Anderson, Zanzibar, 9 October 1859].
85. Ibid.
86. MAHA PD/1859/189/193/97 [Rigby to Anderson, Zanzibar, 9 October 1859].
87. MAHA PD/1859/189/193/97-98 [Rigby to Anderson, Zanzibar, 9 October 1859].
88. MAHA PD/1859/189/193/98 [Rigby to Anderson, Zanzibar, 9 October 1859]; ZZBA AA12/2/3-4 [Seyyid Burghash to Elphinstone, Zanzibar, 31 March 1860].
89. MAHA PD/1859/189/193/99 [Rigby to Anderson, Zanzibar, 9 October 1859].
90. Ibid.
91. MAHA PD/1859/189/193/99-100 [Rigby to Anderson, Zanzibar, 9 October 1859].

92. ZZBA AA12/2/73 [Rigby to Coghlan, Zanzibar, 5 October 1860 (Appendix B: Lieutenant Colonel Rigby's answer to the List of Queries marked A in Brigadier Coghlan's letter to him, No.12 of 1860, 1 October 1860)].
93. MAHA PD/1859/189/193/124 [Rigby to Anderson, Zanzibar, 21 October 1859]; ZZBA AA12/2/72-73 [Rigby to Coghlan, Zanzibar, 5 October 1860 (Appendix B: Lieutenant Colonel Rigby's answer to the List of Queries marked A in Brigadier Coghlan's letter to him, No.12 of 1860, 1 October 1860)].
94. MAHA PD/1859/189/193/112 [Rigby to Anderson, Zanzibar, 21 October 1859].
95. MAHA PD/1859/189/193/112-113 [Rigby to Anderson, Zanzibar, 21 October 1859].
96. MAHA PD/1859/189/193/113 [Rigby to Anderson, Zanzibar, 21 October 1859]. Mājid led almost all the available forces under his command to the camp, thus only about a hundred Baluchis were left in charge of Stone Town (ibid.).
97. MAHA PD/1859/189/193/113 [Rigby to Anderson, Zanzibar, 21 October 1859]; NAUK FO54/17/216 [Rigby to the Secretary of the Admiralty, Zanzibar, 20 October 1859].
98. MAHA PD/1859/189/193/113-114 [Rigby to Anderson, Zanzibar, 21 October 1859].
99. MAHA PD/1859/189/193/114 [Rigby to Anderson, Zanzibar, 21 October 1859].
100. MAHA PD/1859/189/193/114-115 [Rigby to Anderson, Zanzibar, 21 October 1859]; NAUK FO54/17/213-215 [Beckeley to the Secretary of the Admiralty, on board *Lynx*, 10 January 1860].
101. MAHA PD/1859/189/193/115-117 [Rigby to Anderson, Zanzibar, 21 October 1859].
102. MAHA PD/1859/189/193/117 [Rigby to Anderson, Zanzibar, 21 October 1859]; ibid., 171 [Adams to Wellesley, Zanzibar, 19 October 1859].
103. MAHA PD/1859/189/193/118-119 [Rigby to Anderson, Zanzibar, 21 October 1859]; ibid., 171–172 [Adams to Wellesley, Zanzibar, 19 October 1859].
104. MAHA PD/1859/189/193/119 [Rigby to Anderson, Zanzibar, 21 October 1859].
105. Ibid.; MAHA PD/1859/189/193/172 [Adams to Wellesley, Zanzibar, 19 October 1859].
106. MAHA PD/1859/189/193/119-120 [Rigby to Anderson, Zanzibar, 21 October 1859]; ibid., 173 [Adams to Wellesley, Zanzibar, 19 October 1859].

107. MAHA PD/1859/189/193/120 [Rigby to Anderson, Zanzibar, 21 October 1859].
108. MAHA PD/1859/189/193/120-121 [Rigby to Anderson, Zanzibar, 21 October 1859].
109. MAHA PD/1859/189/193/121 [Rigby to Anderson, Zanzibar, 21 October 1859].
110. Ibid.; MAHA PD/1859/189/193/173 [Adams to Wellesley, Zanzibar, 19 October 1859].
111. MAHA PD/1859/189/193/121 [Rigby to Anderson, Zanzibar, 21 October 1859].
112. MAHA PD/1859/189/193/139-140 [Rigby to Adams, Zanzibar, 20 October 1859]; ibid., 161 [Substance of a letter from Syed Burgash son of His Highness the late Imam of Muscat, to the Right Honorable John Lord Elphinstone, Governor of Bombay, dated the 17th Rubbeul Akhir 1276 corresponding with the 13th and received and ordered to be translated on the 19th November 1859]; ibid., 185 [Wellesley to Elphinstone, Bombay, 26 November 1859].
113. OIOC IOR/L/P&S/18/B150/19 [Précis of Correspondence Relating to Zanzibar Affairs, from 1856 to 1872, prepared by Captain P. D. Henderson].
114. For details on this investigation, for example, see MAHA PD/1860/98/41/3-116 [Coghlan to Anderson, Bombay, 4 July 1860].
115. OIOC IOR/L/P&S/18/B150/33-35 [Précis of Correspondence Relating to Zanzibar Affairs, from 1856 to 1872, prepared by Captain P. D. Henderson].
116. NAUK FO881/7427/n.p. [Declaration between Great Britain and France, engaging reciprocally to respect to the independence of the Sultans of Muscat and Zanzibar, signed at Paris, 10 March 1862]. J.A. Kieran, 'The Origins of the Zanzibar Guarantee Treaty of 1862', *Canadian Journal of African Studies* 2, 2 (1968) examines the treaty in the context of diplomatic relationship between Britain and France.
117. Kelly, *The Britain and the Persian Gulf*, 633–634, 746–748; Shelly Johny, 'The Decline of Omans Maritime Empire during the Late Nineteenth Century' (PhD dissertation, Jawaharlal Nehru University, 2010), 143; Landen, *Oman since 1856*, 209; Lorimer, *Gazetteer of the Persian Gulf*, 499–500.
118. Kelly, *The Britain and the Persian Gulf*, 747–749; Landen, *Oman since 1856*, 208–209.
119. The barter had been already planned when Churchill was Consul in Zanzibar during the reign of Mājid (PPEM MH201/4 [Ropes to Secretary of State, Zanzibar, 2 August 1869]). The Sultan of Oman

also signed a treaty to abolish slave trade in 1873 (Landen, *Oman since 1856*, 208–209; Lorimer, *Gazetteer of the Persian Gulf*, 499–500). For involvement of the Indian government, see Robert J. Blyth, *The Empire of the Raj: India, Eastern Africa and the Middle East, 1858–1947*, New York: Palgrave, 2003.

120. Barghash had been in exile in Bombay for 2 years but in 1870 he was allowed to return to Zanzibar and took up residence on the island. For his enthronement, see Sheriff, *Slaves, Spices and Ivory*, 218-221.
121. For example, ZZBA AA12/2/109-110 [Rigby to Bombay Government, Zanzibar, 18 April 1861]; Russell, *General Rigby*, 90.
122. The British Consulate in Zanzibar repeatedly reported that the Consul aggressively requested Mājid to punish Northern Arabs for raiding and kidnapping. See, for example, ZZBA AA12/2/11 [Rigby to Bombay Government, 5 September 1861].
123. The East African coast could not escape from its role as a slave ground after that (Christie, *Cholera Epidemics in East Africa*, 332).

CHAPTER 8

1860: The Rigby Emancipation and the Rise of the Indian Resident Nationality Problem

While the natives of Kutch established in Zanzibar were under our sole protection and jurisdiction, we held the most wealthy and enterprising among the mercantile community, and our influence was in all matters paramount.

NAUK FO881/2314/51 [Kirk to Gonne, s.l., 16 August 1869]

Introduction

This chapter traces the development of the legal status of Indian merchants along the East African coast in the nineteenth century. Legal status is generally understood as something defined and bestowed by states on their citizens or subjects, and it is well known that it has often triggered tensions between states and those citizens or subjects. The remark quoted above is drawn from a letter written in 1869 by John Kirk, British Vice Consul in Zanzibar when Britain finally settled the question concerning the Indian merchants who lived along the East African coast. His proud statement that 'influence was in all matters paramount' might have been somewhat exaggerated, but it was admitted at the time by Edward D. Ropes. As American Consul, Ropes observed that the British Consul's influence was not limited to those under his own official jurisdiction but extended to the Sultan's subjects.[1] Considering the economic and also political influence of Indian merchants in Zanzibar, as well as the fact that Zanzibar became a British protectorate just 21 years

H. Suzuki, *Slave Trade Profiteers in the Western Indian Ocean*, Palgrave Series in Indian Ocean World Studies,
DOI 10.1007/978-3-319-59803-1_8

after Kirk's letter was written, the achievement in 1869 can be regarded as an important milestone on the way to the formal protection that was to come. However, we need to be careful not to assume that the question of the nationality of Indian residents along the East African coast developed as a simple dichotomy between the state—in this case, of course, the British Empire—and its Indian merchant subjects. First of all, an interesting feature of the case is that the Indians were living not in British territory, but in the territory of the Bū Saʿīd. Kirk and other British and Indian officers sought to exert control over people who were actually living outside their control. Indeed, the matter had developed in a complicated way due to the intentions, wishes and strategic requirements of all the various parties in Zanzibar, which must therefore be taken into consideration. This chapter thus looks at how the legal status of the Indian merchants was discussed, challenged and settled as a result of the conjuncture of the interests, cognitions and political intentions of multiple agencies, with slavery acting as the trigger for the whole question. While focusing on the agency of the Indian merchants themselves, we remain alert to the multiple agencies involved besides them.

The legal status of Indian merchants along the East African coast is not an entirely new topic, for it has been referred to often in previous studies, most recently in Chhaya Goswami's *The Call of the Sea: Kachchhi Traders in Muscat and Zanzibar, c.1800–1880*. In Chap. 6 of that book, Goswami traces the development of the question mostly on the basis of sources from the Mahārāshtra State Archives.[2] Although Goswami's use of that particular source makes her almost unique in the field, the source itself does serve rather to limit her insight. In other words, her viewpoint is focused exclusively on the administrative debates between the British Consulate in Zanzibar and the Government of Bombay and, later, that of India. Although Goswami's book has indeed significantly enhanced our understanding of the world of Kachchhī merchants, her contribution to their legal status completely misses its inherent complexity. It is to settle that question that the present chapter goes beyond the dialogue between the British Consulate in Zanzibar and the authorities on the Indian subcontinent.

This introductory section to the chapter is followed by six others. The second section traces how Indian merchants spread along the East African coast, and the next two examine their legal status and commercial activities. The fifth section gives an overview of the so-called 'Rigby emancipation' of 1860, which triggered a British desire to control the legal status of the Indians, and follows the development of the debate around this, and the sixth section concludes.

Indian Merchants along the East African Coast in the Nineteenth Century

There is a fair degree of obscurity surrounding the presence of Indian merchants along the East African coast before the arrival of the Portuguese. Despite this lack of information, it is certain that the nineteenth century marked the highlight of Indian mercantile activity along the coast and adjacent islands governed by the Bū Sa'īd, and that their commercial activity increased rapidly.[3] In 1819, when Albrand visited Zanzibar, he counted 214 Indian residents belonging to several pioneer groups,[4] such as the Kachchhī Bhatiyā who came mainly from Māṇḍvī or Mundrā and who established their business along the coast as late as the beginning of the nineteenth century.[5] In addition to their individual commercial activities, which had been remarkable since the very early part of that century,[6] some of them succeeded in establishing a close relationship with the local authorities. The most remarkable example is that of the Kachchhī Bhatiyā, whose members were first appointed Customs Masters at Stone Town port sometime between the 1820s and 1830s and retained the position until the latter half of the century. They were appointed to the same position at several other ports along the coast.[7]

As to the 1840s, we have the excellent documentation by Loarer, which provides detailed information on Indian natives. Loarer, who was a member of the French naval expedition led by Charles Guillain in the late 1840s, listed a number of Indian individuals as well as group names in his description of commerce in Zanzibar.[8] Among them were 'Banian', 'Hindous', and 'Arabs', and he obviously recognized the superiority of the first two groups over Arab merchants in the commercial life of Zanzibar at that time.[9] Furthermore, he observed that the 'Banian' were building up a commercial network centred on Zanzibar and connected to various ports along the east coast of Africa, and on the Arabian Peninsula, notably Masqaṭ, as well as to ports on the west coast of the Indian subcontinent, including Māṇḍvī and Bombay.[10] Writing in the mid-nineteenth century, Burton noted that:

Table 8.1 Indians residing in Stone Town, Zanzibar, in 1859

Groups	*Population*	*Occupation*	*Remarks*
Kachchhī Bhatiyā	400	Commerce	–
Brahmān	6	–	–
Khatrī	4	Commerce (1), Carpenter (3)	–
Vania	1	–	Apart from them, 3 or 4 half-Lohāna descended from Sind and Kachchh
Lohāna	5	Carpenter, Goldsmith	–
Pārsī	5	Carpenter (2), Watchsmith (1), Agent of company in Bombay (2)	–
Bohra	600–700 in total	–	–
Memmon	(Ismā'īlī Khojah	–	–
Ismā'īlī Khōja	100)	Retail	–

Source Richard F. Burton, *Zanzibar: City, Island, and Coast*, 2 vols, London: Tinsley Brothers, 1872, Vol. 1, 327–339

> Our Anglo-Indian subjects, numbering about 4,000 in the dominions of Zanzibar, some of them wealthy men, are entitled to protection from the Arab, and more especially from the Christian merchants. Almost the whole foreign trade, or at least four-fifths of it, passes through their hands; they are the principal shopkeepers and artisans, and they extend as far South as Mozambique, Madagascar, and the Comoro Islands. During the last few years the number of Indian settlers has greatly increased, and they have obtained possession from the Arabs, by purchase or mortgage, of many landed estates in the Sayyid's dominions.[11]

In addition, Burton gives detailed information on the Indian merchants along the East African coast, which covers several groups, including the Kachchhī Bhatiyā, the Pārsī, the Bohra and and Ismā'īlī Khōja (Table 8.1).

Another detailed study is available in the annual report for 1870 compiled by the British Consul in Zanzibar (Table 8.2). That report reveals the following four remarkable points. First, most of the new arrivals were from the Kachchh region.[12] Second, the number of Ismā'īlī Khōja was increasing rapidly. As Tables 8.1 and 8.2 show, the size of that

Table 8.2 Indians residing in Stone Town, Zanzibar, in 1870

Groups	*Population*	*Number of Houses*
Hindus or Banians	200	80
Bohra	250	40
Ismāʿīlī Khōja	2100	535
Sunnī Muslim	Less than 250	–

Source NAUK FO84/1344/129–132

community, whose main occupation was retail trade, increased nearly 21 times within 15 years. The report noted that there were 700 married women among them, up from the 26 to 30 years previously.[13] Third, various means of migration were identified, not only among the Ismāʿīlī Khōja, but also among communities such as the Bohra, which included 110 children in a community of 250 people.[14] Members of some communities migrated along with their entire households, while other communities, particularly the 'Hindu or Banian' were prohibited by *dharma* (communal law) from taking their wives abroad, so were heavily male-dominated.[15] Lastly, the 1870 report shows the geographical dispersion of several communities. There were 59 Ismāʿīlī Khōja in 28 houses on Pemba Island, 137 in 36 houses in Bagamoyo, and 176 in 77 houses in Kilwa.[16] There were 142 Bohra in 25 houses living in Mombasa, which was their second largest settlement after Zanzibar. The names of 11 towns were mentioned, including Lamu, Malindi and Tanga,[17] while ten more towns are mentioned as places where 'Hindu or Banian' were living.[18]

The first point above, namely that a significant proportion of the Indian population along the East African coast had come originally from Kachchh, makes the question of their legal status problematic, because Kachchh was ruled neither by the British directly nor by the British East India Company. The local ruler of Kachchh, the Rāo, maintained his autonomy, though the East India Company had exercised political control since 1819.[19] Thus, for example, the American Consul in Zanzibar reported in 1850 that vessels sailing from Kachchh to the east coast of Africa carried a certificate issued by the Rāo which stated clearly that its holders were his subjects.[20] As implied by the fact that this point was reported by the American Consul, the legal status of these Indian merchants along the east coast of Africa was a matter involving not just British administrators and the Indian merchants themselves; other parties monitored developments and even intervened from time to time.

Furthermore, this complicated situation actually contributed to the commercial success of the Kachchhīs along the East African coast. The next section examines how the Indian merchants themselves exploited the situation, and the subsequent two sections how their legal status developed, while also considering the recognition, interests and political intentions of the parties surrounding them.

Standing on the Borderline

When a British Consulate was established in Zanzibar in September 1841, Robert B. Norsworthy, one of the pioneer British merchants there,[21] claimed in a communication to the Chairman of the Chamber of Commerce in Bombay that there was ambiguity concerning the legal status of merchants from the Indian subcontinent, namely whether they were British subjects or subjects of the Sultan.[22] At about the same time Hamerton, the first British Consul in Zanzibar, reported the following incident:

> During the conference with His Highness on the 26th just, I took the opportunity of telling him that however unpleasant it might be for him to hear it, that as strict and fearless discharge of my duty, and which government expected from all their servants obliged me to tell him, that his having caused or allowed Jueram Sevvajee the custom master to force the native traders here Banians, Borahs or others, being British subjects to sign a paper or written agreement, stating that they considered themselves citizens, or inhabitants of the city of Zanzibar, and that they were no longer under the Government of England nor would in any wise claim the protection of the British Government has a strange mark of His Highness' respect or friendship for the Government of England, and that it was contrary to the general spirit and intention of the treaty and that the people having been obliged to sign such a paper would not in my opinion deprive any British subject of the protection of Government in the hour of need. His Highness appeared astonished at my telling him this … and then asked me how I knew the people had signed such papers. I told him it was no secret, all Zanzibar knew it and talked of it.[23]

Around the time of Hamerton's arrival in 1841, the Customs Master, more or less by force, obliged the Indian merchants to agree in person to a statement 'admitting' that they belonged to the Sultan and not to Britain. The extent of the Sultan's involvement in the affair is not clear, though the quotation above from Hamerton indicates that he was at least aware of it. According to Hamerton, Jeyram Sivjī, a Kachchhī Bhatiyā and Customs Master at the time, brought two or three Indians at a time to the Sultan and made them sign the statement.[24] Despite the action's forcible nature noted by the British Consul, many 'Banians' refused to sign because their families were still living in British territory on the subcontinent, and some even insisted on being allowed to leave Zanzibar in order to escape from being forced to sign.[25] In the same report, Hamerton gave his own view of the affair:

> [T]he whole of this affair is the act of the custom master Jairam a Banian; a native of Mandavie and no doubt he has done it at the instigation of the American Consul with whom he is connected in the trade, and by doing which; he thinks to have full control over all the travellers; and prevent any complaints in future from British Subjects.[26]

Hamerton was highly suspicious that Jeyram Sivjī and Richard P. Waters, the first American Consul (r.1837–1845) and also a leading American merchant in Zanzibar, were in fact attempting to monopolize trade at Stone Town port, and he was concerned that the relationship between those two parties violated the prohibition of monopolization agreed in the commercial treaty between Britain and the Bū Sa'īd in 1839.[27] For several reasons, Hamerton's suspicions are worth taking seriously. First, much of the trade in Zanzibar at the time was in the hands of the Indian merchants, so Jeyram's initiative might reasonably have been taken as an attempt to assume effective control of all trade. Second, there was evidence of a very close commercial relationship between Jeyram and Waters. For example, a letter from Waters to his brother in 1837 reveals that 90% of his trade in Zanzibar was with Jeyram,[28] and although from the 1840s onwards Waters developed commercial relationships with local merchants other than Jeyram, he maintained close ties with him. Clearly then, Waters too stood to gain from any efforts made by Jeyram to increase his control over Indian merchants and their involvement in Zanzibar's trade.

Jeyram's attempts to force the merchants to renounce their claims to be British subjects failed in the face of strong opposition from Hamerton. However, the ambiguity pointed out by the British merchant Norsworthy as to whether those merchants were British subjects or the Sultan's subjects was never resolved. In fact, the uncertainty worked to the merchants' advantage. Charles Ward, a Salem merchant and the second American Consul in Zanzibar, explained:

> In regard to the Banyans & Hindoos themselves, they claim to be Arab subjects or English subjects as will best suit their purpose. An individual will go to his Highness today with his complaint and is heard, and calls himself the subject of his Highness. Tomorrow the same individual will go to the British Consulate and claim protection as an English subject & he is received. They own Dows and make voyages to Bombay and other parts of India under the British registry & flag, and make their voyages to the coast under the Sultans flag, trade within the restricted limits in the articles of Ivory and Gum Copal, and enter largely into the Slave trade ...[29]

He clearly understood that they exploited their 'mixed' status, which allowed them to choose their protector as the case demanded. However, his reference to their trade is quite significant, for these Indian merchants traded with the mainland as subjects of the Sultan. '[T]he restricted limits in the articles of Ivory and Gum Copal' here can indicate no other place than the Mrima Coast, which was one of the Sultan's most important sources of wealth because several important entrepôts for ivory and copal were located there. However, his control did not extend thoroughly in mainland. That is why, in the commercial treaties Saʿīd signed, he would allow neither British nor French subjects to trade in either ivory or copal there.[30] By contrast, in the commercial treaty with the United States, which was the first commercial treaty he signed, Saʿīd, in what was something of a commercial and diplomatic error of judgement, permitted American subjects to engage in any trade along the Mrima Coast.[31] However, in reality, the American merchants do not seem to have taken full advantage of their entitlement because they came under strong pressure not to do so from the Sultan.[32] However, as subjects of the Sultan,[33] Indian merchants were entitled to trade ivory, copal—and slaves, for that matter—along the Mrima Coast.[34]

Simultaneously, their status as British subjects gave the Indians other privileges of different sorts. First, not only along the East African coast, but wherever they were, they could, as British subjects, request assistance from the British Consulate if they encountered trouble with the local inhabitants, including the local rulers.[35] The status of 'British subject' was also useful in helping them to protect their property back on the subcontinent. Many Indian merchants, especially Hindus, left their families and property at home to go and conduct business along the East African coast. Furthermore, as Hamerton pointed out, if they should die in Zanzibar, the Sultan's officials would often confiscate their property.[36] According to Hamerton, on such occasions their families could rely on British protection through the Consul.

Indian merchants along the East African coast therefore enjoyed the distinct advantages of this 'dual protection'. In that sense, Jagjit S. Mangat's interpretation of the reactions of Indian merchants in the face of demands by the Customs Master to agree to be subjects of the Sultan is incorrect.[37] Mangat suggested that they faced a straight choice between that and British citizenship. In fact, the Customs Master was actually insisting that in becoming subjects of the Sultan they would give up any claim to be British subjects—the reaction of many of the merchants to this was hostile. What they objected to was the requirement to make a binding choice. In other words, they were quite willing to become subjects of the Sultan, but not at the expense of relinquishing their status as British subjects. They wanted to remain in the grey area in-between and continue to exploit this advantage. The strong opposition of the Indians to Jeyram's enforcement was actually, therefore, simple reluctance to lose their 'dual protection'.

Opinions Regarding Indian Merchants Prior to Emancipation

As the previous section shows, in their commercial activities the Indian merchants along the east coast of Africa took advantage of the 'dual protection' that was derived from the uncertainty of their legal status. Despite challenges, they succeeded in preserving this; however, their success was not only due to their own efforts. Rather, their dual status was acknowledged and supported by the conflicts of recognitions, commercial imperatives and political aims of the parties involved. This section describes these in detail.

According to contemporary documents, European and American merchants were the most vocally opposed to the ambiguous legal status of Indian merchants, their principal reason being that, as the previous section shows, they themselves were prohibited from trading along the Mrima Coast, while rival Indian merchants from the subcontinent could do so freely.[38] Furthermore, European and American merchants were often unsure to whom they should bring a claim in the event of conflict with an Indian merchant.[39] The experience of Charles Ward is a case in point.[40]

Ward, the second American Consul in Zanzibar, was asked by Waters, his predecessor, to resolve the following matter. Just before Waters left Zanzibar, a merchant called Calfaun went bankrupt after receiving large investments from merchants on the island. Waters was one who had invested with Calfaun, to the sum of 3000 MT$. Before Waters left, Calfaun had offered to repay half his investment, but Waters was far satisfied with that and asked Ward to pursue the matter on his behalf. Ward was informed by Hamerton, the British Consul, that he, Hamerton, was the man to whom an application should be made for settlement of the case. However, it was the Sultan with whom Ward lodged Waters's complaint. At his interview with the Sultan, Ward asked whether the Indian merchants were subjects of the Sultan or not, to which, according to the documents, the Sultan replied that indeed they were. Ward then pointed out the errors in the accounts of Calfaun, whereupon the Sultan angrily informed Ward that he would force Calfaun to pay twice what Calfaun owed Waters if what Ward claimed was proved correct. With help from other merchants, Ward then assembled evidence to prove his case and submitted it to the Sultan. However, the Sultan subsequently reneged on his promise.

After that, Hamerton repeatedly cautioned Ward that Calfaun was a British subject and any enquiry into this affairs should be carried out by Hamerton, not by the Sultan. Hamerton also explained that he had not hitherto concerned himself with the case because Ward had not yet asked him for official assistance.[41] Despite Hamerton's repeated warnings, Ward again asked the Sultan about the status of Calfaun and the other Indian merchants, but this time the Sultan declined to answer the question quite as categorically as he had done previously. He said that he would answer immediately only if he were asked by the President of the United States himself.[42] In another letter to Ward, the Sultan wrote: '[m]y friend there is no necessity for your asking such a question, for all the people understand who are Arab people and who are English people. If you wish or require anything on my part let me know.'[43] Although Ward sent letters to the American Government, they replied that they were not prepared to intervene in the matter at that stage.[44] Ultimately, Ward agreed on Waters's behalf to a settlement whereby Waters received 70% of his total investment, to be paid to him by the Sultan.[45]

Ward did not therefore submit his case to the British Consul; nor would he have regarded the Indian merchants as British subjects even after the dispute's conclusion,[46] and he had a good reason not to. As he intimated to Ephraim A. Emmerton, under British law the British Government would not accept an application for protection by someone involved in the slave trade or who owned slaves; even at the death of such person who involved slavery and slave trade the British Government would have done nothing to assist.[47] As it was pointed out, Hamerton, the British Consul just suggested Ward that it was better not to become involved in any affair relating to slaves in Zanzibar.[48]

Ward's reasoning was understandable, and convincing enough to make the British Consul hesitate to respond in view of the fact that suppression of the slave trade and slavery was a key policy of the British Government at that time. However, that might not actually have been the real reason. Another of Ward's letters reveals his considerable uncertainty over his own intentions. In a letter to John M. Clayton, US Secretary of State, he anticipated the difficulties of American merchants involved in disputes with Indian merchants if they should sought British protection, because the British Consul would be a more intractable opponent than the Sultan.[49] In the same letter, Ward repeated a view allegedly common among American merchants along the East African coast, which was that while the British Consul considered the Indian merchants to be British subjects, the merchants could not become true British subjects because the Rāo of Kachchh was under the protection of the British East India Company and not of the British Government.[50] That being so, Ward's concern was directed at the future commercial relationship between American merchants and Indian merchants, which at that time was close, with Americans providing short-term finance to the Indians.[51] It was clear to Ward that in future disputes dealing with the Sultan would be far more straightforward than trying to negotiate with the British Consul.

Saʿīd, who was the Sultan of Zanzibar at the time, took a totally different approach to the question from that of the other parties involved. The following exchange between Saʿīd and Ward is crucial to our understanding:

> The Sultan said you have asked me who are my subjects. Now this is my answer; but first answer me one question. According to the English law, can a British subject hold slaves? I said, no your Highness they cannot. The Sultan said now you have answered my question. I tell you that all the people in Zanzibar who hold slaves are my subjects; and those who do not are English subjects; and now my friend I am going to tell you something that perhaps you won't like very well. The English are my best friends, and at one time in Arabia they gave me three thousand men to fight for me and have done me various offices of kindness, and I can never forget them, for it is a custom of the Arabs. If a man gives him a cup of cold water he will always remember it with gratitude; and now if any of these people come to me to settle their business, I will settle it, but if they go to the English

> Consul he will settle it, and it is all the same; for the English people and the Arab people are all one, and if you wish at any time to go with your complaints to the English Consul you can go, or you can come to me; or if any Arab people come to you, you can settle their differences, and I shall be very glad.[52]

Unlike Ward, who distinguished between people strictly according to which group they belonged to and for whom that distinction was the starting point of any discussion of the matter, the Sultan attached no importance to such distinctions: to him what was important was to whom one applied to resolve a dispute.[53] Moreover, he suggested that the American Consul might deal with complaints by Arabs if they asked him for assistance, even though they were the Sultan's subjects. Ward even showed his anxiety that the Sultan dealt with complaints submitted by American and British merchants without any reference to their consulates.[54] The Sultan, in any case, viewed the Indian merchants as being under his special protection because of his treaty with the Rāo.

The British Consuls, another important party to be considered, consistently repeated their opinion that Indian merchants were British subjects. However, that view contained contradictions, as Ward pointed out. Thus, the dispute over the legal status of Indian residents along the east coast of Africa continued between the British Consulate in Zanzibar, the British Government and the Bombay Government. British policy on the question was inconsistent. For example, in December 1845, after Indian merchants had asked the Consul for British protection,[55] the British East India Company schemed to encourage all British subjects to carry a passport whenever they travelled abroad or a certificate acknowledging their entitlement to British protection, and a notice informing them of that was sent to many of the sea ports under British control.[56] However, no definition was given either of the format of the passport or of how the policy was to be communicated, so its actual effect is questionable. A letter written by Ward in 1851, five years after the notice supposedly came into effect, reveals that Kachchh people sailing to Zanzibar were prohibited by the Bombay Government from hoisting the British flag and were instead requested to carry certification issued by the Rāo and to hoist his flag.[57]

While the debates were heated in the 1840s, as this section shows, records from the next decade say very little about the matter—for several reasons. As regards British authority, from around 1853 the

Sultan, who previously had opportunistically handed jurisdiction over Indian merchants to the British Consul,[58] began to make statements which acknowledged such merchants as British subjects.[59] In addition, Ward left Zanzibar in 1852 to return to the United States, and after the Calfaun case no American merchants or Consuls were parties to any major dispute involving bankruptcy and Indian merchants.[60] Nonetheless, such apparent tranquillity does not mean that the legal status of Indian merchants had finally been settled; indeed, the same uncertainty remained throughout the 1850s, as various contemporary documents relating to trade along the Mrima Coast attest.[61]

The uncertainty of the Indians' legal status was a product of the delicate balance among commercial considerations, political aims and the recognition of various parties, and served to support the 'dual protection' claimed and exploited by Indian merchants.

Slave Emancipation in 1860

The uncertain position of the Indian merchants nevertheless remained stable, until, in 1860, it was shaken in what turned out to be the beginning of the end for dual protection. On 10 February 1860, the British Consul informed 'all the British subjects residing in the Zanzibar Dominions' that:

> Whereas by a proclamation issued seventeen years ago, His Highness the late Sultan Syed Said bin Sultan expressly forbid all his subjects to sell any slaves to any natives of India, and also to buy any slaves from any natives of India residing in any part of his Dominions.
>
> And whereas the purchase or sale of slaves by British subjects in any part of the world has been forbidden by the British Government under the severest penalties.
>
> Nevertheless Banians and other natives of India residing in the Zanzibar Dominions have continued to buy and sell slaves up to the present time; I do hereby give notice that if any slaves are found in the possession of any native of India after the expiration of one month from the present date, he will be dealt with as the law directs. All natives of India who now possess slaves are hereby directed to take them before the Cazee [*qāḍī*; magistrate] and procure the legal certificate of emancipation.

> Any native of India who shall bring a slave to Zanzibar from the coast of Africa or from any other country, or who shall in any way assist in the traffic in slaves, by advancing money to slave dealers, or by conveying slaves in their boats or Buggalows, or by receiving slaves in pawn or pledge, will be fined one Hundred Dollars for each offence, and sent as a prisoner to Bombay.[62]

Christopher P. Rigby, the British Consul for Zanzibar, thereby implemented the first British-led emancipation of slaves in the territories of the local polities around the western Indian Ocean.[63] Rigby adopted even stricter measures from February 1860 onwards. In his dispatch of 11 February 1860 to the Secretary to the Bombay Government, he reported on the progress of his operation.[64] First, he had arrested a British subject called Kanoo Munjee for having 69 slaves on his plantation; the slaves were placed under Rigby's protection. Second, he had issued a notice warning all British subjects that if any slaves were found in their possession after the expiry of one month, their owners would suffer a penalty in accordance with the law.[65] Third, Rigby had also requested Mājid to issue a notice similar to that of Saʿīd in 1843, warning all his subjects against trading in slaves with any natives of India.[66] The Sultan had accepted Rigby's request, and following the warning to British subjects, slaves rushed en masse to the British Consulate, where Rigby issued them with certificates of manumission. The actual number of slaves manumitted at that time is difficult to establish with any certainty, but a reasonable estimate would be no more than 5221.[67]

Rigby explained that manumission was in fact a gesture. He noted that if such a large number of slaves had been turned loose at the same time and therefore been required to leave the protection of their owners, it would have been very difficult for them to survive.[68] Recognizing that, Rigby oversaw arrangements between owners and slaves, under which an owner was required to furnish slaves with a part of his plantation for the slaves' own use, where they could cultivate their own piece of land for 3 days a week, and work for their owner on the rest of the plantation for the remaining 4 days.[69] The other reason for the low regard in which Rigby's manumission campaign was held was that it did not last, because as a result of his poor health Rigby could not adequately supervise its progress. After he left Zanzibar, '[t]he whole transaction was found to be a dead letter'.[70]

Although Rigby's manumission campaign was restricted to slaves owned by British Indian subjects and, in the long run, had no great effect on slave-holding, it certainly caused disruption to the local economy. For example, William G. Webb, an American merchant, wrote to a colleague, one Lewis Cass, on 1 September 1860, reporting that Rigby's notice 'has had a very injurious effect upon business having caused a great excitement among the natives'.[71] In fact, the value of plantations on both Zanzibar and Pemba declined dramatically—and both islands were heavily dependent on the plantation economy. The value of a plantation on either island customarily included the slaves living on it,[72] but the notices issued by both Rigby and Mājid strictly prohibited slave trading with Indian residents. Furthermore, the following year Rigby issued another notice, which stated even more precisely that Indian residents were prohibited from owning slaves whom they had purchased along with plantations.[73] With those notices, it became difficult to trade in commercial property in the usual manner, so values collapsed. For example, the value of one such property declined from 30,000 MT$ in February 1860 prior to the issue of the notices, to 8000 MT$ after it.[74] Such a dramatic fall in plantation values affected not only Indian residents but many Arabs too, because they were in the habit of pledging their properties as security to obtain loans from Indian moneylenders.[75]

Moreover, Rigby fined owners between 10 MT$ and 20 MT$ for compensation and expenses after manumission if their slaves claimed they had been badly used or were clearly suffering from hunger or maltreatment.[76] Several individual owners were punished; for example, one Banian merchant was given 40 lashes for selling two female slaves and was subsequently expelled from East African territory of the Bū Saʿīd and ordered to pay 20 MT$ to each of the slaves.[77] At Kwale, another Banian merchant was imprisoned for a year and ordered to pay 150 MT$ for the land given to the slaves because he had purchased four child slaves.[78] Under such circumstances, it is no wonder that many Indians living along the East African coast made haste to ask the Sultan for his protection.[79]

More critical consequences related to the matter of British subjectship. Rigby imposed on all Indian merchants the obligation to accept the jurisdiction of the British Consulate, which, of course, permitted them to claim its protection as British subjects.[80] At the same time, because Rigby tackled the problem of slave ownership by Indian merchants in a much more industrious manner than his predecessor, Hamerton, one criticism made by Ward concerning the contradiction between Indian merchants owning slaves and their seeking British protection was rendered invalid.

After the Slave Emancipation

After the relative tranquillity of the 1850s, the emancipation of 1860 triggered further developments concerning the legal status of Indian merchants along the East African coast. At this stage, one of the most important responsibilities of the British Consulate in Zanzibar was to suppress the slave trade and slavery. This present section therefore discusses the progress made in these areas with regard to Indian traders and owners.

Before Rigby left Zanzibar to receive medical treatment, he asked the American Consul to look after 'British subjects' until his successor arrived.[81] However, soon after Rigby's departure a number of Indian merchants sought and received the protection of Mājid.[82] Although Lewis Pelly (r. 1861–1862) and R. Lambert Playfair (r. 1862–1865), Rigby's successors, seldom referred to the legal status of Indians in their own writings, Mājid wrote that just after arriving at Zanzibar, Pelly summoned all British subjects to the consulate for registration.[83] Playfair too, according to Mājid, drew up another register of British subjects residing in Majid's territory and submitted it to him, informing him that no persons other than those on the register and those born in British territory could receive British protection in Mājid's territory; this was reconfirmed by both parties.[84] Furthermore, this was ratified at the Court of Osborne House on 9 August 1866.[85] The ratification amounted to an official admission by the British Government that Indian merchants along the east coast of Africa whose names were not on Playfair's register would not be regarded as British subjects.

Nonetheless, the merchants maintained the ambiguity of their legal status even after the registers had been compiled. Henry A. Churchill (r. 1865–1870), Playfair's successor, revealed in one of his letters that within two years of Rigby leaving Zanzibar the Indian merchants under the protection of the Sultan had begun to purchase slaves while at the same time bringing their families from India to register as British subjects.[86] In other words, albeit indirectly, they again sought to obtain dual protection. As a consequence, some of those under British protection were prosecuted at the Consular Court for owning slaves, but their cases were rejected because the accused could claim that the slaves did not in fact belong to them but to family members who were under the protection of the Sultan.[87]

That strategy on the part of the Indian merchants must be distinguished from what they did in the 1840s. Then, each of them had dual protection as individuals, now they retained dual protection not as individuals but as family groups. In such circumstances, they were again able to trade in and own slaves, and to trade along the Mrima Coast while enjoying British protection.[88]

Faced with this new strategy, the British Consulate needed to overcome certain legal obstacles to prevent their subjects owning or trading in slaves. First, they had officially acknowledged that Indian merchants whose names were not on the register were not British subjects. (Mājid accordingly refused to submit the Indian merchants under his protection to the jurisdiction of the British Consul.[89]) In addition, it was also officially ruled that several native Kachchh living in Mājid's territory were not British subjects and therefore not entitled to British protection, and even these Kachchhīs were noticed it by the British Consul.[90] Nonetheless, third, according to the criterion of British India, natives of Kachchh were not actually British subjects, but subjects of the Rāo of Kachchh.[91] Therefore, if those Indian merchants who had been forced to release their slaves at Rigby's insistence in 1860 were to realize that, there was every possibility that they would require compensation for their losses.[92] In other words, the British authorities were no longer able to agree with Rigby that all Indian merchants should be regarded simply as 'British subjects' and thus forbidden to own and trade in slaves. However, at the same time, unless Indian merchants were subject to British jurisdiction it would be difficult indeed to control slave ownership and trading among them; even attempting to do so would bring with it the risk of incurring claims for compensation.

The British Consulate on Zanzibar, the Foreign Office in London and the Bombay Government (the Government of India) discussed the matter and resolved the problem in the following way. The British Consul in Bhuj asked the Rāo of Kachchh to deliver the declaration prohibiting the slave trade. On 1 Vaishāf 1925 (according to the Vīkram calendar; 24 April 1869 according to the Gregorian calendar) the Rāo duly declared to his subjects residing along the East African coast and engaging in the slave trade that they should deliver up their slaves to the British Consulate and should not demand any compensation.[93] For the purpose of the declaration, the British argued that the Rāo should not enter into diplomatic relations with other countries because of his treaty with Britain, and also that since the Rāo was himself subject to British control, the British Government could assume responsibility for those of his subjects residing in those territories which the Rāo could not control directly.[94] On this occasion, certain Indian merchants who refused to hand over their slaves declared their allegiance to the Sultan and were later referred to as the 'Sultan's Hindees'.[95]

Conclusion

This chapter directly addresses the question of the legal status of Indian merchants along the East African coast and describes the development of its solution. It soon becomes apparent that it was far from a simple situation with all the power on one side, as might have been expected, nor was any real resolution reached by any attempts at dialogue between the British authorities and the Indian merchants themselves. Instead, the British response was neither unidirectional, nor was Britain's power sufficiently overarching to allow its authorities to reach a resolution alone. Rather, the question developed within a complex pattern of action and reaction by Indian merchants, local rulers, European and American merchants and officials, and the British authorities. In other words, the process reveals the agency of a variety of actors. Of course, we must not ignore the agency of merchants who protested against the efforts of the Customs Master to force them to agree that they were subjects solely of the Sultan or who thought up new strategies to ensure they could retain 'dual protection'. However, nor should we overestimate their role. Continued 'dual protection' was made possible by conflicting commercial aims and the varying political intentions of the involved parties. The British administrative system was not yet firmly established, and it was shaken by those other agencies, one of which was, of course, embodied by the merchants themselves. In other words, this case study shows that the system by which the British Empire was run was far from fully robust, and debates could be triggered among not only imperial officials and their subjects or their supposed subjects, but also those around them, such as the American Consul, American merchants, the sultans of Zanzibar and the Rāo of Kachchh.

To end this chapter, let us return to the statement quoted at the beginning of it. It reflects a sentiment that Kirk will have found agreeable: British 'influence was in all matters paramount'; but as the cases presented here have shown, if that was so it was the result of a conjunction among of multiple agencies in politics and commerce on the East African coast during the nineteenth century.

Notes

1. PPEM MH201/4 [Ropes to Secretary of State, Zanzibar, 2 August 1869].
2. Chhaya Goswami, *The Call of the Sea: Kachchhi Traders in Muscat and Zanzibar, c. 1800–1880*, Hyderabad: Orient Black Swan, 2011, 263–269.
3. For earlier activities of Indian merchants along the coast south of Cape Delgado, see Pedro Machado, *Ocean of Trade*.
4. Albrand, 'Extrait', 73.
5. For Kachchhī Bhatiyā, see Makrand Maheta, *Gujarātīo ane pūrva Āphrikā, 1850–1960: Gujarātīopaānī shodhamām*, Amdāvāda: Darshaka Itihāsa Nidhi, 2001, 63. For the transition among the Indian population in Zanzibar, see Sheriff, *Slaves, Spices and Ivory*, 148, Table 4.8.
6. See, for example, T. Smee, 'Observations during a Voyage of Research on the East Coast of Africa, from Cape Guardafi South to the Island of Zanzibar, in the H.C.'s Cruiser Ternate (Captain T. Smee) and Sylph Schooner (Lieutenant Hardy)', in Burton, *Zanzibar*, Vol. 2, 494.
7. Burton, *Zanzibar*, Vol. 1, 328–329; Jagjit S. Mangat, *A History of the Asians in East Africa c. 1886 to 1945*, Oxford: Clarendon Press, 1969, 2–3, 15–18.
8. CAOM FM/SG/OIND/2/10 (2), No. 4, 49.
9. Ibid., 50–51.
10. Ibid., 50.
11. Burton, *Zanzibar*, Vol. 1, 316–317. See also Mangat, *A History of the Asians*, 7; Cynthia Salvadori, *Through Open Doors: A View of Asian Cultures in Kenya*, Nairobi: Kenway Publications, 1989 (1st. 1983), 8; Sheriff, *Slaves, Spices and Ivory*, 146–148.
12. NAUK FO84/1344/129-132 [Annex No. 1 in Kirk to Secretary of State for Foreign Affairs, Zanzibar, 14 January 1871].
13. NAUK FO84/1344/129 [Annex No. 1 in Kirk to Secretary of State for Foreign Affairs, Zanzibar, 14 January 1871].
14. NAUK FO84/1344/131 [Annex No. 1 in Kirk to Secretary of State for Foreign Affairs, Zanzibar, 14 January 1871].
15. NAUK FO84/1344/132 [Annex No. 1 in Kirk to Secretary of State for Foreign Affairs, Zanzibar, 14 January 1871].
16. NAUK FO84/1344/129 [Annex No. 1 in Kirk to Secretary of State for Foreign Affairs, Zanzibar, 14 January 1871].

17. NAUK FO84/1344/131 [Annex No. 1 in Kirk to Secretary of State for Foreign Affairs, Zanzibar, 14 January 1871].
18. NAUK FO84/1344/132 [Annex No. 1 in Kirk to Secretary of State for Foreign Affairs, Zanzibar, 14 January 1871].
19. James Burnes, *A Sketch of the History of Cutch*, New Delhi: Asian Educational Services, 2004 (1st 1839, Edinburgh: Bell and Bradfute), 57–68; James M. Campbell (ed.), *Gazetteer of the Bombay Presidency, Volume 5: Cutch, Palanpur, Mahi Kantha*, Bombay: Government Central Press, 1880, 157–164. For the articles of the treaty which was concluded on that occasion, see NAUK FO881/2314/3-5.
20. Bennett and Brooks, Jr (eds.), *New England Merchants*, 467 [Ward to Clayton, Zanzibar, 20 July 1850].
21. He served as resident agent for the London firm of Newman, Hunt and Christopher during the 1830s (Reda Bhacker, *Trade and Empire*, 161).
22. MAHA PD/1841/46-1261/316/122 [Norsworthy to Richmond, Zanzibar, 12 September 1841].
23. NAUK FO54/4/187-190 [Hamerton to Willoughby, Zanzibar, 28 September 1841].
24. NAUK FO54/4/191 [Hamerton to Willoughby, Zanzibar, 28 September 1841].
25. NAUK FO54/4/190 [Hamerton to Willoughby, Zanzibar, 28 September 1841]. Apparently, no further enforcement occurred, since it was obvious that revenues would decrease dramatically if they left the island.
26. NAUK FO54/4/190-191 [Hamerton to Willoughby, Zanzibar, 28 September 1841].
27. Following Norsworthy's complaint, Hamerton investigated the close relationship between these two men (MAHA PD/1841/46-1261/316/49-55 [Hamerton to Willoughby, Zanzibar, 13 July 1841]; ibid., 148–152 [Hamerton to Willoughby, Zanzibar, 3 February 1842]).
28. Bennett and Brooks, Jr (eds.), *New England Merchants*, 223 [Waters to Waters, Zanzibar, 17 December 1839].
29. Ibid., 380 [Ward to Buchanan, Zanzibar, 7 March 1847].
30. Ibid., 480 [Ward to Abbot, Kennebunkport, 13 March 1851].
31. For the text, see ibid., 549–551 [The Treaty of 1833 between the United States and Said bin Sultan].
32. For example, the Sultan wrote a letter in 1847 to the President of the United States asking the Americans not to trade along the Mrima Coast (NAUS RG84/Zanzibar/80/n.p. [Buchanan to Ward, Washington, 7 October 1847]). See also AMAE CCC/Zanzibar/1/197 [Romain-Desfossés-MAE, Station navale de Bourbon, 19 November 1844]; NAUK FO54/12/35 [Hamerton to Palmerston, Zanzibar, 15 December 1848]; 'Abd al-Fattāḥ Ḥasan Abū 'Alīyah, *Mukhtārāt min*

wathā'iq tārīkh 'umān al-ḥadīth: qurā'a fī wathā'iq al-arshīf al-amrīkī, al-Riyādh: Dār al-Marrīkh, 1984, 45–46 [McMullan to Marcy, Zanzibar, 21 February 1846]; Bennett and Brooks, Jr (eds.), *New England Merchants*, 381–385 [Ward to Buchanan, Zanzibar, 13 March 1847].

33. According to the letter written by Ward (Bennett and Brooks, Jr (eds.), *New England Merchants*, 467 [Ward to Clayton, Zanzibar, 20 July 1850]), Sa'īd recognized people from Kachchh as subjects of the Rāo and took them under his special protection. Although I have been unable to find any further information on this treaty, an official close to the Rāo clearly mentions that the Rāo's *darbār* could not protect his subjects living on the east African coast. (NAUK FO881/2314/16 [Memorandum on the Connexion of Indian Traders on the Eastern Coast of Africa with the Slave Trade, by Kazi Shahabudin, Dewan of the Rāo of Kutch, London, 14 February 1870]).
34. MAHA PD/1841/46-1261/316/122-123 [Norsworthy to Richmond, Zanzibar, 12 September 1841].
35. See, for example, NAUK FO54/14/119 [Makusbury to Hamerton, s.l., 11 September 1852]. In a letter to his successor, Rigby also mentioned 'a long list' of complaints concerning Arabs made by British subjects to the British Consulate on Zanzibar (NAUK FO800/234/62 [Rigby to anon., Zanzibar, 4 September 1861]).
36. NAUK FO54/10/27 [Hamerton to the Earl of Aberdeen, Zanzibar, 24 September 1846].
37. Mangat, *A History of the Asians*, 4.
38. MAHA PD/1841/46-1261/316/122 [Norsworthy to Richmond, Zanzibar, 12 September 1841]; NAUK FO54/12/35 [Hamerton to Palmerston, Zanzibar, 15 December 1848]; Bennett and Brooks, Jr (eds.), *New England Merchants*, 382–383 [Ward to Buchanan, Zanzibar, 13 March 1847].
39. Bennett and Brooks, Jr (eds.), *New England Merchants*, 377 [Ward to Buchanan, Zanzibar, 7 March 1847].
40. Ibid., 376–381, 413–414 [Ephraim A. Emmerton's Journal, 8 October 1848]; Norman R. Bennett, 'Americans in Zanzibar, 1865-1915: Part II', *Tanganyika Notes and Records* 57 (1961), 122–123.
41. Bennett and Brooks, Jr (eds.), *New England Merchants*, 378 [Ward to Buchanan, Zanzibar, 7 March 1847]; ibid., 414 [Ephraim A. Emmerton's Journal, 8 October 1848].
42. Ibid., 379 [Ward to Buchanan, Zanzibar, 7 March 1847].
43. Ibid., 381 [Said b. Sultan to Ward, Zanzibar, 28 February 1847].
44. NAUS RG84/Zanzibar/80/n.p. [Buchanan to Ward, Washington, 7 October 1847].

45. Ephraim A. Emmerton's journal, which mentions this affair, claims that the Sultan repaid Calfaun's debt (Bennett and Brooks, Jr (eds.), *New England Merchants*, 414 [Ephraim A. Emmerton's Journal, 8 October 1848]).
46. In his letters to the American Government, Ward repeatedly complained about the Sultan's wait-and-see attitude to this affair (ibid., 374 [Ward to Buchanan, Zanzibar, 6 March 1847], 379 [Ward to Buchanan, Zanzibar, 7 March 1847]).
47. Ibid., 414 [Ephraim A. Emmerton's Journal, 8 October 1848].
48. Ibid., 414–415.
49. Ibid., 467–468 [Ward to Clayton, Zanzibar, 20 July 1850], 484 [Ward to Shepard, Kennebunkport, 15 May 1851].
50. Ibid., 467–468 [Ward to Clayton, Zanzibar, 20 July 1850].
51. Ibid., 484 [Ward to Shepard, Kennebunkport, 15 May 1851].
52. Ibid., 383–384 [Ward to Buchanan, Zanzibar, 13 March 1847].
53. CMS missionary Krapf was faced with a similar view. When he met the governor (probably equivalent to *diwani* in Kiswahili) of Buyeni, south of Pangani, in February 1850, he was asked whether only British natives benefited from the protection of the British Consul on Zanzibar, or whether that protection extended to all people who sought his protection (Krapf, *Travels, Researches and Missionary Labours*, 418).
54. Bennett and Brooks, Jr (eds.), *New England Merchants*, 380 [Ward to Buchanan, Zanzibar, 7 March 1847].
55. NAUK FO54/10/111 [Melyn to Addington, India Board, 9 February 1846].
56. NAUK FO54/10/132–136 [Gocelyn to anon., India Board, 26 March 1846].
57. Bennett and Brooks, Jr (eds.), *New England Merchants*, 480 [Ward to Abbot, Kennebunkport, 13 March 1851].
58. For example, ibid., 380 [Ward to Buchanan, Zanzibar, 7 March 1847]; ibid., 414 [Ephraim A. Emmerton's Journal, 8 October 1848].
59. Ibid., 497 [McMullan to Marcy, Zanzibar, 7 December 1853].
60. See, for example, ibid., 490 [Webb, Jelly and Masury to Aulick, Zanzibar, 5 December 1851].
61. See, for example, ibid., 479–480 [Ward to Abbot, Kennebunkport, 13 March 1851].
62. MAHA PD/1860/159/830/251-253 [Notice to All the British Subjects Residing in the Zanzibar Dominions, 10 February 1860]. A typed duplicate is in NAUK FO881/2314/8; it is dated 15 February.
63. For details, see Suzuki, 'Enslaved Population and Indian Owners', 212–217. Also, for a comparison between him and his predecessor, Atkins Hamerton, see Nwulia, *Britain and Slavery in East Africa*, 66–67.

64. MAHA PD/1860/159/830/219-224.
65. This notice was issued on 10 February 1860. It also ordered Indian residents to bring all their slaves to *qāḍī* to be issued with manumission certificates; if involvement in slave dealing were proved the violator would be charged 100 MT$ and sent to Bombay (MAHA PD/1860/159/830/251-253 [Notice to All the British Subjects Residing in the Zanzibar Dominions, 10 February 1860]). NAUK FO881/2314/8 contains a typed duplicate, dated 15 February. Since the document in MAHA is in Rigby's own writing, 10 February must be considered the correct date.
66. See also Russell, *General Rigby*, 86.
67. Suzuki, 'Enslaved Population and Indian Owners', 214.
68. MAHA PD/1860/159/830/205 [Rigby to Anderson, Zanzibar, 21 March 1860]. The same document is located in NAUK FO881/2314/9; ZZBA AA12/2/48.
69. MAHA PD/1860/159/830/205-206 [Rigby to Anderson, Zanzibar, 21 March 1860]. The same document is located in NAUK FO881/2314/9; ZZBA AA12/2/48. The system was quite similar to that of apprenticeship mentioned in Section 5 of the 1833 Abolition Act (3 & 4 Will. 4 c.73), though Rigby did not clearly state the relationship between the two.

    Similar cases where slaves were regularly given days off are frequently noted in documents from a later period. See references in Cooper, *Plantation Slavery*, 159, n. 23. Nonetheless, it was not Rigby's manumission campaign that brought such a custom to this region, for it had existed as early as the mid-1830s when William S.W. Ruschenberger, a surgeon in the US Navy, observed a similar custom on Zanzibar. See William S.W. Ruschenberger, *A Voyage round the World; including An Embassy to Muscat and Siam, in 1835, 1836, and 1837*, Philadelphia: Lea Carey and Blanchard, 1938, 34–35.
70. New, *Life, Wanderings and Labours*, 36. See also NAUK FO881/2314/17-18 [Churchill to Gonne, Zanzibar, s.l., 22 December 1867].
71. Bennett and Brooks, Jr (eds.), *New England Merchants*, 512.
72. ZZBA AA12/29/34 [Hamerton to Secretary to Bombay Government, Zanzibar, 13 July 1841].
73. NAUK FO800/234/83 [Pelly to Forbes, Zanzibar, 12 February 1862]; NAUK FO881/2314/13 [Rigby to Forbes, Zanzibar, 12 July 1861].
74. NAUK FO800/234/83 [Pelly to Forbes, Zanzibar, 12 February 1862]; NAUK FO881/2314/14 [Pelly to the Bombay Government, Zanzibar, 1 February 1862].
75. ZZBA AA12/29/64 [Hamerton to Secretary to Bombay Government, Zanzibar, 9 December 1843].

76. MAHA PD/1860/159/830/206-207 [Rigby to Anderson, Zanzibar, 21 March 1860]. The same document is located in NAUK FO881/2314/9; ZZBA AA12/2/48.
77. MAHA PD/1860/159/830/270 [Rigby to Anderson, Zanzibar, 14 September 1860]. The same document is located in ZZBA AA12/2/57.
78. MAHA PD/1860/159/830/270-271 [Rigby to Anderson, Zanzibar, 14 September 1860]. The same document is located in ZZBA AA12/2/57.
79. OIOC IOR/L/P&S/18/B90/17 [Churchill to Gonne, s.l., 22 December 1867] (the same document is in NAUK FO881/2314/17); NAUK FO84/1325/71 [Churchill to Clarendon, Zanzibar, 18 January 1870]. ZZBA AA12/2/48-9 [Outward letter by Rigby to Bombay, 21 March 1860] states the situation as follows:
The emancipation of so many slaves has caused considerable excitement here, and the owners endeavoured to evade compliance with the order in every way. For some days they threatened to stop all trade if their slaves were emancipated; some denied being British subjects; others disguised themselves as Arabs…
80. As a result, several Indian merchants relinquished their claim to be British subjects (ZZBA AA12/2/49 [Rigby to the Bombay Government, Zanzibar, 21 March 1860]).
81. NAUK FO800/234/65 [Rigby to anon., Zanzibar, 4 September 1861]; NAUS RG84/Zanzibar/12/n.p. [Webb to Rigby, Island of Zanzibar, 5 September 1861]; ibid., n.p. [Webb to Leonard, 19 September 1861].
82. OIOC IOR/L/P&S/18/B90/17 [Churchill to Gonne, s.l., 22 December 1867] (the same document can be found at NAUK FO881/2314/17); NAUK FO84/1325/71 [Churchill to Clarendon, Zanzibar, 18 January 1870]; NAUK FO881/2314/51 [Kirk to Gonne, s.l., 16 August 1869].
83. NAUK FO881/2314/21 [Majid to Churchill, Zanzibar, 23 Shaban 1284/21 December 1867].
84. Ibid., The same fact was repeated by the embassy sent by Mājid to Bombay in 1869 (ibid., 49 [Extract from a translation of a petition from Syud Hamud bin Sooleyman and Shaikh Mahomed bin Shaikh Abdulla, Envoys from His Highness Syud Majid, Sultan of Zanzibar, to his Excellency the Right Honourable Sir Seymour V. Fitzgerald, Governor of Bombay, dated and received 23 June 1869]). Henry A. Churchill, Playfair's successor, criticized his two predecessors for not insisting, as Hamerton and Rigby had done, that the Indian merchants who did not register would still be regarded as subjects entitled to British protection (OIOC IOR/L/P&S/18/B90/18 [Churchill to Gonne, s.l., 22 December 1867]). The same document can be found in NAUK FO881/2314/18. Beachey, *The Slave Trade*, 56–57, also points out the weak policy of Pelly and Playfair in relation to anti-slave trade activities.

85. NAUK FO54/23/88-90 [Extract from the *London Gazette* of Friday, 10 August 1866].
86. OIOC IOR/L/P&S/18/B90/17-18 [Churchill to Gonne, s.l., 22 December 1867]. The same document can be found at NAUK FO881/2314/17-8.
87. OIOC IOR/L/P&S/18/B90/17-18 [Churchill to Gonne, s.l., 22 December 1867]. The same document can be found at NAUK FO881/2314/17-18.
88. Mājid mentioned in the presence of the British Consul that he allowed the Indian merchants under his protection to possess slaves and engage in slave trading (OIOC IOR/L/P&S/18/B90/18-19 [Churchill to Gonne, s.l., 22 December 1867]. See also, ibid., 21 [Majid to Churchill, 16 December 1867)]).
89. OIOC IOR/L/P&S/18/B90/49 [Extract translation of a petition from Syud Hamud bin Sooleyman and Shaikh Mahomed bin Shaikh Abdulla, Envoys from His Highness Syud Majid, Sultan of Zanzibar, to his Excellency the Right Honourable Sir Seymour V. Fitzgerald, Governor of Bombay, dated and received 23 June 1869]; ibid., 52 [Kirk to Gonne, s.l., 16 August 1869].
90. OIOC IOR/L/P&S/18/B90/22 [Gonne to Foreign Secretary, India, Bombay Castle, 31 March 1868].
91. OIOC IOR/L/P&S/18/B90/25 [Churchill to Gonne, s.l., 14 August 1868]; ibid., 29 [Temple to SGB, Fort William, 22 April 1868].
92. OIOC IOR/L/P&S/18/B90/25 [Churchill to Gonne, s.l., 14 August 1868].
93. NAUK FO84/1307/342-4 [Translation of a Proclamation dated 24th April 1869 by His Highness the Rao of Kutch to his subjects]. NAUK FO881/2314/41-42 contains the same document.
94. For the debates preceding the preparation of this declaration, see NAUK FO881/2314/22 [Gonne to the Foreign Secretary, India, Bombay Castle, 31 March 1868]; ibid., 26 [Seton-Karr to Gonne, s.l., 6 November 1868]; ibid., 42 [Shortt to Gonne, Bhooji, 1 February 1869]; ibid., 45 [Gonne to the Political Agent and Consul on Zanzibar, Bombay Castle, 17 April 1869]. See also NAUK FO84/1307/342-4 [Translation of a Proclamation dated 24th April 1869 by His Highness the Rao of Kutch to his subjects]; NAUK FO881/2314/44 [Gonne to the Political Agent, Zanzibar, Bombay Castle, 22 February 1869]; ibid., 49–50 [Gonne to Hamud bin Sooleyman and Shaik Mahomed bin Shaik Abdoolla, Bombay Castle, 28 July 1869]; ibid., 52 [Kirk to Gonne, s.l., 16 August 1869].
95. Thomas R. Metcalf, *Imperial Connections: India in the Indian Ocean Arena, 1860–1920*, Berkeley: University of California Press, 2007, 168.

CHAPTER 9

Beyond the Horizon: The Agency of Dhow Traders, *L'Acte de Francisation* and International Politics in the Western Indian Ocean, c. 1860–1900

Introduction

Confrontation between slave transporters and their suppressors in the western Indian Ocean became rather like a never-ending game of cat and mouse, as the would-be suppressors amended existing treaties and strengthened systems of naval patrol, while the transporters found new ways to evade the meshes of their nets. The latter fully utilized their sailing skills and knowledge of the sea as well as their legal knowledge, and carefully observed international relationships, which changed rapidly. The focus of this penultimate chapter will be the protection afforded the transporters by the French flag. At the end of south–west monsoon season in 1863, British Acting Political Agent in Zanzibar, R. Lambert Playfair, wrote a report to Foreign Minister Lord Russell:

> 1. I have the honor to bring to your Lordship's notice, a new phase in the slave trade on this coast, which threatens to paralize the operations of our cruizers for its suppression.
>
> 2. The Soori Arabs have had recourse to every possible expedient to escape the search of our vessels: last season, instead of coasting northwards, according to their usual custom, they sailed in small fleets and stood out to sea, every eight or ten boats being provided with a person qualified to navigate out of light of land. This will hardly succeed a second year, and of that they are well aware, and some new expedient is necessary.

H. Suzuki, *Slave Trade Profiteers in the Western Indian Ocean*, Palgrave Series in Indian Ocean World Studies,
DOI 10.1007/978-3-319-59803-1_9

> 3. This they have found in the protection of the French flag; they are well aware that under it the right of search is denied to us, and it has now become the great object of their disire to obtain a French register.[1]

The following year, Playfair again cautioned that French flag could be abused to enable the carrying of slaves[2]; his anxiety turned out to be well founded, for the flag proved to be a major obstacle to British anti-slave trade operations right up to the early twentieth century. However, it was also the last remaining effective method for the transporters in their battle against the suppression of the slave trade.

The matter of French registration of vessels has been mentioned in several studies focusing on regions around the western Indian Ocean, particularly in relation to the slave trade and its suppression.[3] However, the problem was not isolated and regional but was truly a western Indian Ocean-wide phenomenon. It was a strategy used off the west coast of Madagascar, in the harbours of the East African coast and off the Horn of Africa as well as in the Gulf of Oman and the Persian Gulf. Nonetheless, the western Indian Ocean seems still small enough to cover the entire mise en scène of this story, the last act of which was played out roughly 6000 km away from Madagascar, in the Permanent Court of Arbitration in Den Haag.

Protection Under the Tricolour: Its Development and Privileges

As an appendix to his letter to the second Earl Russell (John F.S. Russell) quoted at the beginning of this chapter, Playfair attached a list of French flagged ships anchored at Zanzibar at the time of his writing (Table 9.1).

We cannot be sure of the exact date local slavers began to hoist the French flag, but it is practically certain they would have been doing so well before Playfair's report. Indeed, Rigby's journal for 28 February 1861 mentions an Arab ship which had sailed from Mauritius to Kilwa and, according to him,[4] hoisted the French flag 'for facilities of slave trading'.[5] Rigby also frequently reported slave transport by ships flying the French flag around the Comoros Islands,[6] with his report of 4 May 1861 to the Minister of India suggesting that the flag was deliberately being used to facilitate this.[7] Other reports by the Royal Navy show that after the start of the north-east monsoon season in 1858 dhows carried a

Table 9.1 Local ships flying the French flag and anchoring at Stone Town, september 1863

Type of ships	*Owner*	*Origin of owner*	*Note*
Buggalow	Mahommed b. Nasir	Ṣūr	He had never resided in any French colony and had only visited Nosy Be for the purpose of trade
Buggalow	Ahmed b. Saeed	Ṣūr	——
Burden	Ahmed b. Salim	Ṣūr	The owner was known to have taken a cargo of slaves from this coast to Soor in 1860; Colonel Rigby reported this fact to H.M. Seyed Majid
Buggalow	Mahommed Mobarak & Saleem	Ṣūr	The former was a notorious slave dealer and had a contract with Mr. Mas for the supply of slaves for the Cuban market; he had eleven boats engaged in this trade
Buggalow	Mahommed b. Ahmed	Ras al-Ḥadd	——
Ganja	Salim Saeed el-Hajeree	Ṣūr	He was known to have taken a cargo of 200 slaves from Keelwa
Buggalow	Waleed Esh-sheevi	Ṣūr	——
Buggalow	Rashid el-Murzooki	Ṣūr	——
Ganja	Mahommed b. Ahmed Bardthawan	Shiḥr	He was a notorious slave dealer, belonging to an even more notorious slave port
Ganja	The natives of Kutch	——	——

Source MAHA PD/1863/60/1471/155-6 (the same document is available in NAUK F084/1204/355-6)

large number of slaves bound for Madagascar and the Comoros Islands.[8] It is therefore entirely reasonable to surmise that a significant number of ships transporting slaves in the western Indian Ocean—enough to be noticed, at any rate—were hoisting the French flag shortly before 1860.[9] The solid evidence is that after Playfair delivered his report, more and more instances were noted of local ships hoisting the French flag, not only off the East African coast but also in the Gulf of Aden, the Red Sea, ports in Hadramaut, off Madagascar and also along the coast of the Gulf of Oman.[10]

A record entitled 'Memorandum by Mr. Churchill respecting Slave Trade on the east coast of Africa' compiled by Henry A. Churchill states that during his service as British Consul in Zanzibar (1865–1870), 20% of ships anchoring at Stone Town port flying the French flag were owned by Arabs or 'Hindus' under British protection living in Zanzibar.[11] Furthermore, E.S. Meara, captain of the *Nymphe*, which served on patrol to counter the slave trade off the western coast of Madagascar, wrote that in the 1869 season he found at least 50 ships flying the French flag, while during his cruise the previous season he had come across only ten doing so.[12] Of course, it is important not to make the simple mistake of presuming that every ship sailing under the French flag was carrying slaves.

Indeed, there were certain other privileges available to captains or owners of ships in showing the French flag and claiming French nationality for their ships. Before we consider these, however, we must confirm that even prior to 1860, when the French flag began to be seen more often in the western Indian Ocean, shipowners and captains in those waters flew a variety of flags for their own convenience, regardless of whether they were engaged in slave transport. For instance, Hamerton's report of 25 April 1844 to the Secret Committee of the East India Company reveals that a large number of ships from ports like Bombay on the Indian subcontinent or Kachchh entered Stone Town's harbour while hoisting the British flag, but without certification.[13] According to Hamerton, the main purpose was simply to pay less duty,[14] and it was far from unusual for vessels to carry more than one flag in board. Burton, for example, saw ships from Kachchh sailing for the East African coast hoisting several flags together, including the Union Jack, the red flag of the Arabs and the Ottoman crescent and star.[15] A dhow seized off Masqaṭ by the *Clive* in October 1855 with seven slaves on board was also found to be carrying four flags including the Ottoman and Arab flags.[16] As such cases show, a common practice among sailors in those waters simply to select the 'right' one from their stock of flags and run it up the mast as occasion demanded and claim that nationality for the ship.[17] The ensign most frequently reported from the early 1860s was the French one, although there were reports of Ottoman and Qajar flags too.

So, let us now enquire into the privileges available to dhows flying the French flag. An interesting Kiswahili account is found in the text introduced by Katrin Bromber:

> Persons who prefer trade in slaves often use the flag of the French to ship them, because the British are not permitted to enter only any ship that sails under the French flag. This is the reason why some Muslims are under (the protection) of the French nation. If they want to hoist the French flag they need to pay for it every year.... hoist the French flag are many Arabs who are called Wasuri. They frequently ship slaves with their vessels.[18]

It has been pointed out throughout this book that British interference might affect any dhow, regardless of whether or not it had ever had slaves on board. One of the important privileges conferred by the French flag was that it effectively blocked British interference, so it was particularly useful for slave transport, although there were other reasons too for this preference, including its distinctive visual appearance. For example, the basically red flags of the Ottomans and of the Rāo of Kachchh, resembling as they did the flag normally flown by Arab vessels, attracted the attention of both the Indian Navy and the Royal Navy.[19] Therefore, British naval officers took precautions against ships flying red flags because, naturally enough, the navy had suspicions that such ships might be carrying slaves; moreover, they could be seized easily and readily destroyed, if necessary.[20] The following example describes a case of that sort. In 1861, *Sidon* seized what appeared to be a Zanzibari dhow sailing under a red flag. Since *Sidon* had permission to search for Zanzibari ships, she escorted the dhow to Stone Town port where it was investigated thoroughly. It then became clear that the dhow in question was not a Zanzibari, but a dhow to which the Pasha of Jidda (Jeddah) and al-Baṣra had granted formal Ottoman registration.[21] The British Consul at Zanzibar formally admonished the captain of *Sidon*,[22] and eventually the case was settled after the payment of compensation of £5771 10*s.* 6*d.*[23] The captain of the *Sidon* frankly admitted that his mistake was due to the misleading appearance of the vessel's flag.[24] Unsurprisingly, although compensation was paid in this case, the risk of meeting such a difficulty made local captains and sailors reluctant to fly a red-coloured flag, whether or not they had slaves on board or even took part in the trade at all. A leader of the Arab community in Marodoka, on Nosy Be Island, told a French naval officer that seamen there no longer hoisted red flags because British naval patrols so often inspected such vessels, causing the seamen to lose money and goods even when no infringements were discovered.[25]

Another reason to prefer the French flag was the convenient access it gave to effective protection. In the early 1860s, for example, unless they managed to reach al-Baṣra at the very end of the Persian Gulf, Ottoman ships could receive no worthwhile protection from the Ottoman Government except at a few ports around the Gulf of Aden. Similarly, the Qajarid Government was unable to offer proper protection apart from along the Iranian coast of the Persian Gulf, and even along the Arabian side of the Gulf her control was weak and speedy assistance was not to be expected. By contrast, the French had already brought Nosy Be Island and Mahore (Mayotte) Island under their protection by the beginning of the 1840s, and French Consulates were scattered about the western Indian Ocean, such as at Zanzibar, Aden, Masqaṭ and al-Baṣra. So if there were an emergency, dhows with the appropriate registration could seek consular assistance, which was usually forthcoming.

Of course, neither the Ottomans nor the Qajarids allowed the British to exercise unhindered their right of search and seizure of ships under their flags. However, as shown by the case of mistaken identity by the *Sidon* described above, for Royal Navy officers practical considerations often came before strict observance of treaties. The French, however, refused to grant the British any right to search and seize the ships under their protection, even if such ships were engaged in slave transport. The following is from the annex referred to in Article 8 about the right of search and seizure, from a treaty between Great Britain and France signed in London on 29 May 1845:

> You are not to capture, visit, or in any way interfere with vessels of France; and you will give strict instructions to the commanding officers of cruizers under your orders to abstain therefrom. At the same time you will remember that the King of the French is far from claiming that the flag of France should give immunity to those who have no right to bear it; and that Great Britain will not allow vessels of other nations to escape visit and examination by merely hoisting a French flag, or the flag of any other nation with which Great Britain has not, by existing Treaty, the right of search. Accordingly, when from intelligence which the officer commanding Her

> Majesty's cruizer may have received, or from the manoeuvres of the vessel, or other sufficient cause, he may have reason to believe that the vessel does not belong to the nation indicated by her colours, he is, if the state of the weather will admit of it, to go a-head of the suspected vessel, after communicating his intention by hailing, and to drop a boat on board of her to ascertain her nationality, without causing her detention, in the event of her really proving to be a vessel of the nation the colours of which she has displayed, and therefore one which he is not authorized to search...
>
> The commanding officers of Her Majesty's vessels must bear in mind that the duty of executing the instruction immediately preceding, must be discharged with great care and circumspection. For if any injury be occasioned by examination without sufficient cause, or by the examination being improperly conducted, compensation must be made to the party aggrieved; and the officer who may cause an examination to be made without sufficient cause, or who may conduct it improperly, will incur the displeasure of Her Majesty's Government.[26]

As that series of instructions clearly defines, if naval officers realized a vessel could claim French nationality, they must release it even if they found slaves on board. Therefore, when the naval officers of the *Nymphe*, patrolling off the western coast of Madagascar, searched over ten vessels under the French flag and were certain that slaves were on board a number of them, they could neither seize the boats in question nor rescue the slaves solely because the vessels could show proof that they were legitimately under French protection.[27]

In addition, the French were determined opponents of the British anti-slave trade patrols. When French Consulates received reports that vessels holding genuine French registration had been searched or chased by the Indian or Royal Navies, they immediately delivered formal complaints to the nearest British Consuls.[28] Once a British Consulate received an official complaint from its French counterpart, it was obliged to set up an enquiry involving the navy.[29] Individual naval officers were particularly reluctant to embark on such time-consuming investigations, because their patrols were only able to go 'bounty hunting' during a limited period each year. They were therefore reluctant to apprehend ships flying French flags.[30]

The French flag and nationality conferred another advantage, in that French ships were subject to favourable rates of duty at a number of ports on the western Indian Ocean, not only at those under French control like Nosy Be and Mahore (Mayotte), but at others, notably Zanzibar. According to a report in 1870, imported goods from the mainland coast brought by French ships were subject to 5% duty while British ships paid 10 to 15%.[31] Such privileges for ships at Zanzibar naturally made French nationality attractive to Indian merchants there, and they obtained and made use of it in their trade with the mainland. The British Consul at Zanzibar duly complained to the Sultan.[32]

To sum up, the French flag and French nationality conferred privileges which enticed local transporters to western Indian Ocean waters. The question then is: How could individuals who were clearly not French citizens obtain French protection? Playfair wanted to know the same thing.[33] He wondered whether claims of French nationality were genuine; that is, he wondered if vessels were in the habit of simply hoisting the French flag without authorization from the French. Such fraudulence and disguise are indeed frequently to be seen in documents related to the western Indian Ocean at that time.[34] Thus, I find we cannot presume that all cases reported in the sources were indeed genuine. However, as to the dhows met by the *Nymphe*, as mentioned above, many of them had in fact obtained the proper permission to fly the French flag from the French authorities and were therefore genuine. The next section explores the system concerning French nationality and reveals how it could be obtained.

L'Acte de Francisation

The reply of the French Consul at Zanzibar to the enquiry from Playfair about the boats shown in Table 9.1, stated:

> All the boats which carry the French flag are furnished with papers in proper order, delivered to them in our colonies and stating that they belong to Frenchmen (Français). Their papers are all viséd at this consulate on arrival and departure.
>
> It is true that the proprietors and commanders of these boats are all of Arab or Sowaheli origin, but I have the honor to make you aware that the condition of French citizen is obtained not only by birth, but by benefit of the law, namely by naturalization, and that a stranger, associated with a Frenchman may be the proprietor of a French ship.[35]

The 'papers in proper order' refers to the so-called *acte de francisation* which guaranteed the French nationality of local ships and authorized them to hoist the French flag.

The *acte de francisation* originated in *l'acte de navigation*, which was proclaimed on 21 September 1793 and became effective on 1 January 1794 under the First Republic. The Act was modelled on the British Navigation Acts in 1651,[36] and its main purpose was to restrict shipping between France and its colonies conducted by foreign ships. The second article of *l'acte de navigation* is about the nationality of ships:

> After 1st of January 1794, no vessel shall be deemed French, will be entitled to the privileges of the French ship, if it has not been originally built France, or in the colonies and other possessions of France, declared or made lawful prize from the enemy, or confiscated for contravention of the laws of the Republic, if it is not entirely in French, and if the officers and three quarters of the crew are not French.[37]

That Act went through various amendments and additions of articles of exception,[38] especially notable is an amendment of 1818, stating ships built outside French territory—if owned by a French citizen—could obtain French nationality under special government determination.[39] Discussions went on between colonies and protectorates and the French Government about the increase in the number of grants and the simplicity of the procedure for obtaining them.[40] Eventually, the debate led to discussion about repeal of the second article mentioned above.[41] Other restrictions on the granting of French nationality to ships were moderated; for example, in August 1861, the French Foreign Ministry sent a notice to its consulates allowing the granting of French nationality—for a fee—to ships built in the United States which had previously sailed under the American flag.[42] In French colonies and protectorates, local ships had been granted French nationality since the 1840s as long as they fulfilled certain requirements, such as the owner being a French citizen (which could include inhabitants of French colonies and protectorates), payment of a registration fee according to the weight of the ship and subject to annual renewal, and that such ships were intended for coastal navigation.

It is unclear exactly when the certification programme began to be applied to local ships in Nosy Be and Mayotte, but the earliest such document I have yet found was issued on 14 April 1861 at Helleville, the port of Nosy Be, to the *Fatalaher* (122 tons), owned by Salim b. Rashid and numbered 'Nosy Be, Mayotte and its attachment No. 172'.[43]

The main places issuing certificates of French nationality to ships in the western Indian Ocean region were Mahore (Mayotte) and Nosy Be Islands.[44] Surviving documents show that grants there were made according to the instructions of the French Government. Thus, anyone wishing to obtain such a certificate had to be a French citizen even if a local inhabitant or native of those islands. However, Table 9.1 contains individuals clearly not in that category, so grants not strictly in accordance with French law do seem to have been made. It appears, therefore, that even non-French citizens could, in certain circumstances, obtain proper French registration for their ships. It was in fact possible to obtain French registration for a ship even without taking the step of becoming naturalized French, if a French citizen who would be willing to act as co-owner of the vessel could be found. Clear evidence of this strategy can be found in an interview between Playfair and a Kachchhī who owned the last of the ships mentioned in Table 9.1. The record of interviews of non-French owners of French ships is rather exceptional. The following is the testimony of one Sewjee Mahommed:

> I am a British subject and reside usually in Kutch in Hindostan. I have lately come from the French colony of Nossé Bé. The Kanja [sic. =Ganja] *Baroongoo* now in the harbour of Zanzibar under French colors belongs half to me, and half to Suleiman Jooma, also a resident of Kutch, and as Sepoy of the Rao. The share of Suleiman was purchased with the money of a Bhattia named Keta Ludda also a resident of Kutch, and therefore I presume the last mentioned is the real owner of the second half of the Kanja. No other party has any share or interest in it. Suleiman has a wife belonging to the French settlement of Nossé Bé, but he himself is not a French subject, Suleiman obtained a French register for the said Kanja in Nossé Bé.[45]

To judge the accuracy of Sewjee Mahommed's testimony, Playfair summoned another man called Khimjee Lamjee, who was a friend of Keta Ludda, and interviewed him.[46] After all, the *Baroongoo* in question appeared to have two owners: Sewjee and Suleiman. While Suleiman had not actually spent any of his own money purchasing the vessel, for Keta Ludda had paid for it, he had a wife resident at the time on Nosy Be, so through her he had been able to obtain genuine French registration for the vessel.

Sewjee's statement is unusual in providing details of the way in which one could obtain registration. However, this case was only one of many similar cases. A letter sent from Guillois to the duc de Broglie in September 1873 implies this.[47] Guillois's letter can be summarized as follows. First, there was a high demand among Arab sailors for French ships. Second, the regulation restricting French registration to inhabitants of French colonies was easily overcame by purchasing ships after registration, by marriage with local inhabitants or by impersonating local inhabitants. Thus, non-French citizens were able to obtain genuine French registration for their vessels. Sailors even came to Nosy Be and Mahore (Mayotte), for the purpose of obtaining registration, from as far away as Baraawe.[48]

The Permanent Court of Arbitration in Den Haag

The French flag and French registration offered sailors in that area of the ocean protection from the British campaign which intended to suppress the slave trade but affected all maritime transport in the western Indian Ocean. The British Consulate at Zanzibar did his best to discuss the state of affairs both with the neighbouring French Consulate on the spot and with the French Government at home; however, far from fruitful outcomes resulted, despite the fact that some French Consuls supported the British endeavour.[49] Abolition of the slave trade in Zanzibar in 1873 did not prevent slave transport under the French flag on the western Indian Ocean. For example, over a hundred ships were confiscated off Mozambique by the Portuguese Government for slave transportation in 1902.[50] However, circumstances had changed dramatically since 1899. The changes were not triggered by events on Nosy Be, Mahore (Mayotte) or even in Zanzibar, but at Masqaṭ.[51]

At the end of 1890s, the French Government had managed to win over Sayyid Fayṣal b. Turkī, current sultan of Oman (r. 1888–1913), to their own side, and planned to construct a coaling depot near Masqaṭ and establish it as their naval base in Oman and the Persian Gulf. If the French plan had come to fruition, the British Government would have been in danger of losing control over the Gulf, especially since, simultaneously, the Ottomans were expanding their influence over the Qaṭar Peninsula.[52] The British Government was therefore fiercely opposed to this plan, not least because it was in contradiction of a joint statement acknowledging the Canning Arbitration of 1862, which recognized both the branches of the Bū Saʿīd family in Zanzibar and Oman as governing independent states. At the end, the British offer to share al-Makallā cove was accepted by the French, and the scheme to establish a naval base in Oman did not succeed.[53]

Concurrently, the British Government had not overlooked the fact that the French Consul at Masqaṭ had begun to issue French registration to local ships. To the British this was more evidence of a clear violation of Oman's independence, which, of course, also challenged the British position in the Persian Gulf. In 1899, the British Consul at Masqaṭ advised the Sultan to use his own ensign and allow his subjects to use that flag instead of the simple red flag which was common among Arab seafarers in the Persian Gulf, the intention being to signify Oman's independence. The Sultan, however, rejected the Consul's advice, although he did send an instruction to seafarers in Ṣūr not to hoist the French flag as was common practice. The British Consul too complained to the French Consul that protection of Omani subjects hoisting the French flag was against the joint statement of 1862. That series of exchanges in turn prompted a debate between Britain and France about whether Omani ships could legitimately sail under the French flag. Eventually, in March 1904, the French Government demanded arbitration at the Permanent Court of Arbitration in Den Haag, and both sides signed an agreement to abide by the Court's judgement the following October.

The British claims can be summarized as follows. First, without the Sultan's agreement, his subjects could not benefit from the French maritime registration rules; if the Sultan and the French Government had concluded their own treaty to allow this, that might have been acceptable, but there was no such treaty. Moreover, ships flying the French flag and protected by French registration were engaging in the slave trade, which was prohibited by a General Act of the Brussels Conference relating to the African Slave Trade in 1890. In addition, the General Act contained the limitation that only French citizens and citizens under French protection were permitted to be French-registered; despite this, Omani shipowners who met neither condition were to be found with French registrations. Furthermore, in providing registrations to Omani subjects the French were acting against the settled will of the Sultan, while effectively removing such subjects from Omani jurisdiction was a violation of Omani independence and likewise contrary to the joint statement in

1862. Even if conferment of French privileges on Omani subjects were permitted, such individuals would remain under Omani jurisdiction within the Sultan's territory. Finally, such registration was the property of a particular individual and not heritable, nor was registration transferrable between ships.

Four main counter arguments came from the French side. In the opinion of the French, Oman was not yet fully established as modern nation so the question of its citizenship was vague. Then, according to a treaty of friendship concluded between the French Government and Sa'īd b. Sulṭān in 1844, the French Government undertook to guarantee to the Sultan's subjects protection equal to that of French citizens. In addition, the French side regarded the Bū Sa'īdi Government as the government which offered formal capitulation, such as the Ottoman Government. It was the Sultan of the Bū Sa'īd who granted the French the right to offer French citizenship to his subjects, thus, for the French side, there was no reason to reject this and potentially lose the Sultan's favour. Lastly, holders of the registration in question were sailors constantly travelling at sea, and belonged to polygamous societies, so had stronger connections to French colonies than to Oman.

After hearing the claims of both parties, the Permanent Court of Arbitration handed down the following judgements. About the first question, the Court began by stating that:

> Whereas generally speaking it belongs to every Sovereign to decide to whom he will accord the right to fly his flag and to prescribe the rules governing such grants, and whereas therefore the granting of the French flag to subjects of His Highness the Sultan of Muscat in itself constitutes no attack on the independence of the Sultan,
>
> Whereas nevertheless a Sovereign may be limited by treaties in the exercise of this right ...[54]

The full decision consists of six points. First, it was accepted that 'before the 2nd January 1892 (the day on which the Brussels Act was ratified) France was entitled to authorize vessels belonging to subjects of His Highness the Sultan of Muscat to fly the French flag, only bound by her own legislation and administrative rules', therefore, second, owners granted authorization by France before 1892 retained that authorization as long as France renewed it. However, as to the third point, authorizations approved after 2 January 1892 became invalid unless their proprietors could establish that they had been considered and treated by France as her 'protégés' before 1863 (when the Ottoman law of 23 Sefer 1280 (August 1863) and French-Moroccan Treaty (19 August 1863) restricted the scope of the term 'protégés'; this was largely acceded to by European countries). Fourth, dhows of Masqaṭ authorized to fly the French flag were granted inviolability in the territorial waters of Masqaṭ under the French-Masqaṭ Treaty of 17 November 1844. Fifth, authorization to fly the French flag could not be transferred to any other person, nor vessel, even if owned by the same person. Lastly, even owners authorized to fly the French flag enjoyed no rights of extraterritoriality which could exempt them from the sovereignty, and especially from the jurisdiction, of the Sultan of Masqaṭ.[55]

The judgement of the Permanent Court of Arbitration at Den Haag limited the future increase in numbers of local ships permitted to fly the French flag and any extension of the usage. Eventually, by 1917, only 12 dhows sailed under the French flag.[56]

Conclusion

What then does the progress of the issue of French registration tell us about the history of the western Indian Ocean? First, the hoisting of the French flag by local dhows was generally not fallacious but indicated a proper registration had been granted to a vessel by the competent French authority. As a result, the British anti-slave trade campaign could do almost nothing to directly interfere in their activities.

Second, a French flag and registration provided various general privileges to dhows in that part of the ocean, not only because without it dhows tended to be victims of the suppression campaign, but also because it allowed lower port taxes to be paid at certain ports. We can see in this another aspect of the inseparable nature of the slave trade from the rest of the region's trading activity. In fact, between the very end of the nineteenth century and the beginning of the twentieth century, while French-flagged dhows with French nationality were criticized as being engaged in slave transport in the Gulf of Oman, they also conveyed a certain amount of rice and sundries from Bombay to Mirbāt, Ṣūr and Maṣīra Island, for example.[57] They were not only slave transporters as the British Government claimed at the Permanent Court, rather, they were also general trade carriers within the bounds of the wider western Indian Ocean.

The third point concerns the role of Nosy Be and Mahore Islands in this story. Nosy Be in particular had not been involved in the western Indian Ocean exchange network before France took it under its protectorate in 1841,[58] while the Comoros Islands, including Mahore (Mayotte), had functioned as a part of a wide maritime exchange network since very early times. But regardless of that, the important element that enabled them to play a part of this story was their new attribute of being under French protection. This is clearly at odds with the traditional view, notably espoused by Kirti N. Chaudhuri, which emphasizes the collapse of the maritime network when it encountered European colonialism.

The final point this chapter highlights is the fact that the matter was concluded at Den Haag, so far away from the ocean where dhows actually sailed under the French flag. The arbitration was between the British and French Governments and was focused on the treatment of Omani subjects, although, of course, neither these Omani subjects nor even representatives of the Sultan were in court. They were completely excluded, and the British Government appointed Melville W. Fuller, the Director General of the Supreme Court of the United States, as its arbitrator, while Alexander. F. de Savolnin Lohman, former Minister of Domestic Affairs of the Netherlands and a Doctor of Law, took the same role for the French Government. The judge, appointed by King Vittorio Emanuele III of Italy, was Heinrich Lammasch, a professor from Vienna and a member of the Upper House of Austria.[59] Simultaneously, Ottoman and Moroccan cases were taken into consideration as part of the question of the power of protection—the actual focus of the arbitration process.[60] These actors and the referred cases show clearly that the fate of the transporters was no longer in their own hands, nor even in those of the Sultan of Oman.

Notes

1. MAHA/PD/1863/60/1471/153-154 [Playfair to Russell, Zanzibar, 20 September 1863]. The same document is found in NAUK/FO84/1204/355.
2. MAHA PD/1864/54/942/13 [Playfair to Havelock, Zanzibar, 1 May 1864].

3. Jean Martin, 'L'affranchissement des esclaves de Mayotte, décembre 1846 juillet-1847', *Cahiers d'Etudes Africaines* 16 (1976), 224; Campbell, *An Economic History of Imperial Madagascar*, 227.
4. Russell, *General Rigby*, 90.
5. Ibid.
6. MAHA PD/1860/159/12/22-23 [Rigby to Anderson, Zanzibar, 3 January 1860]; NAUK FO84/1146/241 [Rigby to Bart, Zanzibar, 4 May 1861]. The same document is found in ZZBA AA12/2/27.
7. NAUK FO84/1146/241 [Rigby to Bart, Zanzibar, 4 May 1861]; The same document is in ZZBA AA12/2/27.
8. NAUK ADM123/179/n.p. [Extract from Letter No 63 of 21st of March 1859 from Sir. Fred Grey to Secretary of the Admiralty]; ibid., n.p. [Half Yearly Report on Slave Trade on the east coast of Africa, Walker to the Secretary of the Admiralty, Simon's Bay, 20 November 1861]; ibid., n.p. [Crawford to Walker, H.M.S. *Sidon* at Mauritius, 30 June 1861].
9. Sulṭān b. Muḥammad al-Qāsimī claims the first case was in 1845 with OIOC IOR/R/15/1403/230 as a reference (al-Qāsimī, *Les relations entre Oman et la France (1715–1905)*, tr. Abdeljelil and Mireille Temimi, Paris: L'Harmattan, 1995, 140). However, he does not mention its source and I have yet to confirm this reference.
10. For example, AMAE CP/Zanzibar/3/127 [Mémorandum remis par Mr. Grey, 14 septembre 1863]; *BPP*, Vol. 49, Class D, 125–126 [Playfair to Russell, *Pleiad*, 26 April 1864]; CAOM FM/SG/MAD/240/530/n.p. [Notes pour la direction des colonies, Versailles, 13 novembre 1873]; MAHA PD/1864/54/407/344-345 [Playfair to Russell, Zanzibar, 30 December 1863]; MAHA PD/1864/54/942/13 [Playfair to Havelock, Zanzibar, 1 May 1864]; NAUK FO84/1204/358 [Playfair to Jabłoński, Zanzibar, 14 September 1863]; ibid., 369–370 [Chapman to Playfair, H.M.S. *Ariel* at Sea, 14 October 1863]; ibid., 399 [Playfair to Russell, Zanzibar, 30 December 1863]; NAUK FO84/1374/58 [Humpage to anon., on board *Daphne*, 14 February 1873]; ibid., 88–91 [Humpage to Bateman, on board *Daphne*, 5 March 1873]; NAUK FO84/1389/342-350 [Frere to Granville, Mombasah, 24 March 1873]; OIOC IOR/L/P&S/18/B84/66 [Civil Commissioner of Seychelles to Barkly, s.l., 6 May 1869]; ibid., 79 [Murdoch to Rogers, Emigration Office, 19 July 1869]; OIOC IOR/L/P&S/18/B85/93 [Heath to the Secretary to the Admiralty, *Forte* at Aden, 7 June 1869]; OIOC IOR/R/20/A1A/579/12 [Prideaux to the Political Resident at Aden, Aden, 2 December 1872] (the same document can be found in D. Ingrams and L. Ingrams (eds.), *Records of Yemen, 1798–1960*, 16 vols, London: Archives Editions, 1993, Vol. 3, 557); OIOC IOR/R/20/A1A/579/39 [Ross to Pelly, Muskat, 25 July 1872] (the same document also in ibid.,

44); Raymond W. Beachey *The Slave Trade of Eastern Africa: A Collection of Documents*, London: Rex Collings, 1976, 99–102; Devereux, *A Cruise in the 'Gorgon'* 138–139.

11. OIOC IOR/L/P&S/18/B84/85 [Memorandum by Mr. Churchill respecting the Slave Trade on the east coast of Africa, s.l., n.d.].
12. OIOC IOR/L/P&S/18/B84/93 [Maera to Heath, *Nymphe* at Aden, 5 June 1869].
13. ZZBA AA12/29/65 [Hamerton to Secretary to Bombay Government, Zanzibar, 25 April 1844].
14. ZZBA AA12/29/65 [Hamerton to Secretary to Bombay Government, Zanzibar, 25 April 1844].
15. Burton, *Zanzibar*, Vol. 1, 321.
16. MAHA PD/1855/70/1457/113-117 [Manners to Leeke, at anchor off Muscat, 10 October 1855]; MAHA PD/1856/93/28/187-8 [Manners to Leeke, Bombay, 11 January 1856]; ibid., 203 [Extract Paras: 16 and 17 from a letter to the Court of Directors dated the 18th March 1856 No. 27].
17. For other cases, see ZZBA AA3/20/664 [Crawford to Walker, Simon's Bay, 25 October 1861]; ZZBA AA12/29/60 [Hamerton to Christopher, Zanzibar, 3 February 1843].
18. Katrin Bromber (ed. and tr.), *The Jurisdiction of the Sultan of Zanzibar and the Subjects of Foreign Nations*, Wurzburg: Ergon Verlag, 2001, 25.
19. The Third Article of General Maritime Treaty in 1820 also defines the flag of the ships under the shaykhs who signed this treaty as red with a white border (Aitchison, *A Collection of Treaties*, Vol. 7, 249).
20. MAHA PD/1864/54/435/361-362 [Playfair to Havelock, Zanzibar, 16 December 1863]; ZZBA AA2/4/226 [Rigby to Walker, Zanzibar, 8 May 1861]; ZZBA AA3/20/665 [Crawford to Walker, Simon's Bay, 25 October 1865].
21. NAUK FO54/19/13-14 [Rigby to Russell, Rectory, 10 March 1862]; NAUK FO84/1179/251-252 [Rigby to Bart, Zanzibar, 14 May 1861]; ZZBA AA2/4/217 [Rigby to Crawford, Zanzibar, 6 May 1861]; ibid., 225–235 [Rigby to Walker, Zanzibar, 8 May 1861]; ZZBA AA3/20/659-679 [Crawford to Walker, Simon's Bay, 25 October 1861].
22. ZZBA AA2/4/218-220 [Rigby to Crawford, Zanzibar, 7 May 1861].
23. MAHA PD/1864/54/407/326 [Playfair to Russell, s.l., 1 June 1864].
24. ZZBA AA3/20/659-679 [Crawford to Walker, Simon's Bay, 25 October 1861].
25. CAOM FM/SG/MAD/240/530/n.p. [le commandant la division navale des côtes orientales d'Afrique to Etat major, mouillage de Nossi-bé, 6 septembre 1873]. The Governor of Kilwa made a similar statement

(NAUK FO84/1389/344-345 [Frere to Granville, Mombasah, 24 March 1873]). See also a story of anonymous 'Jack' quoted in Chap. 4.

26. Lewis Hertslet, Edward Hertslet, Cecil Hertslet et al. (eds.), *A Complete Collection of the Treaties and Conventions, and Reciprocal Regulation, at present submitting between Great Britain and Foreign Powers, and of the Laws, Decrees, and Orders in Council, concerning the same; so far as They relate to Commerce and Navigation; to the Repression and Abolition of the Slave Trade; and to the Privileges and Interests of the Subjects of the High Contracting Parties*, 31 vols, London: Henry Butterworth and James Bigg and Sons, 1840–1925, Vol. 7, 345–346.
27. NAUK FO84/1389/343 [Frere to Granville, Mombasah, 24 March 1873]; OIOC IOR/L/P&S/18/B85/93 [Meara to Heath, *Nymphe* at Aden, 5 June 1869].
28. For example, a letter sent from Henryk Jabłoński, French Consul at Zanzibar, to Playfair, the British Consul there, on 6 October 1863 refers to the case of *Noussoura*. That vessel had been inspected by the Royal Navy's ships five times during her voyage from Mahore Island to Zanzibar, via Mohilla Island and Kilwa, between 7 August 1863 and 3 October 1863. And some of the inspections were even done by the same officer of the Royal Navy (NAUK FO84/1204/366 [Jabłoński to Playfair, Zanzibar, 6 Octobre 1863]). For another similar case, see NAUK FO84/1292/228-289 [Bure to anon. (Churchill), Zanzibar, 24 août 1868].
29. For example, NAUK FO84/1204/369 [Playfair to Chapman, Zanzibar, 7 October 1863]; ibid., 369–370 [Chapman to Playfair, H.M.S. *Ariel* at Sea, 14 October 1863]; NAUK FO84/1292/230-2 [Churchill to Bure, Zanzibar, 25 August 1868]; ibid., 234–236 [Heath to Churchill, H.M.S. *Octavia*, 27 August 1868].
30. OIOC IOR/L/P&S/18/B84/67 [Otway to the Secretary to the Admiralty, Foreign Office, 21 July 1869]; OIOC IOR/L/P&S/18/B150a/123 [Chapter VI: Slave Trade, pp. 87–88]. See also, Colomb, *Slave-Catching*, 63.
31. NAUK FO84/1325/97 [Kirk to Chief Secretary to Government, Bombay, Zanzibar, 4 March 1870]. For superiority of French ships to British ships in terms of port tax along the East African coast, see ibid., 102.
32. NAUK FO84/1325/104 [Extract of letter from the Sultan of Zanzibar to Mr. H. A. Churchill, C. B., dated Zanzibar 20th Sharban 1285 equal to the 6th December 1868]; ibid., 105–106 [Kirk to Sheikh Suliman b. Ali, Zanzibar, February 1870].

33. MAHA PD/1863/60/1471/160-161 [Playfair to Jabłoński, Zanzibar, September 1863]. The same document is found in AMAE CP/Zanzibar/3/153-154 and NAUK FO84/1204/358.
34. For example, MAHA PD/1856/93/28/188-189 [Manner to Leeke, Bombay, 11 January 1856]; NAUK ADM123/179/n.p. [Extract of Sir Fred Grey's Letter to Secretary of the Admiralty dated 11th February 1858 No. 9. Report on the State of the Slave Trade on the East Coast African Station to 31st December 1857]; NAUK FO84/1224/207 [Playfair to Russell, on board H.M.S. *Pleiad*, 26 April 1864]; Devereux, *A Cruise in the 'Gorgon'*, 138–139.
35. MAHA PD/1863/60/1471/167-168 [Jabłoński to Playfair, Zanzibar, 15 September 1863]. Original French version is on AMAE CP/Zanzibar/3/156.
36. CAOM FM/SG/MAD/240/530/n.p. [David, Paris, 28 mai 1818].
37. Philippe-Joseph-Benjamin Buchez and Pierre-Célestin Roux, *Histoire parlementaire de la révolution française; ou joural des assemblées nationales*, 40 vols, Paris: Libraire Paulin, 1834–1838, Vol. 32, 481.
38. For example, CAOM FM/GEN/641/2766/n.p. [le vice-amiral, sénateur, ministre de la marine et des colonies to Messieurs les gouverneurs et commandants des colonies, Paris, 29 mars 1878]; CAOM FM/SG/MAD/240/530/n.p. [David to anon., Paris, 28 mai 1818].
39. CAOM FM/GEN/641/2766/n.p. [Projet de loi destiné a régler la police et les droits de navigation, dressé par ordre du Conseiller d'Etat, Directeur général des Douances, mai 1818].
40. For example, CAOM FM/GEN/599/2666/n.p. [Circulaire du 22 juin 1833, N.1387, Paris]; ibid., n.p. [le Ministre to les Gouverneurs de la Martinique, Guadaloupe, Guyane française, Bourbon, Sénégal, Paris, 12 mars 1844]; CAOM FM/SG/MAD/240/530/n.p. [la direction des colonies, Versailles, 13 novembre 1873].
41. CAOM FM/GEN/297/1976/n.p. [*Courrier du Havre* du 3 avril 1845].
42. CAOM FM/GEN/641/2766/n.p. [MAE, Paris, septembre 1861].
43. OIOC IOR/L/P&S/18/B84/67 [Papers given to Arab Dhows]. This was obtained by the captain of *Nymphe* (ibid., 66 [the Civil Commissioner of Seychelles to Barkly, s.l., 6 May 1869]).
44. MAHA PD/1863/60/1471/156 [Playfair to Russel, Zanzibar, 20 September 1863] (The same document is found in NAUK FO84/1204/355-6); MAHA PD/1864/54/942/13 [Playfair to Havelock, s.l., 1 May 1864]; NAUK FO84/1389/343 [Frere to Granville, Mombasah, 24 March 1873]. Also, some obtained registration at Djibouti (Sultān b. Muḥammad al-Qāsimī(ed.), *Wathā'iq al-'arabīya al-'umānī fī marākiz al-arshīf al-faransīya*, s.l., 1993, 291).

45. MAHA PD/1863/60/1471/164-165 [Playfair to Jabłoński, Zanzibar, 14 September 1863].
46. MAHA PD/1863/60/1471/165-166 [Playfair to Jabłoński, Zanzibar, 14 September 1863].
47. CAOM FM/SG/MAD/240/530/n.p. [Guillois to le Duc de Broglie, Zanzibar, 24 septembre 1873].
48. CAOM FM/SG/MAD/240/530/n.p. [Guillois to le Duc de Broglie, Zanzibar, 24 septembre 1873]. See also, NAUK FO84/1389/342-343 [Frere to Granville, Mombasah, 24 March 1873].
49. For example, NAUK FO84/1204/398 [Playfair to Layard, s.l., 30 December 1863]; NAUK FO84/1392/217-218 [Rémusat to l'ambassadeur, Versailles, 7 avril 1873]; ibid., 219 [anon. to Granville, Paris, 9 April 1873]; ibid., 221–223 [Lyons to anon., s.l., 11 April 1873]; Reginald Coupland, *The Exploitation of East Africa: The Slave Trade and the Scramble 1856–1890*, Evanston: North Western University Press, 1967, 218.
50. OIOC IOR/R/15/1/406/51.
51. Lorimer, *Gazetteer of the Persian Gulf*, 561–570; Briton C. Busch, *Britain and the Persian Gulf, 1894–1914*, Berkeley and Los Angeles: University of California Press, 1967, 154–186; Y.A. al-Ghailani, 'Oman and the Franco-British Rivalry: The Bandar al-Jissah Crisis, 1898–1900', *Adab* 29 (2009).
52. For Ottoman expansion to the Persian Gulf and its influence, see Frederick F. Anscombe, *The Ottoman Gulf: The Creation of Kuwait, Saudi Arabia, and Qatar*, New York: Columbia University Press, 1997, 54–90; Zekeriya Kurşun, *The Ottoman in Qatar: A History of Anglo-Ottoman Conflicts in the Persian Gulf*, Istanbul: The Isis Press, 2002, 49–110.
53. Lorimer, *Gazetteer of the Persian Gulf*, 561; al-Ghailani, 'Oman and the Franco-British Rivalry', 13.
54. George G. Wilson, *The Hague Arbitration Cases : Compromise and Awards, with Maps, in cases decided under the Provisions of the Hague Conventions of 1899 and 1907 for the Pacific Settlement of International Disputes and Texts of the Conventions*, Boston: Ginn and Companies, 1915, 70–73.
55. Wilson, *The Hague Arbitration Cases*, 76–81.
56. Martijn Th. Houtsma, T.W. Arnold, R. Basset et al. (eds.), *Encyclopaedia of Islām: A Dictionary of the Geography, Ethnography and Biography of the Muhammadan Peoples*, 9 vols, Leiden: E.J Brill, 1991 (1st. 1913–1938), Vol. 8, 976, s.v. 'Omān.
57. OIOC IOR/R/15/1/406/74.

58. For the integration of Nosy Be in the western Indian Ocean network, triggered by the French protectorate, see Hideaki Suzuki, '19 seiki Nosy Be de karamariau tayouna kankeisei', in Taku Iida (ed.), *Madagasukaru chiiki bunka no dōtai*, Osaka: National Ethnographical Museum, 2012.
59. OIOC IOR/R/15/1/406/85.
60. OIOC IOR/R/15/1/406/85-87.

CHAPTER 10

General Conclusion: Slave Trade Profiteers

From Burgash bin Saeed,

To all our subjects who may see this, and also to others, may God save you!

Know that we have prohibited the transport of raw slaves by sea in all our harbours, and have closed the markets which are for the sale of slaves through all our dominions. Whosoever, therefore, shall ship a raw slave after this date, will render himself liable to punishment, and this he will bring upon himself. Be this known.

Dated 12 Rabi el Akhr, 1290 (June 8, 1873)[1]

The Inseparable Nature of the Slave Trade from Other Trades

In the context of the western Indian Ocean, as repeated throughout this book, a significant point is the inseparable nature of the slave trade there from other trades. The slave trade was in fact part of a complex western Indian Ocean trade system.

The slave trade in this region was not specialized, being spread as widely throughout individual traders as it was geographically. Traders were of very varied status and might come from all social ranks. Low entry barriers was one of characteristic features of the trade in this region. In most cases, slave trading required no large amount of capital,

H. Suzuki, *Slave Trade Profiteers in the Western Indian Ocean*, Palgrave Series in Indian Ocean World Studies,
DOI 10.1007/978-3-319-59803-1_10

nor a specially adapted vessel, unlike in the Atlantic trade. There are a number of reasons for this, including considerations of the sailing distances involved, which were much shorter than those of the Atlantic trade. Unlike ships carrying slaves in the Atlantic, which were required to sail almost directly across the whole Atlantic Ocean from West Africa, ships of the western Indian Ocean had many of ports of call if they adopted coastal sailing routes, which meant too that they could disembark slaves anywhere on their way to their final destinations. Demand for slaves was widespread. Consequently, traders were in a position to effectively reduce their transport costs, which relieved them of having to make a large capital investment in their business. Indeed, around the rim of the western Indian Ocean—apart from plantations in Zanzibar, Pemba, the Mascarene Islands and Nosy Be—the demand for slaves was not concentrated in any particular place, but was present more or less everywhere. This also meant that slaves were sometimes forced to travel around the vast sphere of the western Indian Ocean region from place to place, once they were sold, in order to find a new master, as several individual cases show in Chap. 5. Slave trading had existed since time immemorial in the western Indian Ocean, but a large proportion of the slaves traded had always been destined for domestic service. Large scale slave-holding was not common; rather than that, its scale was small but widely distributed. Even in Zanzibar, which was the centre of the plantation economy along the East African coast, a list made by Rigby of slaves in the possession of Indian residents shows that the majority of owners owned fewer than five slaves, with nearly a third owning only a single slave.[2] Slave transactions therefore tended to be of relatively small scale throughout history, carried out at the individual rather than mass level.

In the context of individual transactions, we cannot ignore the fact that there was a chain of reselling in which non-professional individuals were involved alongside professional traders. Chapter 5 discusses this and reveals the societal importance of slave dealings. In addition, dealing in slaves as well as owning them were not limited to individuals of higher social status. Indeed, there were slave masters who were themselves slaves.[3] Slavery had in fact become so deeply rooted in societies around the western Indian Ocean that blocking the channels of supply had a profound impact on the region.

To consider the overall effect of the suppression campaign, we must therefore recognize that the slave trade cannot be separated from other trades, but has to be regarded as part of complex commercial whole.

Slaves were only one type of cargo that might be taken on board a vessel, and all cargoes, including the slaves themselves, were items that connected remote regions, creating and maintaining some sort of connectedness across the western Indian Ocean. Thus, control over slave transport indirectly implied control over all transport, and affected the whole maritime world. The significance of the suppression campaign with regard to western Indian Ocean history should be seen in that context.

Political Interference in Maritime Communication

Undoubtedly, the greatest change brought to the region by the series of events related to slave trade, particularly those covered by this book, was political intervention in maritime commerce. Unlike inhabitants of the East Asian Seas, for example, historically people in the western Indian Ocean had too little experience of facing political interference in their maritime activities.[4] In the East Asian Seas, authorities showed great interest in and aptitude for controlling maritime traffic, and, although it took time, were eventually able to exert control over these seas at a certain degree. The maritime bans of the Ming and Qing dynasties as well as the so-called *sakoku* ('locked country') policy during the Tokugawa Shogunate are good examples. By contrast, in the western Indian Ocean, strong political control of maritime trade had rarely taken place before the suppression campaign began. For example, Michael N. Pearson tells us that fifteenth-century rulers of ports in South and Southeast Asia never tried to force merchants to make use of their facilities or pay customs duties.[5] Of course, as is the case everywhere, straits were always the focus of tensions, as polities around the western Indian Ocean tried to establish control of them, such, as for example, when the Rasūlid sultans attempted to control the Bāb al-Mandab strait, the entrance to the Red Sea. After their rise in 1229, the Rasūlid constantly sent out sea patrols in the strait and placed commercial ships under an obligation to call at their ports.[6] However, such strictly local attempts at control were usually temporary and sporadic over the long history of the western Indian Ocean.

It was in fact generally true that local powers surrounding the western Indian Ocean were historically less persistent than those of the East Asian Seas in trying to take control of maritime commercial activities, and that large empires such as the Ottoman, the Qajar or even the Mughals were generally not interested in it.[7] Polities around the western Indian Ocean began to communicate with maritime transporters only if they entered their particular ports, and showed very little concern with what happened on the open sea. The high seas were little known and seen as a somewhat marginal zone where local polities rarely ventured, so any political intervention that did occur was always incidental. Indeed, the same observation applies to trading ships operating under the Portuguese *cartaz* system of licensing. The Portuguese required local ships to purchase a permit which guaranteed them protection by the Portuguese; otherwise they would be attacked.[8] Local ships were further placed under an obligation to call at Portuguese-controlled ports and pay duty. The Portuguese *cartaz* system can in fact be regarded as the earliest attempt by a European power to profit from controlling maritime trade in the western Indian Ocean, although again the crucial point here is that while the Portuguese wished to get profit from local traders their system was by no means intended to stop any aspect of the trade. So, it may be fair to regard the western Indian Ocean as an ocean of traders who were largely untroubled by political powers.

Of historical significance in the British suppression campaign in the western Indian Ocean context is the fact that the British tried to directly control and even to stop a part of its maritime trade. Interestingly, it was not only British Empire that was behind this move, but also various polities, even local polities such as the Bū Saʿīd. In the story of the development of the struggles against the suppression campaign between the 1820s and the 1870s, we can discern gradual changes in the methods of resistance adopted by the transporters. Chapter 3 looks at how they made increasingly sophisticated use of their own abilities, knowledge and skill, finally managing to infiltrate their suppressors' own legal web and exploiting their international relationships.

Clearly, the transporters were never really entrapped at the beginning; in fact, they ventured quite voluntarily into that complex web. For instance, they soon hit upon the idea of using the French flag as a sort of 'special pass' at sea, and on land the story was similar. What might have been intended as restrictions were actually recognized by the traders and the transporters almost as what we might think of as a sort of asylum. For example, Indian merchants exploited the 'dual protection' available to them, under which they could both profit from continued legal possession of slaves and enjoy the privileges of remaining British subjects. However, traders were all proved to have been deluded in the end, like fish apparently swimming freely in the net until gradually it closes in on them. The 'special pass' might be withdrawn at any time with a change in French policy on the slave trade and France's political relationship with Britain. After all, licence holders cannot determine the validity of their own papers, because, of course, licences are issued by third parties who actually hold the power. These licence holders had no power of redress, and no French register holders, nor any sultan or his representatives, were ever present at the Permanent Court of Arbitration in Den Haag. The system of 'dual protection' followed almost the same path, with Indian merchants delicately balanced on a very fine border line created by the relationship between nations. The sense of balance, the sure-footedness, the merchants showed is remarkable—that is, their skill and ingenuity in response to the circumstances they found themselves in, which they cleverly saw as an opportunity. However, as they discovered an opportunity but had not created it themselves, the British response (detailed in Chap. 8) meant that the merchants immediately lost their 'dual protection'. Released slaves, of course, gained their freedom, but traders and transporters were now absorbed into a system of political control under which they were forced to register themselves as well as their ships with a controlling power. So they were forced to relinquish a great deal of their freedom, and that is the significant conclusion of this story. Traders and transporters in the western Indian Ocean became tightly bound in a new web of political control in which they could no longer make effective use of their abilities, knowledge and skill in resistance, developed throughout their long history of communications by sea. However, this did not mean the collapse of the commercial connectedness of the western Indian Ocean. Neither connection necessarily repelled the other. What is clear is that the western Indian Ocean was then no longer only an ocean of traders.

The Other Slave Trade Profiteer

But let us look at the situation from the other side, too. However much we try to emphasize all the political connections, it is obvious that the British occupied the most powerful and significant position and that they profited most from the campaign of suppression. The Royal Navy managed to establish solid control over the slave trade in the western Indian Ocean, at least over its major route, which led from East Africa. It was not only the major route but also the most troublesome to control, because unlike other important routes, such as the one across the Gulf of Aden or the Mozambique Channel, the trade route from the

East African coast covered vast space of waters, which therefore needed to be extensively—and expensively—patrolled. However, for the British the effort must have seemed worthwhile at the end, because the same vastness and complexity of trade on the ocean which made it so difficult to control meant that once they had succeeded they could influence the entirety of trade in the region. This would not be an intended conclusion by anyone, even the British officials, rather than that, conjunction of various actors and events consequently led it. However, here, we can observe that British supremacy has been solidly established. In other words, we have found the other profiteer of the slave trade.

Notes

1. Hertslet et al. (eds.), *A Complete Collection of the Treaties and Conventions*, Vol. 15, 492.
2. Suzuki, 'Enslaved Population and Indian Owners', 233–234.
3. PPEM Log1827 A3B9F1/116.
4. Chaudhuri, *Trade and Civilisation in the Indian Ocean*, 14–16; Masashi Haneda, 'Canton, Nagasaki and the Port Cities of the Indian Ocean: A Comparison', in Masashi Haneda (ed.), *Asian Port Cities, 1600–1800: Local and Foreign Cultural Interactions*, Singapore and Kyoto: NUS Press and Kyoto University Press, 2009, 21–22; Philip E. Steinberg, *The Social Construction of the Ocean*, Cambridge: Cambridge University Press, 2001, 44–52.
5. Michael N. Pearson, *Merchants and Rulers in Gujarat: The Response to the Portuguese in the Sixteenth Century*, Los Angeles and Berkeley: University of California Press, 1976, 15.
6. Yajima, *Umi ga tsukuru bunmei*, 196–222; Hikoichi Yajima, *Kaiiki kara mita rekishi: Indoyō to chicyūkai wo musubu kōryūshi*, Nagoya: Nagoya University Press, 2006, 311–332.
7. Masashi Haneda, 'Mittsu no 'Isulamu kokka'', in Masashi Haneda (ed.), *Islamu, Kan Indoyō sekai, 16–18 seiki*, Tokyo: Iwanami Shoten, 2000; Masashi Haneda, *Higashi indo-kaisya to Ajia no umi*, Tokyo: Kōdansha, 2007, 98–100, 110. Also, see Pearson, *Merchants and Rulers in Gujarat*, 132.
8. Pearson, *Merchants and Rulers in Gujarat*, 40–44.

Appendix: Note on Archival Documents

This book relies heavily on documents from a number of different archives—a multi-archival approach proved to be key for seeing the shape of slave traders in the western Indian Ocean. Slave traders had few opportunities to leave any written record of their own, so their existence is recorded only in documents written by others, more precisely in the records compiled by Europeans and Americans. However, each single document, of course, reveals only a fragment of the information available to us. In fact, such sources are rather like a jigsaw puzzle, in which a picture emerges clearly only when a number of pieces—that is to say documents extracted from the sources—are put together. In other words, the greater the number and variety of sources selected the more clearly we can see the slave traders and their activities. The documents used in the book range across government records, private papers and the reports of religious missionaries. The three major government records used in this book are those of the British, the French and the Americans, and there are clear differences between them. As to France, rivalry with the British was not only limited by the competition for hegemony in the western Indian Ocean, but also grounded in different national policies on the slave trade. While, for the British, the abolition of slavery and the slave trade were established policy, the French, who ruled Bourbon Island, opposed abolition because of their critical need for labour. So we learn different things from British and French records, which approach the slave trade from different angles. Furthermore, it is worth

H. Suzuki, *Slave Trade Profiteers in the Western Indian Ocean*, Palgrave Series in Indian Ocean World Studies, DOI 10.1007/978-3-319-59803-1

remarking on the considerable internal variation of British documents. Indian Political Service officers were posted to the British Consulate in Zanzibar, but because Zanzibar was not under British protection, they reported to both the Indian Foreign Department and the Foreign Office in London.[1] Because of the different interests of both parties,[2] the Consulate at Zanzibar often sent varying information on the same subject. For example, on the matter of the Indian residents, the consulate sent detailed reports to Bombay, but often only cursory ones to London. Similarly, certain details were available only locally, such as Rigby's list of slaves, made at the time of his emancipation of them in 1860–1861, which is only available in Zanzibar's National Archives.

On the other hand, unlike both the British and the French, the foremost motivation of the Americans in the western Indian Ocean was not political but commercial,[3] and American Consuls in Zanzibar were often influential merchants. A large proportion of the American documents relate to some commercial matter or other, even though naturally most of them were reports of purely consular business, and although the Americans did not involve themselves in the suppression campaign they monitored it carefully. I also consulted the National Archives for official documents and the Phillips Library of the Peabody and Essex Museum for private documents while researching for this book. Private documents naturally tend to contain more details of the social conditions of Zanzibar and the western Indian Ocean, and the American documents provide a quite different insight into the relationships between slave traders and the campaign to suppress them.

This appendix, then, is a brief introduction to each of the archives I consulted and a list of the series which this book uses.

AMAE: Archives de Ministère des Affaires Étrangères, Paris, France. This is an archive of communications between the Ministry of Foreign Affairs and its consulates, including consular reports from Zanzibar. They are sorted according to consulate and the documents are divided into economic and political matters. In addition, Sulṭān b. Muḥammad al-Qāsimī (ed.), *Wathā'iq al-'arabīya al-'umānī fi marākiz al-arshīf al-faransīya*, s.l., 1993, is a selected collection of Arabic documents held in this archives.

AMAE CCC/Zanzibar/volume no./page no.: Documents on commerce received and dispatched from Masqaṭ and Zanzibar Consulates.

AMAE CP/Zanzibar/volume no./page no.: Documents on politics received and dispatched from Masqaṭ and Zanzibar Consulates.

CAOM: Centre des Archives d'Outre-Mer, Aix-en-Provence, France.
The French, who possessed Bourbon Island and several other colonies in the western Indian Ocean, left a number of documents related to this region. CAOM mainly holds the documents related to French overseas territories. In addition, reports from expeditions conducted by the French Navy in the nineteenth century around the western Indian Ocean are also held in these archives.

CAOM FM/GEN/box no./file no./page no.: General reports related to the Ministry of Foreign Affairs.

CAOM FM/SG/MAD/box no./file no./page no.: Reports and letters related to Madagascar and its adjacent islands.

CAOM FM/SG/OIND/box no./file no./page no.: Reports and letters related to the Indian Ocean and its surrounding regions.

MAHA: Mahārāshtra State Archives, Mumbai, India.
This archive holds the documents received and dispatched by the Political Department of the Bombay Government, which was in charge of most of the regions surrounding the western Indian Ocean.

MAHA PD/year/volume no./compilation no./page no.: Documents received and dispatched by the Political Department of Bombay Government.

MLUB: Main Library, University of Birmingham, Birmingham, UK.
This library preserves the documents of CMS, which sent missionaries to various places in the western Indian Ocean during the nineteenth century. The documents include communications between missionaries and CMS headquarters as well as certain private documents such as diaries. The library possesses the copies which were made by CMS headquarters, but this book relies only on original material.

MLUB CMS/CA5/O24/file no./page no.: Documents related to the missionary Johannes Rebmann, who was stationed at Rabai Station near Mombasa.

NAUK: National Archives, Kew, UK.

FO84/file no./page no.: This series contains documents relating to slave trade sent from consulates all over the world.

NAUK ADM1/file no./page no.: Official correspondence directed to the Secretary of the Admiralty, including materials for Vice-Admiral Court.

NAUK ADM123/file no./page no.: Documents related to Africa Station between 1797 and 1932. It includes communications between the ships engaged in the suppression campaign and the shore station, as well as between patrols and consulates.

NAUK FO54/file no./page no.: Documents related to Masqaṭ and Zanzibar between 1834 and 1905. However, most of those related to the slave trade are to be found in FO84.

NAUK FO78/file no./page no.: Documents related to the Ottomans between 1780 and 1905.

NAUK FO84/file no./page no.: Documents related to the slave trade between 1816 and 1892. Documents are sorted by year and country. The archive covers not only reports on the slave trade but also documents on its suppression, relating to the Indian Navy.

NAUK FO800/file no./page no.: Secret documents related to the Foreign Ministry between 1824 and 1968.

NAUK FO881/file no./page no.: Confidential printed papers of the Foreign Ministry between 1827 and 1914.

NAUS: National Archives, College Park, USA.
As already stated, American documents have an enormous advantage in that they provide a different perspective on the situation of the western Indian Ocean from both British and French documents. Many of the American documents are lodged in both the NAUS and Phillips Library. The NAUS preserves consular records. The records from Zanzibar contain not only dispatches to Washington, but also communications with the Bū Saʿīd. Furthermore, it contains miscellaneous shipping records

from consulates other than the American Consulate; some of them are not available in other archives. I also referred to the compilation of the documents related to the Bū Saʿīd, ʿAbd al-Fattāḥ Ḥasan Abū ʿAlīyah (ed.), *Mukhtārāt min wathā'iq tārīkh ʿumān al-ḥadīth qirā'a wathā'iq al-arshīf al-amrīkī*, al-Riyāḍ: Dār al-Marīkh, 1984.

NAUS RG84/Zanzibar/volume no./page no.: Documents sent and received by the Zanzibar Consulate between 1846 and 1912.

OIOC: Oriental and India Office Collection, British Library, London, UK.
This collection, formerly held at the India Office Library, contains documents from the India Office (later the Indian Government) as well as consular correspondence from Oman and the Persian Gulf.

OIOC IOR/F/volume no./page no.: Documents dispatched from the British East India Company to the Board of Control between 1784 and 1858.
OIOC IOR/L/P&S/volume no./page no.: Documents related to the Public and Judicial Department of the Indian Government between 1795 and 1950.
OIOC IOR/R/15/volume no./page no.: Documents related to agents and Consuls stationed at Bandar-e Būshehr, Baḥrayn, Kuwayt, Masqaṭ, Trucial Coast between 1763 and 1951.
OIOC IOR/R/20/volume no./page no.: Documents related to the Aden protectorate between 1837 and 1967.

PPEM: Phillips Library, Peabody Essex Museum, Salem, MA, USA.
The collection includes private documents of Salem merchants, which were donated to the Peabody Museum as well as the Essex Institute. Private documents are sorted by individuals and families. They include not only correspondence with family members and other merchants but also numerous commercial contracts made in Zanzibar, Madagascar Island, Aden and so on, as well as various log books from so-called eastern voyages. For this current book I have used the papers of Richard P. Waters, who served as the first American Consul in Zanzibar, as well as being the most influential American merchant in the island, and those of E.D. Ropes and J. Bertram, both engaged in commercial activity

around the western Indian Ocean. Several documents relating to Africa are collected in Norman R. Bennett and George E. Brooks, Jr (eds.), *New England Merchants in Africa:A History through Documents, 1802 to 1865*, Boston: Boston University Press, 1965, which is also widely used in this book.

PPEM MH14/box no./folder no.: Richard P. Waters Papers.
PPEM MH201/box no.: Edward D. Ropes Papers.
PPEM Log1827 A3B9F1/page no.: Bark *La Plata*, Bart William Schroder, seaman's journal.

ZZBA: Zanzibar National Archives, Zanzibar, Tanzania.
This archive holds consular records from various consulates in Zanzibar as well as documents locally collected by colonial officers between 1888 and 1963. The most important collection in the archive for this book is Consular Records, which contains documents sent and received by the British Consulate.

ZZBA AA2/file no./page no.: Collection of communications with individuals and administrators except those in the British Foreign Ministry and the Governments in India between 1837 and 1890.
ZZBA AA3/file no./page no.: Collection of communications between the British Consulate and the Bombay Government between 1840 and 1884.
ZZBA AA7/file no./page no.: Civil and criminal court records of the British Consulate between *c.*1855 and 1891. It contains records of the maritime court, which dealt with cases related to the slave trade.
ZZBA AA12/file no./page no.: Miscellaneous, between 1837 and 1914.

In addition to these, *British Parliamentary Papers*, Slave Trade, 95 vols, Shannon: Irish University Press, 1968–1971, has been used.
BPP, volume no., class, page no.

Notes

1. James Onley, *The Arabian Frontier of the British Raj: Merchants, Rulers, and the British in the Nineteenth-Century Gulf*, Oxford: Oxford University Press, 2007, 14–15.
2. For example, see Johny, 'The Decline of Omans Maritime Empire', 142.
3. Sheriff, *Spice, Slaves and Ivory*, 260.

Bibliography

Abū ʻAlīyah, ʻAbd al-Fattāḥ Ḥasan, *Mukhtārāt min wathā'iq tārīkh ʻumān al-ḥadīth: qurā'a fī wathā'iq al-arshīf al-amrīkī*, al-Riyādh: Dār al-Marrīkh, 1984.

Adam, William, *Law and Custom of Slavery in British India, in A Series of Letters to Thomas Fowell Buxton, Esq.*, Boston: Weeks, Jordan and Co., 1840.

Admiralty, *Instructions for the Guidance of Her Majesty's Naval Officers employed in the Suppression of the Slave Trade*, London: T.R. Harrison, 1844.

Agius, Dionisius A., *In the Wake of the Dhow: The Arabian Gulf and Oman*, Ithaca: Reading, 2002.

Ahmad, Abdussamad H., 'Ethiopian Slave Exports at Matamma, Massawa and Tajura, c.1830–1885', in Clarence-Smith (ed.), *The Economics of the Indian Ocean Slave Trade*, 93–102.

Aitchison, Charles U., *A Collection of Treaties, Engagements and Sunnuds: Relating to India and Neighbouring Countries*, 8 vols, Calcutta: Savielle and Cranenburgh, 1862–1866.

Albrand, Fortuné, 'Extrait d'une mémoire sur Zanzibar et Quiloa', *Bulletin de la société de géographie* 2, 10 (1838), 65–84.

Allen, Richard B., *Slaves, Freedmen, and Indentured Laborers in Colonial Mauritius*, Cambridge: Cambridge University Press, 1999.

———, 'The Mascarene Slave-Trade and Labour Migration in the Indian Ocean during the Eighteenth and Nineteenth Centuries', in Campbell (ed.), *The Structure of Slavery*, 33–50.

———, 'Satisfying the "Want for Laboring People": European Slave Trading in the Indian Ocean, 1500–1850', *Journal of World History* 21, 1 (2010), 45–73.

H. Suzuki, *Slave Trade Profiteers in the Western Indian Ocean*, Palgrave Series in Indian Ocean World Studies,
DOI 10.1007/978-3-319-59803-1

———, *European Slave Trading in the Indian Ocean, 1500–1850*, Athens: Ohio University Press, 2014.

Alpers, Edward A., *Ivory and Slaves: Changing Pattern of International Trade in East Central Africa to the Later Nineteenth Century*, Berkeley: University of California Press, 1975.

———, 'The Story of Swema: Female Vulnerability in Nineteenth-Century East Africa', in Robertson and Klein (eds.), *Women and Slavery in Africa*, 185–219.

———, 'Recollecting Africa: Diasporic Memory in the Indian Ocean World', *African Studies Review* 43, 1 (2000), 83–99.

———, '"Moçambiques" in Brazil: Another Dimension of the African Diaspora in the Atlantic World', in José C. Curto and Renée Soulodre-La France (eds.), *Africa and the Americas: Interconnections during the Slave Trade*, Trenton and Asmara: Africa World Press, 2005, 43–68.

———, *The Indian Ocean in World History*, Oxford: Oxford University Press, 2014.

———, 'The African Diaspora in the Indian Ocean: A Comparative Perspective', in Jayasuriya and Pankhurst (eds.), *The African Diaspora*, 19–50.

———, 'The Other Middle Passage: The African Slave Trade in the Indian Ocean', in Christopher, Pybus and Rediker (eds.), *Many Middle Passages*, 20–38.

Alpers, Edward A. and Mattherw S. Hopper, 'Parler en son nom? Comprendre les témoignages d'esclaves africains originaires de l'océan Indien (1850-1930)' *Annales* 63, 4 (2008), 799–828.

Anscombe, Frederick F., *The Ottoman Gulf: The Creation of Kuwait, Saudi Arabia, and Qatar*, New York: Columbia University Press, 1997.

Austen, Ralph A., 'From the Atlantic to the Indian Ocean: European Abolition, the African Slave Trade, and Asian Economic Structures', in Eltis and Walvin (eds.), *The Abolition of the Atlantic Slave Trade*, 117–139.

———, 'The 19th Century Islamic Slave Trade from East Africa (Swahili and Red Sea Coasts)', in Clarence-Smith (ed.), *The Economics of the Indian Ocean Slave Trade*, 21–44.

Banaji, Dady R., *Slavery in British India*, Bombay: D.B. Taraporevala Sons, 1933.

Basu, Helen (ed.), *Journey and Dwellings: Indian Ocean Themes in South Asia*, Hyderabad: Orient Longman, 2008.

Baxter, H.C., 'Pangani: the Trade Centre of Ancient History', *Tanganyika Notes and Records* 17 (1944), 15–25.

Beachey, Raymond W., *The Slave Trade of Eastern Africa*, London: Rex Collings, 1976.

———, *The Slave Trade of Eastern Africa: A Collection of Documents*, London: Rex Collings, 1976.

Beaujard, Philippe, *Les mondes de l'océan indien*, 2 vols., Paris: Armand Colin, 2012.

———, 'The Indian Ocean in Eurasian and African World-Systems before the Sixteenth Century', *Journal of World History* 16, 4 (2005), 411–465.

———, 'The Worlds of the Indian Ocean', in Pearson (ed.), *Trade, Circulation, and Flow*, 15–26.

Behnaz A. Mirzai, Ismael Musah Montana and Paul E. Lovejoy (eds.), *Slavery, Islam and Diaspora*, Trenton: Africa World Press, 2009.

Bellagamba, Alice, Sandra E. Greene and Martin Klein (eds.), *African Slaves, African Masters: Politics, Memories, Social Life*, Trenton: Africa World Press, 2017.

———, ——— and ——— (eds.), *African Voices on Slavery and the Slave Trade*, Cambridge: Cambridge University Press, 2013.

Bennett, Norman R., 'Americans in Zanzibar, 1865–1915: Part II', *Tanganyika Notes and Records* 57 (1961), 121–138.

———, *A History of the Arab State of Zanzibar*, London: Methuen, 1978.

———, *Arab versus European: Diplomacy and War in Nineteenth-Century East Central Africa*, New York and London: Holmes and Meier, 1986.

——— and George E. Brooks, Jr (eds.), *New England Merchants in Africa: A History through Documents, 1802 to 1865*, Boston: Boston University Press, 1965.

Berg, Fred J., 'Mombasa under the Busaidi Sultanate: The City and its Hinterlands in the Nineteenth Century' (Ph.D dissertation, University of Wisconsin, 1971).

Bertz, Ned, 'Indian Ocean World Travellers: Moving Models in Multi-Sited Research', in Basu (ed.), *Journey and Dwellings*, 21–60.

Blyth, Robert J., *The Empire of the Raj: India, Eastern Africa and the Middle East, 1858-1947*, New York: Palgrave, 2003

Bose, Sugata, 'Space and Time on the Indian Ocean Rim: Theory and History', in Fawaz and Bayly (eds.), *Modernity and Culture*, 365–388.

Boyer-Rossol, Klara, 'L'histoire orale de Makoa: un pont entre les deux rives du canal de Mozambique', paper presented at Tales of Slavery Conference, University of Toronto, 20–23 May 2009.

———, 'Le stigmatisation des *Makoa* ou *Masombika*: les séquelles de l'esclavage à Madagascar (XIXe-XXe siècles)', in Médéa (ed.), *Kaf*, 31–37.

Braudel, Fernand, *Civilisation matérielle, économie et capitalisme: XVe-XVIIIe siècle*, 3 vols, Paris: Armand Colin, 1979.

Bromber, Katrin (ed. and tr.), *The Jurisdiction of the Sultan of Zanzibar and the Subjects of Foreign Nations*, Wurzburg: Ergon Verlag, 2001.

Buchez, Philippe-Joseph-Benjamin and Pierre-Célestin Roux, *Histoire parlementaire de la révolution française; ou journal des assemblées nationales*, 40 vols, Paris: Libraire Paulin, 1834–1838.

Buckingham, James S., 'Voyage from Bushire to Muscat, in the Persian Gulf, and from thence to Bombay', *Oriental Herald* 67 (1829), 79–103.

Burnes, James, *A Sketch of the History of Cutch*, New Delhi: Asian Educational Services, 2004 (1st 1839, Edinburgh: Bell and Bradfute).

Burton, Richard F., 'Zanzibar, and Two Months in East Africa', *Blackwood's Edinburgh Magazine* 133 (1858), 200–224, 276–290.

———, *The Lake Regions of Central Africa: A Picture of Exploration*, 2 vols, California: The Narrative Press, 2001 (1st 1860, London: Longman, Green, Longman, and Roberts).

———, *Zanzibar; City, Island, and Coast*, 2 vols, London: Tinsley Brothers, 1872.

———, *Personal Narrative of A Pilgrimage to Mecca and Medina*, 3 vols, Leipzig: Bernhard Tauchnitz, 1874.

———, *The Book of the Thousand Nights and a Night*, ed. Leonard C. Smithers, 12 vols, London: H.S. Nichols, 1894.

Busch, Briton C., *Britain and the Persian Gulf, 1894–1914*, Berkeley and Los Angeles: University of California Press, 1967.

Campbell, Gwyn, 'Madagascar and Mozambique in the Slave Trade of the Western Indian Ocean, 1800–1861', in Clarence-Smith (ed.), *The Economics of the Indian Ocean Slave Trade*, 166–193.

——— (ed.), *The Structure of Slavery in Indian Ocean Africa and Asia*, London and Portland: Frank Cass, 2004.

———, 'Introduction: Slavery and Other Forms of Unfree Labour in the Indian Ocean World', in Campbell (ed.), *The Structure of Slavery*, vii–xxxii.

———, *An Economic History of Imperial Madagascar, 1750–1895: The Rise and Fall of an Island Empire*, Cambridge: Cambridge University Press, 2005.

———, 'Slave Trade and the Indian Ocean World', in Hawley (ed.), *India in Africa, Africa in India*, 17–51.

———, Suzanne Miers and Joseph C. Miller (eds.), *Children in Slavery though the Ages*, Athens: Ohio University Press, 2009.

Campbell, James M. (ed.), *Gazetteer of the Bombay Presidency, Volume 5: Cutch, Palanpur, Mahi Kantha*, Bombay: Government Central Press, 1880.

Capela, José, *O tráfico de escravos nos portos de Moçambique; 1733–1904*, Porto: Edições Afrontamento, 2002.

Chaudhuri, Kirti N., *Trade and Civilisation in the Indian Ocean: An Economic History from the Rise of Islam to 1750*, Cambridge: Cambridge University Press, 1985.

———, *Asia before Europe: Economy and Civilisation of the Indian Ocean from the Rise of Islam to 1750*, Cambridge: Cambridge University Press, 1990.

Chittick, Neville H. and Robert I. Rotberg (eds.), *East Africa and the Orient: Cultural Synthesis in Pre-Colonial Times*, New York: Africana Publishing, 1975.

Christie, James, *Cholera Epidemics in East Africa: An Account of the Several Diffusions of the Disease in that Country from 1821 till 1872*, London: Macmillan, 1876.

Christopher, Emma, Cassandra Pybus and Marcus Rediker (eds.), *Many Middle Passages: Forced Migration and the Making of the Modern World*, Berkeley, Los Angeles and London: University of California Press, 2007.

Clarence-Smith, William G., 'The Economics of the Indian Ocean and Red Sea Slave Trades in the 19th Century', in Clarence-Smith (ed.), *The Economics of the Indian Ocean Slave Trade*, 1–20.

——— (ed.), *The Economics of the Indian Ocean Slave Trade in the Nineteenth Century*, London: Routledge, 1989.

———, *Islam and the Abolition of Slavery*, New York: Oxford University Press, 2006.

Colin, Épidariste, 'Notice sur Mozambique', *Annales des voyages, de la géographie et de l'histoire* 9 (1809), 304–328.

Colomb, Philip H., *Slave-Catching in the Indian Ocean: A Record of Naval Experiences*, New York: Negro Universities Press, 1873.

Cooper, Frederick, *Plantation Slavery on the East Coast of Africa*, Portsmouth: Heinemann, 1997 (1st 1977, New Haven: Yale University Press).

Cooper, Joseph, *The Lost Continent or Slavery and the Slave Trade in Africa 1875, with Observations on the Asiatic Slave Trade Carried on under the Name of Labour Traffic, and Some Other Subjects*, London: Frank Cass, 1968.

Coupland, Reginald, *The Exploitation of East Africa: The Slave Trade and the Scramble 1856–1890*, Evanston: North Western University Press, 1967.

Das Gupta, Ashin, 'Introduction II: The Story', in Das Gupta and Pearson (eds.), *India and the Indian Ocean*, 25–45.

——— and Michael N. Pearson (eds.), *India and the Indian Ocean*, Calcutta: Oxford University Press, 1987.

Deutsch, Jan-Georg, *Emancipation without Abolition in German East Africa c.1884–1914*, Oxford: James Curry, 2006.

Devereux, William C., *A Cruise in the 'Gorgon'; or, eighteen months on H. M. S. 'Gorgon', engaged in the suppression of the slave trade on the east coast of Africa. Including a trip up the Zambesi with Dr. Livingstone*, London: Dawsons, 1869.

Doulton, Lindsay, 'The Royal Navy's Anti-Slavery Campaign in the Western Indian Ocean, c.1860–1890: Race, Empire and Identity' (PhD dissertation, University of Hull, 2010).

Drescher, Saymour, *Abolition: A History of Slavery and Antislavery*, Cambridge: Cambridge University Press, 2009.

Dubuisson, Patricia R., 'Qāsimī Piracy and the General Treaty of Peace (1820)', *Arabian Studies* 4 (1978), 47–57.

Edwardes, Stephen M., *The Gazetteer of Bombay City and Island*, 3 vols, Bombay: Time Press, 1909.

Eltis, David, 'Construction of the Trans-Atlantic Slave Trade Database: Sources and Methods', available on http://www.slavevoyages.org/voyage/understanding-db/methodology-2 (last viewed 8 February 2017).

——— and James Walvin (eds.), *The Abolition of the Atlantic Slave Trade: Origins and Effects in Europe, Africa and the Americas*, Madison: University of Wisconsin Press, 1981.

Ewald, Janet J., 'The Nile Valley System and the Red Sea Slave Trade 1820–1880', in Clarence-Smith, *The Economics of the Indian Ocean Slave Trade*, 71–92.

al-Farsī, 'Abd Allāh b. Ṣāliḥ, *Al-bū saʿīdiyūn: Ḥukkām zanjibār*, Masqaṭ: Wizāra al-turāth wa al-thaqāfa, 2005.

Fawaz, Leila Tarazi and Christopher A. Bayly (eds.), *Modernity and Culture: From the Mediterranean to the Indian Ocean*, New York: Columbia University Press, 2002.

Floor, Willem M., *Bandar Abbas: The Natural Trade Gateway of Southeast Iran*, Washington: Mage, 2011.

Fontanier, Victor, *Voyage dans l'Inde et dans le Golfe Persique par l'Égypte et la Mer Rouge*, 2 vols, Paris: Paulin, 1844.

Frank, Andre Gunder, *ReOrient: Global Economy in the Asian Age*, Berkeley, Los Angeles and London: University of California Press, 2000.

Freeman-Grenville, G.S.P., *The East African Coast: Selected Documents from the First to the Earlier Nineteenth Century*, Oxford: Oxford University Press, 1962.

Fuma, Sudel, *L'esclavagisme à La Réunion 1794–1848*, Paris: L'Harmattan, 1992.

Gaüwère, Bernard-Alex and Pierre Aubry, 'Histoire des épidémies et des endémoépidémies humaines dans le sud-ouest de l'océan Indien', *Médecine et Santé Tropicales* 23 (2013), 145–157.

al-Ghailani, Y.A., 'Oman and the Franco-British Rivalry: The Bandar al-Jissah Crisis, 1898–1900', *Adab* 29 (2009), 1–17.

Gibb, Hamilton A.R., J.H. Kramers, E. Lévi-Provençal et al. (eds.), *Encyclopaedia of Islām*, new ed., 12 vols, Leiden: E.J. Brill, 1960–2005.

Gilbert, Erik, 'The Zanzibar Dhow Trade: An Informal Economy on the East African Coast, 1860–1964' (Ph.D dissertation, Boston University, 1997).

———, *Dhows and the Colonial Economy of Zanzibar, 1860–1970*, Oxford: James Curry, 2004.

Glassman, Jonathan, *Feasts and Riots: Revelry, Rebellion, and Popular Consciousness on the Swahili Cost: 1856–1888*, London: James Currey, 1995.

Goody, Jack, 'Slavery in Time and Space', in Watson (ed.), *Asian and African Systems of Slavery*, 16–42.

Goswami, Chhaya, *The Call of the Sea: Kachchhi Traders in Muscat and Zanzibar, c.1800–1880*, Hyderabad: Orient Black Swan, 2011.

Graham, Gerald S., *Great Britain in the Indian Ocean 1810–1850*, Oxford: Clarendon Press, 1967.
Guillain, Charles, *Documents sur l'histoire et le commerce de l'Afrique Orientale*, 2 parts, Paris: Arthus Bertrand, 1856–1885.
Haneda, Masashi (ed.), *Islamu, Kan Indoyō sekai, 16–18 seiki*, Tokyo: Iwanami Shoten, 2000.
———, 'Mittsu no "Isulamu kokka"', in Haneda (ed.), *Islamu, Kan Indoyō sekai*, 3–92.
———, *Higashi indo-kaisya to Ajia no umi*, Tokyo: Kōdansha, 2007.
——— (ed.), *Asian Port Cities, 1600–1800: Local and Foreign Cultural Interactions*, Singapore and Kyoto: NUS Press and Kyoto University Press, 2009.
———, 'Canton, Nagasaki and the Port Cities of the Indian Ocean: A Comparison', in Haneda (ed.), *Asian Port Cities*, 13–23.
Harris, William C., *The Highlands of Æthiopia, described, during 18 months' residence of a British Embassy at Christian Court of Shoa*, 3 vols, London: Longman, Brown, Green, and Longmans, 1844.
Hawley, John (ed.), *India in Africa, Africa in India: Indian Ocean Cosmopolitanisms*, Bloomington: Indiana University Press, 2008.
Hertslet, Lewis, Edward Hertslet, Cecil Hertslet et al. (eds.), *A Complete Collection of the Treaties and Conventions, and Reciprocal Regulation, at present submitting between Great Britain and Foreign Powers, and of the Laws, Decrees, and Orders in Council, concerning the same; so far as They relate to Commerce and Navigation; to the Repression and Abolition of the Slave Trade; and to the Privileges and Interests of the Subjects of the High Contracting Parties*, 31 vols, London: Henry Butterworth and James Bigg and Sons, 1840–1925.
Heude, William, *A Voyage up the Persian Gulf and a Journey Overland from India to England in 1817*, London: Longman, 1819.
al-Ḥijjī, Ya'qūb Yūsuf, *Ṣinā'a al-sufun al-sharā'īya fī al-Kuwayt*, Kuwayt: Markaz al-Buḥūth wa al-Dirāsāt al-Kuwaytīya, 2001.
Ho, Hai Quang, *Histoire économique de l'île de la Réunion (1849–1881): Engagisme, croissance et crise*, Paris: L'Harmattan, 2004.
Hopper, Matthew S., 'The African Presence in Arabia: Slavery, the World Economy, and the African Diaspora in Eastern Arabia, 1840–1940' (PhD dissertation, University of California, Los Angeles, 2006).
———, 'East Africa and the End of the Indian Ocean Slave Trade', *Journal of African Development* 13, 1 (2011), 39–66.
———, *Slaves of One Master: Globalization and Slavery in Arabia in the Age of Empire*, New Haven and London: Yale University Press, 2015.
Horton, Mark and John Middleton, *The Swahili: The Social Landscape of A Mercantile Society*, Oxford: Blackwell Publishers, 2000.

Houtsma, Martijn Th., T.W. Arnold, R. Basset et al. (eds.), *Encyclopaedia of Islām: A Dictionary of the Geography, Ethnography and Biography of the Muhammadan Peoples*, Leiden: E.J Brill, 9 vols, 1991 (1st 1913–1938).

Ibn Ruzayq, Ḥamīd ibn Muḥammad, *Al-fataḥ al-mubīn fī sīra al-sāda al-bū saʿīdiyīn*, ed. ʿAbd al-Munʿim ʿĀmir and Muḥammad Mursī ʿAbd Allāh, Masqaṭ: Wizāra al-turāth wa al-thaqāfa, 2001.

Iida, Taku (ed.), *Madagasukaru chiiki bunka no dōtai*, Osaka: National Ethnographical Museum, 2012.

Ingrams, D. and L. Ingrams (eds.), *Records of Yemen, 1798–1960*, 16 vols, London: Archives Editions, 1993.

Ingrams, William H., *Zanzibar: Its History and its People*, London: Taylor & Francis, 1967.

al-Ismaily, Issa bin Nasser, *Zanzibar: Kinyang'anyiro na utumwa*, Ruwi: Issa bin Nasser al-Ismaily, 1999.

Jayasuriya, Shihan de S., 'Identifying Africans in Asia: What's in a Name?' *African and Asian Studies* 5, 3–4 (2006), 275–303.

——— and Richard Pankhurst (eds.), *The African Diaspora in the Indian Ocean*, Trenton: Africa World Press, 2003.

——— and ———, 'On the African Diaspora in the Indian Ocean Region', in Jayasuriya and Pankhurst (eds.), *The African Diaspora*, 7–17.

Johny, Shelly, 'The Decline of Omans Maritime Empire during the Late Nineteenth Century' (PhD dissertation, Jawaharlal Nehru University, 2010).

Jwaideh, Albertine and James W. Cox, 'The Black Slaves of Turkish Arabia during the 19th Century', in Clarence-Smith (ed.), *The Economics of the Indian Ocean Slave Trade*, 45–59.

Kamioka, Ko'ichi and Hikoichi Yajima, *Indo-yō nishi-kaiiki ni okeru chiikikan kōryū no kōzō to kinō: Dau chōsa hōkoku 2*, Tokyo: Institute for the Study of Languages and Cultures of Asia and Africa, 1979.

Kearney, Milo, *The Indian Ocean in World History*, New York and London: Routledge, 2004.

Keita, Maghan (ed.), *Conceptualizing/Re-Conceptualizing Africa: The Construction of African Historical Identity*, Leiden: Brill, 2002.

Kelly, John B., *Britain and the Persian Gulf 1795–1880*, Oxford: Clarendon Press, 1968.

Kemball, Arnold B., 'Paper Relative to the Measures Adopted by the British Government, between the Years 1820 and 1844, for Effecting the Suppression of the Slave Trade in the Persian Gulf', in Thomas (ed.), *Arabian Gulf Intelligence*, 635–687.

Khalidi, Omar, 'The Habshis of Hyderabad', in Robbins and McLeod (eds.), *African Elites in India*, 245–253.

Khalilieh, Hassan S., *Islamic Maritime Law: An Introduction*, Leiden: Brill, 1998.

Kieran, J.A., 'The Origins of the Zanzibar Guarantee Treaty of 1862', *Canadian Journal of African Studies* 2, 2 (1968), 147–166.
Klein, Herbert S., *The Atlantic Slave Trade*, Cambridge: Cambridge University Press, 2010 (1st 1999).
Kjekshus, Helge, *Ecology Control and Economic Development in East African History: The Case of Tanganyika 1850-1950*, London: Heinemann, 1977.
Krapf, Johann L., *Travels, Researches and Missionary Labours during an Eighteen Years' Residence in Eastern Africa: together with Journeys to Jagga, Usambara, Ukambani, Shoa, Abessinia, and Khartum; and a Coasting Voyage from Mombaz to Cape Delgado*, London: Trubner, 1860.
Kurşun, Zekeriya, *The Ottoman in Qatar: A History of Anglo-Ottoman Conflicts in the Persian Gulf*, Istanbul: The Isis Press, 2002.
Landen, Robert G., *Oman since 1856: Disruptive Modernization in a Traditional Arab Society*, Princeton: Princeton University Press, 1967.
Lane, Paul J. and Kevin C. Macdonald (eds.), *Slavery in Africa: Archaeology and Memory*, Oxford: Oxford University Press, 2012.
Larson, Pier M., 'Enslaved Malagasy and "Le Travail de la Parole" in the Pre-Revolutionary Mascarenes', *Journal of African History* 48 (2007), 457–479.
Lloyd, Christopher, *The Navy and the Slave Trade: The Suppression of the African Slave Trade in the Nineteenth Century*, London: Longmans, Green, 1949.
Lorimer, John G., *Gazetteer of the Persian Gulf, 'Oman and Central Arabia*, London: Archive Editions, 1986 (1st 1808–1815, Calcutta: Superintendent Government Printing).
Lovejoy, Paul E., *Transformations in Slavery: A History of Slavery in Africa: Third Edition*, Cambridge: Cambridge University Press, 2012.
Low, Charles R., *History of the Indian Navy 1613–1863*, 2 vols, Delhi: Manas Publications, 1985 (1st 1877, London: Richard Bentley).
Lyne, Robert R., *Zanzibar in Contemporary Times: A Short History of the Southern East in the Nineteenth Century*, New York: Negro Universities Press, 1969 (1st 1905, London: Hurst and Blackett).
McCalman, Iain, 'The East African Middle Passage: David Livingstone, the Zambezi Expedition and Lake Nyassa, 1858–1866', in Christopher, Pybus and Rediker (eds.), *Many Middle Passages*, 39–51.
Machado, Pedro, 'A Forgotten Corner of the Indian Ocean: Gujarati Merchants, Portuguese India and the Mozambique Slave-Trade, *c.*1730–1830', in Campbell (ed.), *The Structure of Slavery*, 17–32.
———, *Ocean of Trade: South Asian Merchants, Africa and the Indian Ocean, c.1750–1850*, Cambridge: Cambridge University Press, 2014.
McMahon, Elisabeth, *Slavery and Emancipation in Islamic East Africa: From Honor to Respectability*, Cambridge: Cambridge University Press, 2013.
McMaster, D.N., 'The Ocean-Going Dhow Trade to East Africa', *East African Geographical Review* 4 (1966), 13–24.

McPherson, Kenneth, *The Indian Ocean: A History of People and the Sea*, Oxford; Oxford University Press, 1993.

Madan, Arthur C., *Kiungani; or, Story and History from Central Africa*, London: George Bell and Sons, 1887.

Maheta, Makrand, *Gujarātīo ane pūrva Āphrikā, 1850–1960: Gujarātīpaānī shodhamām*, Amdāvāda: Darshaka Itihāsa Nidhi, 2001.

Major, Andrea, *Slavery, Abolitionism and Empire in India, 1772–1843*, Liverpool: Liverpool University Press, 2012.

Malcolm, John, *Sketches of Persia*, 2 vols, London: J. Murray, 1849.

Mangat, Jagjit S., *A History of the Asians in East Africa c.1886 to 1945*, Oxford: Clarendon Press, 1969.

Manning, Patrick, *Slavery and African Life: Occidental, Oriental, and African Slave Trades*, New York: Cambridge University Press, 1990.

Martin, Bradford G., *Muslim Brotherhoods in Nineteenth Century Africa*, New York: Cambridge University Press, 2003 (1st 1976).

Martin, Esmond B., *The History of Malindi: A Geographical Analysis of an East African Coastal Town from the Portuguese Period to the Present*, Nairobi: East African Literature Bureau, 1973.

——— and Chryssee P. Martin, *Cargoes of the East: The Ports, Trade and Culture of the Arabian Seas and Western Indian Ocean*, London: Elm Tree Books, 1978.

——— and T. C. I. Ryan, 'A Quantitative Assessment of the Arab Slave Trade of East Africa, 1770–1896', *Kenya Historical Review* 5 (1977), 71–91.

Martin, Jean, 'L'affranchissement des esclaves de Mayotte, décembre 1846 juillet–1847', *Cahiers d'Etudes Africaines* 16 (1976), 207–233.

Martin, Vanessa, *The Qajar Pact: Bargaining, Protest and the State in Nineteenth-Century Persia*, London and New York: I.B. Tauris, 2005.

Mateer, Samuel, *Native Life in Travancore*, London: W.H. Allen, 1883.

Maurizi, Vincento, *History of Seyd Said, Sultan of Muscat; together with an Account of the Countries and People on the Shores of the Persian Gulf, particularly of the Wahabees*, London: John Booth, 1819.

Médard, Henri and Shane Doyle (eds.), *Slavery in the Great Lakes Region of East Africa*, Oxford: James Curry, 2007.

Medard, Henri, Marie-Laure Derat, Thomas Vernet et al (eds.), *Traites et esclavages en Afrique orientale et dans l'océan Indien*, Paris: Karthala, 2013.

Médéa, Laurant (ed.), *Kaf: Etude pluridisciplinaire*, Sainte-Clotilde: Zarlor éditions, 2009.

Metcalf, Thomas R., *Imperial Connections: India in the Indian Ocean Arena, 1860–1920*, Berkeley: University of California Press, 2007.

Mignan, Robert, *Winter Journey through Russia, the Caucasian Alps, and Georgia; thence across Mount Zagros, by the Pass of Xenophon and the Ten Thousand Greeks, into Koordistaun*, 2 vols, London: Richard Bentley, 1839.

Milburn, William, *Oriental Commerce: Containing a Geographical Description of the Principal Places in the East Indies, China, and Japan, with their Produce, Manufactures, and Trade*, 2 vols, London: Black, Parry, and Co., 1813.

Miles, Samuel B., *The Countries and Tribes in the Persian Gulf*, London: Bentley, 1919.

Miller, Joseph, 'A Theme in Variations: A Historical Schema of Slaving in the Atlantic and Indian Ocean Regions', in Campbell (ed.), *The Structure of Slavery*, 169–194.

Minorsky, Vladimir, *Sharaf al-Zamān Ṭāhir Marvazī on China, the Turks and India*, London: Royal Asiatic Society, 1942.

Mirza, Sarah and Margaret Strobel (eds.), *Three Swahili Women: Life Histories from Mombasa, Kenya*, Bloomington and Indianapolis: Indiana University Press, 1989.

Mirzai, Behnaz A., 'Slavery, the Abolition of the Slave Trade, and the Emancipation of Slaves in Iran (1828–1928)' (PhD dissertation, York University, 2004).

Mirzai, A. Behnaz, Ismael Musah Montana and Paul E. Lovejoy (eds.), *Slavery, Islam and Diaspora*. Trenton: Africa World Press, 2009.

Morton, Fred, 'Small Change: Children in the Nineteenth-Century East Africa Slave Trade', in Campbell, Miers and Miller (eds.), *Children in Slavery*, 55–70.

Moyse-Bartlett, Hubert, *The Pirates of Trucial Oman*, London: Macdonald, 1966.

al-Mughayrī, Saʿīd b. ʿAlī, *Juhayna al-akhbār fī tārīkh Zanjibār*, ed. ʿAbd al-Munʿim ʿĀmir, Masqaṭ: Wizāra al-turāth al-qawmī, 1979.

New, Charles, *Life, Wanderings and Labours in Eastern Africa: With an Account of the First Successful Ascent of the Equatorial Snow Mountain, Kilima Njaro, and Remarks upon East African Slavery*, London: Frank Cass, 1971 (1st 1873, London: Hodder & Stoughton).

Nicholls, Christine S., *The Swahili Coast: Politics, Diplomacy and Trade on the East African Littoral, 1798–1856*, London: George Allen & Unwin, 1971.

Nicolini, Beatrice, *Il Sultanato di Zanzibar nel XIX secolo: Traffici commerciali e relazioni internazionali*, Torino: L'Harmattan Italia, 2002.

Nwulia, Moses D.E., *Britain and Slavery in East Africa*, Washington: Three Continents Press, 1975.

Nyanchoga, Samuel A., Herman O. Kiriama, Patrick Abungu, Marrie Pierre Ballarin and Samson O. Moenga (eds.), *Slave Heritage and Identity at the Kenyan Coast*, Nairobi: CUEA Press, 2014.

Onley, James, 'Britain's Informal Empire in the Gulf, 1820–1971', *Journal of Social Affairs* 87 (2005), 29–45.

———, *The Arabian Frontier of the British Raj: Merchants, Rulers, and the British in the Nineteenth-Century Gulf*, Oxford: Oxford University Press, 2007.

Osgood, Joseph B.F., *Notes of Travel or Recollections of Majunga, Zanzibar, Muscat, Aden, Mocha, and Other Eastern Ports*, Salem: George Creamer, 1854.

Parthasarathi, Prasannan and Giorgio Riello, 'The Indian Ocean in the Long Eighteenth Century', *Eighteenth-Century Studies* 48, 1 (2014), 1–19.

Pearson, Michael N., *Merchants and Rulers in Gujarat: The Response to the Portuguese in the Sixteenth Century*, Los Angeles and Berkeley, University of California Press, 1976.

Pearson, Michael (ed.), *Trade, Circulation, and Flow in the Indian Ocean World*, New York: Palgrave, 2015

———, *The Indian Ocean*, London and New York: Routledge, 2003.

Pelly, Lewis, 'Remarks on the Tribes, Trade and Resources around the Shore Line of the Persian Gulf', *Transaction of Bombay Geographical Society* 17 (1863), 32–112.

Pomeranz, Kenneth, *The Great Divergence: China, Europe and the Making of the Modern World Economy*, Princeton: Princeton University Press, 2000.

Pouwels, Randall L., *Horn and Crescent: Cultural Change and Traditional Islam on the East African Coast, 800–1900*, Cambridge: Cambridge University Press, 1987.

Prestholdt, Jeremy, *Domesticating the World: African Consumerism and the Genealogies of Globalization*, Berkeley: University of California Press, 2008.

Prins, Adriaan H.J., *Sailing from Lamu: A Study of Maritime Culture in Islamic East Africa*, Assen: Van Gorcum, 1965.

Prior, James, *Voyage along the Eastern Coast of Africa to Mosambique, Johanna, and Quiloa: to St. Helena; to Rio de Janeiro, Bahia, and Pernambuco in Brazil in the Nisus Frigate*, London: Richard Phillips, 1819.

al-Qāsimī, Sulṭān b. Muḥammad (ed.), *Wathā'iq al-'arabīya al-'umānī fī marākiz al-arshīf al-faransīya*, s.l., 1993.

———, *Les relations entre Oman et la France (1715–1905)*, tr. Abdeljelil and Mireille Temimi, Paris: L'Harmattan, 1995.

Reda Bhacker, Mohamed, 'Family Strife and Foreign Intervention: Causes in the Separation of Zanzibar from Oman: A Reappraisal', *Bulletin of the School of Oriental and African Studies* 54, 2 (1991), 269–280.

———, *Trade and Empire in Muscat and Zanzibar: Roots of British Domination*, London: Routledge, 1992.

Reilly, Benjamin, *Slavery, Agriculture, and Malaria in the Arabian Peninsula*, Athens: Ohio University Press, 2015.

Ricks, Thomas M., 'Slaves and Slave Traders in the Persian Gulf, 18th and 19th Centuries: An Assessment', in Clarence-Smith (ed.), *The Economics of the Indian Ocean Slave Trade*, 60–70.

———, 'Slaves and Slave Trading in Shi'i Iran, AD 1500–1900', in Keita (ed.), *Conceptualizing/Re-Conceptualizing Africa*, 77–88.

Robbins, Kenneth X. and John McLeod (eds.), *African Elites in India: Habshi Amarat*, Ahmedabad: Mappin Publishing, 2006.

Roberts, Edmund, *Embassy to the Eastern Courts of Cochin-China, Siam, and Muscat; in the U.S. Sloop-of-War Peacock, David Geisinger, Commander, during the years 1832-3-4*, Wilmington: Scholarly Resources, 1972 (1st 1937, New York: Harper).

Robertson, Claire C. and Martin A. Klein (eds.), *Women and Slavery in Africa*, Madison: University of Wisconsin Press, 1983.

Ruete, Emilie, *An Arabian Princess between Two Worlds: Memoirs, Letters Home, Sequels to My Memories: Syrian Customs and Usages*, ed. and intro. E. van Donzel, Leiden: Brill, 1993.

al-Rūmī, Aḥmad al-Bishr, *Mu'jam al-muṣṭalaḥāt al-baḥrīya fī al-Kuwayt*, Kuwayt: Markaz al-buḥūth wa al-dirāsāt al-Kuwaytīya, 2005.

Ruschenberger, William S.W., *A Voyage round the World; including An Embassy to Muscat and Siam, in 1835, 1836, and 1837*, Philadelphia: Lea Carey and Blanchard, 1938.

Russell, Charles E.B., Mrs, *General Rigby, Zanzibar and the Slave Trade: With Journals, Dispatches, etc.*, London: Allen & Unwin, 1935.

Saadi, Amur Omar, 'Mafia: History and Traditions', tr. D.W.I. Piggott, *Tanganyika Notes and Records* 12 (1941), 23–27.

Saldanha, Jerome A. (ed.), *The Persian Gulf Précis*, 8 vols, Gerrards Cross: Archive Editions, 1986 (1st in 18 vols, 1903–1908, Calcutta and Simla).

Salim, Ahmed, *The Swahili-Speaking Peoples of Kenya's Coast, 1895–1965*, Nairobi: East African Publishing House, 1973.

Salvadori, Cynthia, *Through Open Doors: A View of Asian Cultures in Kenya*, Nairobi: Kenway Publications, 1989 (1st 1983).

Shahriyār, Buzurg b., Pieter A. van der Lith and L. Marcel Devic, *Livre des merveilles de l'Inde= Kitāb 'ajā'ib al-Hind*, Leiden: Brill, 1883–1886.

Sheriff, Abdul, *Slaves, Spices and Ivory in Zanzibar: Integration of an East African Commercial Empire into the World Economy, 1770–1873*, Oxford: James Curry, 1987.

———, 'Localisation and Social Composition of the East African Slave Trade, 1858–1873', in Clarence-Smith (ed.), *The Economics of the Indian Ocean Slave Trade*, 131-145.

Smee, T., 'Observations during a Voyage of Research on the East Coast of Africa, from Cape Guardafi South to the Island of Zanzibar, in the H.C.'s Cruiser Ternate (Captain T. Smee) and Sylph Schooner (Lieutenant Hardy)', in Burton, *Zanzibar*, Vol. 2, 458–513.

Stanziani, Alessandro, *Sailors, Slaves, and Immigrants: Bondage in the Indian Ocean World, 1750-1914*, New York: Palgrave, 2014.

Steinberg, Philip E., *The Social Construction of the Ocean*, Cambridge: Cambridge University Press, 2001.

Strobel, Margaret, 'Women and Slavery on the East African coast', in Tominaga (ed.), *Rethinking African History*, 45–65.

Sullivan, George L., *Dhow Chasing in Zanzibar Waters*, Zanzibar: The Gallery Publications, 2003.

Suzuki, Hideaki, 'Enslaved Population and Indian Owners along the East African Coast: Exploring the Rigby Manumission List, 1860–1861', *History in Africa* 39 (2012), 209–239.

———, '19 seiki Nosy Be de karamariau tayouna kankeisei', in Iida (ed.), *Madagasukaru chiiki bunka no dōtai*, 241–258.

———, 'Baluchi Experiences under Slavery and the Slave Trade of the Gulf of Oman and the Persian Gulf, 1921–1950', *Journal of the Middle East and Africa* 4, 2 (2013), 205–223.

———, 'Tracing their "Middle" Passages: Slave Accounts from the Nineteenth-Century Western Indian Ocean', in Bellagamba, Greene and Klein (eds.), *African Voices on Slavery and the Slave Trade*, Cambridge: Cambridge University Press, 2013, 307–318.

———, 'Distorted Variation: Reconsideration of Slavery in the Nineteenth Century Swahili Society from Masters' Perspective', in Bellagamba, Greene and Klein (eds.), *African Slaves, African Masters*, 221-236.

Taylor, William E., *African Aphorisms; or, Saws from Swahili-land*, London: Society for Promoting Christian Knowledge, 1891.

Teelock, Vijaya, *Bitter Sugar: Sugar and Slavery in 19th Century Mauritius*, Moka: Mahatma Gandhi Institute, 1998.

Thomas, R. Hughes (ed.), *Arabian Gulf Intelligence*, Bombay: Bombay Education Society's Press, 1856.

Tinker, Hugh, *A New System of Slavery: The Export of Indian Labour Overseas 1830–1920*, London: Hansib, 1993 (1st 1974, London: Oxford University Press).

Toledano, Ehud R., *Slavery and Abolition in the Ottoman Middle East*, Seattle: University of Washington Press, 1998.

Tominaga, Chizuko (ed.), *Rethinking African History from Women's/Gender Perspectives: Slavery, Colonial Experience, Nationalist Movement and After*, Osaka: National Museum of Ethnology, 2004.

Toussaint, Auguste, *Histoire de l'Océan Indien*, Paris: Presse Universitaires, 1961.

———, *History of the Indian Ocean*, tr. June Guicharnaud, London: Routledge and Kegan Paul, 1966.

UNESCO (United Nations Educational, Scientific and Cultural Organization) (ed.), *Historical Relations across the Indian Ocean: Report and Papers of the Meeting of Experts Organized by UNESCO at Port Louis, Mauritius, from 15 to 19 July, 1974*, Paris: UNESCO, 1980.

Vernet, Thomas, 'Slave Trade and Slavery on the Swahili Coast (1500–1750)', in Mirzai, Montana and Lovejoy (eds.), *Slavery, Islam and Diaspora*, 37–76.

———, 'The Deep Roots of the Plantation Economy on the Swahili Coast: Productive Functions and Social Functions of Slaves and Dependents, Circa 1580–1820', in Weldemichael, Lee and Alpers (eds.), *Changing Horizons*, 51–100.

Villiers, Alan, 'Some Aspects of the Arab Dhow Trade', *Middle East Journal* 2, 4 (1948), 399–416.

———, *Sons of Sinbad; An Account of Sailing with the Arabs in their Dhows, in the Red Sea, around the Coasts of Arabia, and to Zanzibar and Tanganyika; Pearling in the Persian Gulf; and the Life of the Shipmasters, the Mariners, and Merchants of Kuwait*, New York: Scribner, 1969.

Vink, Markus P.M., 'Indian Ocean Studies and the "New Thalassology"', *Journal of Global History* 2 (2007), 41–62.

Wallerstein, Immanuel, *The Modern World-System*, 3 vols, New York: Academic Press, 1974–1989.

Walz, Terence, 'Sketched Lives from the Census: Trans-Saharan Africans in Cairo in 1848', paper presented at Tales of Slavery Conference, University of Toronto, 20–23 May 2009.

Watson, James L. (ed.), *Asian and African Systems of Slavery*, Berkeley and Los Angeles: University of California Press, 1980.

Weldemichael, T. Awet, Anthony A. Lee and Edward A. Alpers (eds.), *Changing Horizons of African History*, Trenton: Africa World Press, 2017.

Wellsted, James R., *Travels in Arabia*, 2 vols, London: J. Murray, 1838.

Wilkinson, John C., *The Imamate Tradition of Oman*, London: Cambridge University Press, 1987.

Wilson, David, 'Memorandum Respecting the Pearl Fisheries in the Persian Gulf', *Journal of Royal Geographical Society of London* 3 (1833), 283–286.

Wilson, George G., *The Hague Arbitration Cases: Compromise and Awards, with Maps, in Cases Decided under the Provisions of the Hague Conventions of 1899 and 1907 for the Pacific Settlement of International Disputes and Texts of the Conventions*, Boston: Ginn and Companies, 1915.

Wink, André, *Al-Hind, the Making of the Indo-Islamic World, Volume 1: Early Medieval India and the Expansion of Islam 7th–11th Centuries*, Leiden: Brill, 1996 (1st 1990).

Wong-Hee-Kam, Edith, *La diaspora chinoise aux Mascareignes: le cas de la Réunion*, Paris: L'Harmattan, 1996.

Wong, Roy Bin, *China Transformed: Historical Change and the Limits of European Experience*, Ithaca: Cornel University Press, 1997.

Wright, Marcia, *Strategies of Slaves and Women: Life-Histories from East/Central Africa*, New York: Lillian Barber Press, 1993.

Yajima, Hikoichi, *The Arab Dhow Trade in the Indian Ocean: Preliminary Report*, Tokyo: Institute for the Study of Languages and Cultures of Asia and Africa, 1976.

———, *Umi ga tsukuru bunmei: Indo-yō kaiiki sekai no rekishi*, Osaka: Asahi shinbunsha, 1993.

———, *Kaiiki kara mita rekishi: Indoyō to chicyūkai wo musubu kōryūshi*, Nagoya: Nagoya University Press, 2006.

Ylvisaker, Marguerite H., 'The Political and Economic Relationship of the Lamu Archipelago to the Adjacent Kenya Coast in the Nineteenth Century' (PhD dissertation, Boston University, 1975).

Yokoi, Katsuhiko, *Ajia no umi no dai-ei-teikoku: 19seiki kaiyō shihai no kōzō*, Tokyo: Kōdansha, 2004 (1st 1988, Tokyo: Dōbunkan).

Yule, Henry and Arthur C. Burnell, *Hobson-Jobson: A Glossary of Colloquial Anglo-Indian Words and Phrases, and of Kindred Terms, Etymological, Historical, Geographical and Discursive*, London: James Murray, 1903 (1st 1886).

Index

H. Suzuki, *Slave Trade Profiteers in the Western Indian Ocean*, Palgrave Series in Indian Ocean World Studies,
DOI 10.1007/978-3-319-59803-1